ONE MORE KISS

The Broadway Musical in the 1970s

THE GOLDEN AGE OF THE BROADWAY MUSICAL

AVAILABLE:

MAKE BELIEVE: THE BROADWAY MUSICAL IN THE 1920s
BEAUTIFUL MORNIN': THE BROADWAY MUSICAL IN THE 1940s
COMING UP ROSES: THE BROADWAY MUSICAL IN THE 1950s
OPEN A NEW WINDOW: THE BROADWAY MUSICAL IN THE 1960s
ONE MORE KISS: THE BROADWAY MUSICAL IN THE 1970s

FORTHCOMING:

SING FOR YOUR SUPPER: THE BROADWAY MUSICAL IN THE 1930s

The Broadway Musical in the 1970s

ETHAN MORDDEN

ONE MORE KISS

palgrave
macmillan

ONE MORE KISS: THE BROADWAY MUSICAL IN THE 1970s
© Ethan Mordden, 2003

All rights reserved. No part of this book may be used or reproduced in any manner whatsoever without written permission except in the case of brief quotations embodied in critical articles or reviews.

First published in hardcover in 2003 by Palgrave Macmillan
First PALGRAVE MACMILLAN™ paperback edition: June 2004
175 Fifth Avenue, New York, N.Y. 10010 and
Houndmills, Basingstoke, Hampshire, England RG21 6XS
Companies and representatives throughout the world.

PALGRAVE MACMILLAN is the global academic imprint of the Palgrave Macmillan division of St. Martin's Press, LLC and of Palgrave Macmillan Ltd. Macmillan® is a registered trademark in the United States, United Kingdom and other countries. Palgrave is a registered trademark in the European Union and other countries.

ISBN 1-4039-6539-0

Library of Congress Cataloging-in-Publication Data is available from the Library of Congress.

A catalogue record for this book is available from the British Library.

First PALGRAVE MACMILLAN paperback edition: June 2004

10 9 8 7 6 5 4 3 2 1

Printed in the United States of America.

Contents

Acknowledgments	VIII
Conclusion	1
1. The Age of Sondheim	8
2. All Those Glittering Years: *Follies*	34
3. If Everyone Got What They Wanted: Musical Comedy I	48
4. Decca Broadway: Americans in London	79
5. Why Can't We All Be Nice?: The Dark Musical	87
6. Nobody Does It Like Me: *Pippin* and *Seesaw*	107
7. It's a Bore: The Dreary Musical	114
8. Keep It Hot: The Concept Musical	127
9. I Could Be at Home with My Seven Maids: The Revival	140
10. Were You Saying Something?: Off-Broadway	161

11. Haven't We Met?: The Revue　167

12. I Really Don't Want to Write a Musical About Some Man Who Is Running from the Nazis. I Want to Do Something with Showgirls: Musical Comedy II　177

13. Evolution Papa: Three "Don't" Musicals　207

14. Don't Pop the Head, Cassie!: Three Classics　217

15. Please Sign the Book on Your Way Out the Door: The 1979–80 Season　233

Index　254

To Gregg

Acknowledgments

To my dynamite agent, Joe Spieler; to my friend and colleague Ken Mandelbaum for his endless generosity; and, at Palgrave, to Alan Bradshaw, Doric Wilson, the populous copy editing team of Benjamin Dreyer, esquire, and to my editor, Michael Flamini, who eagerly awaits the reunion of Jerry Bock and Sheldon Harnick in a followup to *The Rothschilds*, this time about America's great poultry dynasty: *The Perdues*.

CONCLUSION

This is the sixth and culminating volume in a chronicle of the American musical's Golden Age. In one way, it is the most important of the six: for here we learn why the Golden Age ended.

We know why it began. Composers Jerome Kern and Irving Berlin, listening to trends in the writing of popular music, listening to the types of singer available, and listening above all to each other, invent a new style of song with an American voice, suitable for theatrical adaptation. This happens around 1915.

Meanwhile, Berlin the lyricist develops a playfully demotic tone; his colleagues Henry Blossom and Anne Caldwell feature slang and wordplay; and P. G. Wodehouse, especially with Kern, introduces wit into the musical. By about 1920, Cole Porter, George and Ira Gershwin, Vincent Youmans, Richard Rodgers and Lorenz Hart, and Oscar Hammerstein II become prominent. It is the time of American culture's great efflorescence: in film, the spoken theatre, literature. Just as America's immigrant population has been blending into the native stock, the popular and the élite are merging in America's arts—in *Krazy Kat*, Louis Armstrong, Eugene O'Neill, *Rhapsody in Blue*, Jay Gatsby.

Naturally, this alchemy favors the musical theatre, at once so demanding of its creators yet so accommodating of its public. The Golden Age lasts for decades, surviving the death or retirement of its begetters with a second generation of creators. Secure as a mainstay of American civilization, profitable and prestigious, the musical rides through the 1960s. Yet by the end of the 1970s, the Golden Age is finished.

To understand why, let us start at the beginning. I chart the musical's history in four Ages. The First Age, in the nineteenth century, finds it vital but primitive. The music is often a hodgepodge of "arrangements." Songs and dances are inserted on pretexts. The performing styles comprise a miscellany of the amateur, the freak, the imitator. The art is so rudimentary that no inspiring genius—had one been available—could have taught it anything. In fact, the available genres were so unimprovable that they died out early, the very terms all but meaningless today.

There was first of all pantomime, utilizing but not given over entirely to dumb show and somewhat related to the English form still in use today as family Christmas fare. Pantomimes were retellings from storybookland featuring a star clown: most notably *Humpty Dumpty* (1868) and its many sequels built around George L. Fox.

There was also burlesque, a spoof of, usually, some lofty or upper-middle literary work with pride to be needled: *Evangeline* (1874) and *Hiawatha* (1880), both from Henry Wadsworth Longfellow, with their trouser-role leading ladies and pun-obsessed humor. Many shows were really just plays with a few songs and dance specialties. Many other shows were hybrids of uncertain flavor, including the title often cited as the first musical, *The Black Crook* (1866), a demonic thriller containing hunks of ballet and vaudeville.

Not the first, but the first influential musical, *The Black Crook* shows how loose format was in the First Age. Originally, the show belonged to the form called "extravaganza," indicating spectacular visuals, a big cast, and, usually, a supernatural or around-the-world plotline. *The Black Crook* was of the supernatural variety, reminiscent of the pact-with-the-devil theme of Carl Maria von Weber's opera *Der Freischütz*.

Constantly revived throughout the First Age and sporadically for a generation after, *The Black Crook* was never the same show twice. Numbers were replaced, new scenic "transformations" and dances added, new roles interpolated for available talent. The revisions visited upon this all but quintessential American musical do not betoken a wish to perfect the art, however. The show had no center, no substance. What was *The Black Crook*? Whatever its latest producer said it was. Yes, the audience could expect that true-love-versus-the-devil's-minion plot, and the ballerinas, and some of the more popular music. But everything else was opportunistically variable; and by the late 1800s even the ballet girls in tights might be replaced by something racier.

So there was no consistency in musicals, even as the works of Jacques Offenbach, Gilbert and Sullivan, and Johann Strauss were teaching the

Virtuous Show: unified in both composition and performing style. But the Second Age, from 1900 to 1920, stabilized the musical. The nineteenth-century genres were largely retired in favor of two newish forms: comic opera (i.e., operetta) and musical comedy.

The former emphasized music. The latter emphasized fun. Both proved resourceful and versatile, learning from each other. And a completely new form was developed—the revue, a variety show devoted to ironic commentary on the current cultural scene.

"Variety" had been an important feature of American show biz throughout the nineteenth century—but only as a collection of unrelated specialty acts or, in the minstrel show, a stereotypical mélange on southern black life. Florenz Ziegfeld's pioneering *Follies* annuals opened up a major possibility for writers and performers: topical satire. This was to permeate every sort of musical, even provisioning evening-length spoofs such as *Of Thee I Sing* (1931), *Louisiana Purchase* (1940), *Finian's Rainbow* (1947), *Li'l Abner* (1956), *Hallelujah, Baby!* (1967), *Chicago* (1975), and *Urinetown* (2001).

Looking back on the Second Age, historians note only two authors of lasting prominence, the composer Victor Herbert and the all-around thespian George M. Cohan. However, the musical counted at the time twelve major composers besides these two, all but four from Central Europe. The four, like Cohan native-born Americans, were Reginald De Koven, Louis Hirsch, Raymond Hubbell, and A. Baldwin Sloane.* Herbert, of Irish family, was raised and educated in Germany, as were Gustave Kerker and Gustav Luders. Ludwig Englander came from Austria, Sigmund Romberg and Jean Schwartz from Hungary, Rudolf Friml and Karl Hoschna from Bohemia, and Ivan Caryll from Belgium.

So Jerome Kern and Irving Berlin—the latter also from Europe—had not yet created Tin Pan Alley. They were working on it. Kern's music was first published in 1902 and Berlin's (after he started as a lyricist for other composers) in 1909. Still, for the time being, musicals really were derivative in musical style—of the Gilbert and Sullivan echoes in such English works as *Florodora* (1899; on Broadway in 1900) and *The Arcadians*

---

* Some readers may miss the name of John Philip Sousa, born in Washington, D.C. Sousa is known mainly for his marches, however. He had but middling success in the theatre, at that mostly during the end of the First Age.

(1909; 1910); of the brisk marches and droopy waltzes of the continental European approach, especially in *The Merry Widow* (1905; 1907); of older American forms, deadening the ear with front-parlor musicale.

Yet a native energy kept slipping in. An encompassingly typical Broadway offering of the Second Age was *King Dodo* (1902), by Gustav Luders and Frank Pixley. This team brought forth three outstanding hits, especially popular on the midwest touring circuit: *The Burgomaster* (1900), in which Pieter Stuyvesant visits modern-day New York; *The Prince of Pilsen* (1903), whose score could be heard on radio into the 1940s and was still in print a generation later; and *Woodland* (1904), in which all the characters are birds.

King Dodo's slight plot starts in Dodo Land, where a venturesome hero fascinates the king with report of a fountain of youth in Spoojus Land. The Spoojus queen has sworn to wed the first king she meets, and when Dodo shows up, it's a royal romance; then the king finds the fountain and drinks. Unfortunately, the queen's taste runs to venerable sages, and the king has dropped thirty years! What next?

Obviously, the story line was of no moment. *King Dodo* was goofs, tricks, and comic Raymond Hitchcock's folksy turn in the title role. But note that the music and lyrics were of the old type, with the bustling yet vapid choruses, the one-joke patter songs, and mushy love duets that had long outstayed their effectiveness. The young hero was played by a soprano in tights, his romantic interest was the usual convenient "ward" popularized in Gilbert and Sullivan, and the chorus was comprised of loons obsessively repeating whatever the principals have just sung.

Worst of all are Pixley's monotonous rhymes and merrily worthless verses, tuned in High Middle Cliché. Consider the heroine's entrance:

CITIZEN: (in recitative) But see, here comes the fair Annette!
    A jolly girl is she.
CHORUS: (as the orchestra perks up) Yes! Here she comes,
    'Tis Annette,
    Ah! She's the girl for me.
ANNETTE: (in a thrill of coloratura) Joy rules the day,
    Care flies away.
    Let's all be gay.
    We'll sing and dance the hours away.

Still, amid all the foolish European markdowns, *King Dodo* could slip in something fresh. "The Tale of a Bumble-Bee" is generically routine, a mild exposé of a bee that won't make a commitment to a lovesick clover blossom. Animal fables were the rage, especially with garrulous rum-ti-tum verses, as here. But the refrain suddenly goes into a pure $\frac{4}{4}$ with a melody that looks forward to Jerome Kern. True, the lyrics are in the "tears in thine eyes" mode. But the music has ring and power, even honesty.

Even better is "Diana," setting up a romantic tryst with the usual diaphanous corn:

If you listen, my dear,
Magic strains you will hear.
All the fairies are singing to the moon.

Yet the lively music borders on ragtime here and there, as if trying to pull the whole of *King Dodo* out of the nineteenth century into something like last week.

All that was needed was an expansion of this sort of writing: and that will be New Music. It was the songs that must break the ground, creating the need for the kinds of shows that could sing them, with new characters, new stories. *Jazzy* stories, leaving Dodo Land for New York City and its characteristic talents: the high-tech sweetheart Marilyn Miller, those wiseacres in dance Fred and Adele Astaire, the gentleman-bum Bert Lahr, that broad of broads Ethel Merman. Some were of New York and some came to it. But their innovative energy all but drove the Raymond Hitchcocks off the stage.

So the Third Age cut off relations with the past. Most Second Age shows ran on First Age equipment to an extent. But the first entries in the *Greenwich Village Follies* series (1919–24) or *Lady, Be Good!* (1924) were inconceivable in 1910. Then, too, the equipment was constantly being reinvented. There were technical advances, for example in set design in the revolving stage and in the use of "wagons" to roll pieces in from the wings. These freed the eye of the banal side-frames-and-backdrop combinations in use for centuries. Or in lighting, to guide the eye on darkened stages to the separate pools of action so useful to the modern "concept show."

The aesthetic advances centered on the use of musical scenes, with dialogue spoken over music between the vocal paragraphs to develop situation and character. Choreography underwent an evolution, from hoofing to ballet to Dance, without which the musical of the 1940s would have consisted exclusively of *Sons O' Fun* (1941) and *Laffing Room Only* (1944).

One extremely telling aspect of the Third Age is the discovery of the Classic. The First Age counts a few historical titles but almost nothing that could draw a public a decade or so after. One can't revive a footnote. The Second Age at least introduces the musical's first enduring scores, by Herbert, Cohan, and Kern. But they don't belong to truly great *shows*, in the line of *Show Boat* (1927), *My Fair Lady* (1956), *Cabaret* (1966). A Third Age show of lesser quality that nevertheless claims a popular score may do well in revival—*Anything Goes* (1934) or *Babes in Arms* (1937), say. But it's hard to imagine any Second Age work going for a long run on Broadway today. *Naughty Marietta* (1910)? *Little Johnny Jones* (1904)? *Oh, Boy!* (1917)?

No, it is the Third Age that creates the genuinely deathless title. The Third Age even claims works whose greatness is debatable but whose influence is not—*Lady, Be Good!* again, but also *Pal Joey* (1940), *Love Life* (1948), *Redhead* (1959).

With so much *there* there, why did the Golden Age give out? Some of the explanation is obvious. First of all: money. The capitalization and maintenance of a good-sized show has grown out of all proportion to the potential gross. Thus, in the Second Age, a show doing good business could pay off literally within a few weeks of opening night. (This is why historians always hasten to remind readers that a run of 200 performances was very satisfying for, say, 1915 or so. By 1925, when smash hits ran a year in New York and then toured for perhaps two years and a half, forty-one of those forty-two months were profitable.)

By 1965, however, a year's run sometimes meant a loss of some of the investment. One reason for this is that sets and costumes are the most expensive items in a show's production budget, and the rich variety of subject matter in the post-*Oklahoma!* (1943) era virtually impelled many a piece to the spendthrift in duplicating monarchical Siam, Voltairean Europe and America, or Arthurian England. After all, when your show is set in Spoojus Land, your cast can wear almost anything, including costumes recycled from storage. But narrative verisimilitude can be expensive.

Another reason is that *every* aspect of production was costing more; but the audience was not expanding in proportionate support. Yes, the biggest hits were attracting vast publics of returnees, tourists, the curious, and the usual "me, too" schmengies. But the bread-and-butter entries between failure and classic—*Rio Rita* (1927) or *Plain and Fancy* (1955)—could no longer be hits in the commercial sense.

Music itself, the very essence of the musical, also contributes to the breakdown of the Golden Age: because it changes from Tin Pan Alley to rock. Americans as a whole cease to take their hit parade from Broadway, while attempts to infuse the musical with contemporary pop—as we shall see in the first chapter—mostly fail. At the same time, some composers reinstruct traditional theatre music, sophisticate it till the average ear cannot readily accommodate it.

Money and music. But there are many other reasons why the Third Age ends somewhere in the 1970s. We shall have to watch for revelations as the years pass—and for signs as well that this once all-basic Great American Thing refuses to cede pride of place to inferior forms of art. If the American musical is becoming the Willy Loman of entertainment, attention must be paid.

I

THE AGE OF SONDHEIM

It is the arrogance of certain critics to believe that their job lies less in assessing an art than in guiding and even bullying it. But art can properly appear only as the product of the free artist. Telling a painter to use a trendier shade of red or a novelist to lay his action in San Diego instead of Altoona is stupid: so why were people who don't write musicals telling writers what kind of songs to write?

Part of it lay in the wish to appear trendy. It looks hip to dismiss traditional work as "old-fashioned." It makes one feel so young. But note that theatre critics of the 1920s, 1930s, 1940s, and 1950s did not consider *passéiste* writing as ineffective. Any era of theatre history naturally enjoys a mixture of the old stuff and innovation, because there is no one theatregoing audience, no consensus of taste. The 1920s played host to something as newfangled as the mixed-race operetta *Deep River* (1926) yet something as old hat as the George M. Cohan imitation *The Gingham Girl* (1922), complete with Eddie Buzzell doing Cohan. George M. himself was originating the new style of hot-tempo dance musical, albeit with astonishingly outdated songs, in *Little Nellie Kelly* (1922). This was a forward-backward genre all at once, looking ahead to the work of the director-choreographers of two generations after yet making do with the same old mother songs, Irish songs, flag songs, girl's-name songs. There were twenties shows in the outmoded one-set-per-act look, shows carefully moved from one set to a second set with a change-of-décor interlude downstage of the traveler curtain, and shows whose action led them from one to many other places within a single act. Everything was happening at once, including, almost incredibly, the last productions in the old pantomime-extravaganza genre (they had merged by 1900) in the vehicles of Fred Stone. And they were smash hits, too.

What made some critics suddenly impatient for sweeping change in the late 1960s? Rock was taking over radio, edging out not only Broadway and easy-listening but classical stations as well. Did rock have to seize the stage, too? Why, because it's there?

Then, too, intellectuals had finally taken notice of the musical, and not positively. Before *Oklahoma!*, a founding title in so many ways, those who wished to could ignore the musical or enjoy it, condescendingly, as a few hours of refreshing nonsense. But once narratives became realistic and characters substantial and music strove for expressive power, the musical could irritate the unbeliever. Worse, it could turn up where intellectuals had to deal with it, as cinema. Reviewing the movie version of the Tommy Steele English show *Half a Sixpence* for *The New York Times*, Renata Adler called the songs "trite, gay, and thoroughly meaningless" and added that they "make absolutely no concessions to anything that has happened in popular music in the last ten years."

What should a musical set in England in the year 1900 sound like? *Revolver*? And if the score is "trite and gay," it is certainly not meaningless. Aside from a few scene-setters, it means what its characters say and how they feel at the moment the music hits in. Or try Pauline Kael on *1776*: "Yocks and uplift—that's the formula."

Only someone who had never seen a stage musical would sniff out a formula in *1776*, a show without precursor or successor. Kael was the one who, reviewing the film of *Fiddler on the Roof*, blithely admitted that she had never seen the show. (No wonder; it closed so quickly.) Could it be that what we really have here is people who Don't Do Theatre and Don't Get Music? I mean *any* theatre and *any* music—so, again, why are they offering opinions on what Broadway is using for music?

It may be that rock not only overwhelmed theatre music as the national sound but gave intellectuals something to feel hip about. Rock critics are like movie critics in their distaste for established art forms like the novel and, say, Shakespeare and Schiller. Normally, rock writers deal with nothing but rock. Yet every so often, a work of some relevance to the rock scene forces them to consider the musical—the *West Side Story* film, the *Porgy and Bess* question, or perhaps *The Rocky Horror Picture Show*. At such times, their loathing of Golden Age Broadway is unmistakable.

Why the attitude? Are they defensive because Rodgers and Hart, Cole Porter, and their colleagues were consistent in melodic and lyrical content, exactly where rock is erratic? And, after all, it is their father's music—their grandfather's, by now.

So were *Two Gentlemen of Verona* (1971), *Dude* (1972), and *Via Galactica* (1972) going to please these skeptics? All three were the work of composer Galt MacDermot, all were immediately typed as "rock musicals," and while the first was a hit, the other two count among the biggest bombs of all time. Yet the trio did unquestionably mark the eruption of contemporary American pop on Broadway.

Two Gentlemen, from one of Shakespeare's earliest comedies, is one of those epochal titles, so full of the views of its day that it cannot properly be enjoyed thereafter. The look was Elizabethan hippie in a three-tiered unit set, the cast was racially so mixed that there were almost no white principals at all, and the score was so *now!* that the Duke of Milan, in a two-faced grin, led the chorus in a semi-gospel piece called "Bring All the Boys Back Home."

Is this Pauline Kael's idea of a musical? It sounds like Joseph Papp's: and it was. He produced it first in Central Park side by side with a non-singing *Timon of Athens* and *Cymbeline*, the book adapted by John Guare and the show's director, Mel Shapiro, and the lyrics by Guare. With Raul Julia, Jonelle Allen, Clifton Davis, Carla Pinza, Frank O'Brien, Jerry Stiller, and Norman Matlock, the show proved at once a zany stunt, a feel-good musical comedy, and a bit of social engineering. It did what the traditional musical did, yet with people that one didn't normally see in a musical and in sounds unfamiliar to the stage.

Rock? By 1971, what *was* rock? It was "Wake Up, Little Susie" but also "Eleanor Rigby," with its string octet; black harmony groups but also the Steve Miller Band; Bob Dylan but also the Grateful Dead; and Elvis. Like Walt Whitman, rock contains multitudes. Thus, any music whose lineage owes more to Louis Armstrong than to Victor Herbert, set into a theatre context, can be a rock score. *Two Gentlemen*'s musical style is limitless, indescribable. I'd call it Funky Mandolin with a Latin Pulse, keeping in mind that the evening began with O'Brien coming out alone in his white suit, the tunic smothered in medals, to scream, in his freaky soprano, the first half of the old Tin Pan Alley hit "Love in Bloom."

All the principals but Pinza and Stiller reappeared when the show began its Broadway previews at the St. James in November. John Bottoms took Stiller's role, which was sound casting, but Pinza was replaced, in a daring coup, by the Hispanic pop singer La Lupe. Famed for her riches-to-rags cabaret performances in which she used the power of song to devolve from glamour to an almost animalistic earthiness, La Lupe simply didn't suit the more amiable style of the other actors. She was also somewhat unintelligible, and had to relinquish her part to Diana Davila.

"Cultural vandalism" was the opinion of *Time*'s T. E. Kalem; but then, he thought as much of Peter Brook's *A Midsummer Night's Dream*, the production that defined this era of theatre history. *Two Gentlemen* was not so influential—and, strangely, its busily tuneful score threw off no hits on even the most modest level. Perhaps there was too much music. The work is nearly opera, singing at any moment, every moment, making music out of not only Shakespeare but also the many isms of the day, all of which were love. Remember "the summer of"? "All you need is"? "Make, not war"? *Two Gentlemen*'s last line is "You can't love another without loving yourself," and note how many of the song titles treat it: "I Love My Father," "I Am Not Interested in Love," "What Does a Lover Pack?," "Love's Revenge"—set to the shuffling beat of the fifties group dance the Stroll—"Hot Lover," "Love Me," "Love, Is That You?," whose reprise creates the at-first-sight pairing of O'Brien with Alix Elias, which helps resolve the love plot.

Guare's lyrics seemed to egg on MacDermot's prankish side, now digging into feeling, now riding a pun, now just being silly in an adamant way. Only grouches didn't like the show, perhaps especially when Jonelle Allen's boy friend (Alvin Lum) made his entrance late in the action. Lum was Asian, so he showed up in one of those holiday dragon heads with the long train—why? because he could—and the finale found the cast on bicycles, blowing soap bubbles, skipping rope, snapping yo-yos, and throwing Frisbees.

Okay, it wasn't *Carousel*. It was the other kind of musical, the happy-crazy kind, with a lot of ingenuity in the way the score threaded the needle of Shakespeare. What seventies show was older, and newer?

But *Dude*, a follow-up not to *Two Gentlemen* but to MacDermot's *Hair* (1967), was the useless kind of musical, what happens when those lacking in fundamental capability chance into a fluke hit and are consequently given a theatre to play in and a limitless budget. The villain in the case was Gerome Ragni, author of *Dude*'s book and lyrics, though

MacDermot did not distinguish himself, either. Ragni had co-written (with James Rado) *Hair*'s book and lyrics and had played its outstanding hippie, Berger. So Ragni was now the fair-haired boy of the rock musical.

And a rock musical *Dude* absolutely was. Not an everything musical like *Two Gentlemen of Verona* or, for that matter, *Hair*. *Dude* was R&B with piano shavings, Motown group harmony, and a shoo-fly-lazy country band. As well, *Dude* embodied that resenting dismissal of tradition that we have noted in trendy voices of the time. But Pauline Kael merely scorned the musical. *Dude* hated it.

Think, first, of its very title. It's like *Lewd*. Like *Turd*. Think of the poster, a rear view of a long-haired male clad in denim, as if this in itself meant something. Think of the reconstitution of the Broadway Theatre's auditorium into an arena-style "space," with the instrumentalists broken into winds here and strings there and the performers running in from somewhere else with mike wires trailing behind them. This in itself meant something, in a way: the physical trashing of the legitimate theatre. Think of the only veteran pros in the cast, Michael Dunn (who left during previews; congratulations, Miss Logan), and Rae Allen and William Redfield, who played Dude's parents; or were they supposed to be broken-down actors?

It wasn't clear, but then *Dude* was apparently more hallucinated than written, in the hope that some of *Hair*'s good Zen would amplify the images. There was no plot per se, but rather a premise. Like *Cabin in the Sky* (1940), *Dude* proposed a contest between angels of light and darkness for the hero's soul. He, the title character, was to be a kind of twenty-something rover; the show's subtitle was *The Highway Life*. But when the actor playing Dude was fired during previews, the producers brought in an eleven-year-old *and* a grown-up to share the role. This suited the "metaphysical quest" nature of the show, perhaps. More likely, the show was gasping for talent and a kid turned up who had some. (He was Ralph Carter, soon to move on to a lead in *Raisin*, thence to a television series.) Other characters included Mother Earth, Bread, Sissy, Electric Bill, Suzie Moon (an on-the-rise Nell Carter), and World War Too. As with *Hair*, there was a huge tunestack filled with wiseacre titles, such as "Eat It," "I Love My Boo Boo," "Air Male," and "Jesus Hi."

Dude was directed by Rocco Bufano, choreographed by Louis Falco, and physically designed by Eugene Lee, Roger Morgan, and Franne Lee.

Three people collaborating on scenery for a show that had none suggests the amorphous nature of the project, the sheer lack of narrative material for anyone to work with.* Previews had to be suspended during the first week as Tom O'Horgan replaced Bufano and Falco to try to turn *Dude* into *Hair*. After all, it was O'Horgan who turned *Hair* into *Hair* in the first place. But how is one to transform something that never existed except as a fancy in the minds of idiot critics who think they know better than theatre people what theatre is? In the end—from the very start, in fact—*Dude* was something never before attempted, not even in the days of *The Black Crook*: an absolutely unintegrated musical.

Dude closed two weeks after it opened, and five weeks after that came *Via Galactica*. Unfortunately, the earlier show's notoriety proved contagious, and those who skipped the second show assumed that it was another inane attempt to duplicate *Hair*. And little Ralph Carter was in this one, too.

However, *Via Galactica* was not entirely inane and certainly no duplication. "For a long time," the PR handouts read, "there hasn't been a musical that isn't a remake of a remake... but this is it: VIA GALACTICA, road to the stars." Yes, this was the outer-space musical, and one of the first of the so-called pop operas, because MacDermot set virtually every line written by Christopher Gore and Judith Ross. British eminences Peter Hall and John Bury respectively directed and designed it, and unlike *Dude*, *Via Galactica* gave one much to look at: life on earth in the year 2972, a trip by spacecraft to an asteroid ruled by a disembodied head, and a spectacular backdrop made of some 350,000 tennis balls hanging on lines running from the flies down to the stage floor and shimmering against a weird blue light. *Via Galactica* was something of an event, too, in that it put a brand-new auditorium into rotation, the Uris Theatre.

Put simply, the piece told how Raul Julia escapes the insipid conformity of "perfected" life on earth. Julia sails off to the asteroid Ithaca, ruled by that head (Keene Curtis), which flies around on a kind of Mr. *Wizard* science-project doohickey. Curtis' wife (Virginia Vestoff) and Julia mate,

---

* Let no one blame the designers for Ragni's decision to play *Dude* on a dirt floor, which soiled those in the front rows. A coagulating solution only turned the dirt to mud; and all Broadway was laughing. Eventually, the problem was solved—but this is the level of professionalism that one gets when tradition allows itself to be mugged by trendy novelty.

but in the end their offspring descend a huge ladder, beginning a journey back to earth.

I say "put simply," but the show's producers thought the action so tangled that they provided a summary in the program. Wouldn't it have been smarter to clarify the writing of the show itself? In truth, the action wasn't tangled, just screwy. For instance, the relative lack of gravity on Ithaca was suggested by the actors' bounding about on trampolines. After the first minute or two of startled amusement, the public found it monotonous. So was the relentless singing, at least for some. On CBS, critic Leonard Harris voiced what was to become a standard complaint as the book material in musicals began to contract and even disappear. "Galt MacDermot has written some fine melodies," Harris allowed. "But we need some rest between them."

The combined debacles of *Dude* and *Via Galactica* (which closed a week after it opened) all but ended MacDermot's potential as the voice of the New Music. But Andrew Lloyd Webber was just getting started, with the first of the pop operas to be generally referred to as such, *Jesus Christ Superstar* (1971). Here was a resourceful composer paired with a clever lyricist, Tim Rice. So was this to be Broadway's new pop sound? Certainly, the Lloyd Webber shows and those of the French team of Claude-Michel Schönberg and Alain Boublil were, at first, anything but debacles. To twist George S. Kaufman's famous line about satire, pop opera is what closes Saturday night . . . twenty years later.

Or is it "rock opera"? That was the original term, because The Who's *Tommy* had appeared on a two-disc set in 1969, and the band performed it live in its complete form only in opera places, first at the English National Opera's new home in the London Coliseum and then in New York's Metropolitan Opera House. The Who was utterly rock, and their piece was totally opera, even specified as such on the album: "Opera by Pete Townshend."

Some there are that resist the application of this culturally prestigious word to works by musical primitives, with their hooks and riffs and punk etiquette. Opera is educated, not to mention drug-free. But genius needs no diploma: it strikes in crazy venues. And "opera" simply denotes theatre that is not spoken but sung. "Opera" has no qualification clause requiring a music degree or opening-night top hats or Renata Tebaldi. If it's through-sung, it's opera.

For all that, Lloyd Webber belongs to an educated musical family. The classical stuff: cellos and sonata-allegro movements. This is crucial in understanding why the now rather unappreciated *Jesus Christ Superstar* had such impact when it was new. It marked a wedding of the sacred and the profane, and not only in the use of the pop idiom to narrate the last seven days in the life of Christ. No, the lyrics themselves mix genres, blending poetry and slang. The music sends woodwinds pirouetting over bass guitar lines, or slips difficult counts of $\frac{7}{8}$ and $\frac{5}{4}$ into R&B's traditional $\frac{4}{4}$. Simply the line "Jesus is cool" in an *opera* was revolutionary, because the action is drawn so closely from the Bible. *Tommy* had no such effect, because its Savior-like hero never registers as anything but a symbol in a parable. But *Jesus Christ Superstar* uses pop to bring us back to the most influential week in the history of Western Civilization with sweetness and brutality combined with a disturbing brilliance. It is almost as if the music were sacred and the subject profane.

That's partly why the work so outraged some at the time. It substantiates the ineffable, dramatizes belief. It presents Pilate as fair-minded, even more reluctant to order the Crucifixion than in the Gospels. The apostles are opportunistic toads. Judas is ambivalent, knowledgeable, even *sensible*! Remember when "Judas Priest" was the meanest curse available? Lloyd Webber and Rice give us a villain who seems to comprehend— fighting it all the way—that he is Christianity's enabler *because* he is Christ's betrayer. Note also that while Jesus has the title role, Judas has the Point of View, taking the first vocal, "Heaven on Their Minds," and the last, "Superstar."

The whole saga began with Murray Head's 45 single of the latter, backed by the instrumental number "John 19:41" (which treats the Burial "in a new sepulchre, wherein was never man yet laid"). This led to a full-scale double album, featuring Head's Judas, Ian Gillan's Jesus, and Yvonne Elliman's Mary Magdalene, accompanied by rock sextet, Moog synthesizer, church organ, and a symphony orchestra big enough for Mahler. Tremendous sales in America especially prompted all sorts of groups to rush the piece into halls and theatres, setting off an avalanche of lawsuits from Robert Stigwood, the putative producer of the work's authorized staging. Even nuns got sued. Stigwood's plan was to launch the live *Superstar* with a concert tour, Elliman performing with Jeff Fenholt (who would again sing Jesus on Broadway) and Carl Anderson (who would play

Judas in the 1973 film). Now came the tricky part, finding the director with the right concept for *Superstar* in the theatre.

With no dialogue, the narrative is presented in gobs of music, giving it the abstract quality of ballet. Then, too, what should ancient Israel look like? How much acting can rock singers be asked to do? How does one stage the Crucifixion?

Hal Prince was interested, but his letter to Lloyd Webber didn't reach him in time. Meanwhile, Stigwood made, at first, an arresting choice: Frank Corsaro, a veteran theatre director leaning to the Actors Studio side of things but also an experienced naturalizer of the music theatre's least naturalistic form in his work at the New York City Opera. In Corsaro's *Rigoletto*, one truly believed that the baritone was the soprano's father; his helpless disgust after the tenor ravished her was worthy of O'Neill.

It was Corsaro's intention to stage the piece somewhat simply, using projections and also television monitors, emphasizing the show-biz stardom hysteria that runs through Rice's contemporary spin. It may be that Stigwood became concerned that Corsaro would bring out the tale's gruesome beauty at the expense of its pageantry, for when Corsaro suffered an automobile accident, Stigwood quickly replaced him with our old friend Tom O'Horgan, giving *Superstar* a link with *Hair* and *Dude* in the cycle of New Music on Broadway.

The cast that opened the show was Fenholt and Elliman, with Ben Vereen's Judas and the Pilate of Barbra Streisand's former boy friend Barry Dennen. Vereen in particular won réclame for his baffled, raging portrayal, but it almost didn't matter who played the parts because of O'Horgan's overwhelming production. With his designers, Robin Wagner and Randy Barcelo, O'Horgan brought forth an opening in which the "curtain" did not rise but inclined backward to become the stage floor as three choristers clambered about on top; an entrance for Jesus out of a great grooved calyx; a construction of dinosaur bones lowered from above for the Jewish clerics to spy and conspire on in their white robes and oversized crazyhats; the materialization of Herod (Paul Ainsley) out of a dragon's head in full drag, from platform heels to pearl-string earrings; and the most famous moment of all, when Fenholt rose from the stage floor on a hidden elevator as his twenty-thousand-dollar golden robe expanded till it filled the Mark Hellinger's playing area.

At that, O'Horgan's mad shivaree almost didn't matter, either, for *Superstar* had become such an Event that attending it was more important than seeing it. The atmosphere on West Fifty-first Street became Warholian, not only in the word "superstar" and the kooky costumes of some of the audience, but in the "everything is nothing but nothing is everything" attitude that the show seemed to strike. Seemed to, I repeat: if one didn't listen to what it said. And most people weren't listening: they just wanted to get into the party. When the first preview was canceled at the last minute, there was, if not a riot, a very stubborn ticket holders' resistance. Opening night knew a crass hoopla on a scale beyond recollection. And while the reviews were very mixed, the hype was all raves.

What was this show? The critics cited Radio City spectaculars, Cecil B. DeMille, *Fellini Satyricon*, Luna Park, the Folies Bergère. What was this music? Prokofyef, *Carmina Burana*, Grieg's Piano Concerto, Ligeti, Hindu ragas, Honegger, and Copland were among the sources subject to detection. Someone heard *Bye, Bye, Birdie* in it, others silent-movie piano scoring, synthesizer pinball toccata, Erich Wolfgang Korngold Warner Bros. main title. Was this because *Superstar* was an amalgam of old sounds, or because of the pretentious need to defame anything new by "unmasking" it?

What few if any noticed, at least in 1971, was Lloyd Webber's system of Leitmotiven. His later works would use recurring themes sometimes indiscriminately; here, there is a program. Also, the scenes are laid out in vigorous structures that instantly reveal who the principals are and how they react to one another, a quality that marks all the great operas from Wagner to Britten.

A scene called "The Last Supper" typifies the work's discernment, giving the apostles merry-men lines over a blithe piccolo. These aren't fanatics. They aren't even advocates. They're idiot teens looking forward to fame. "Look at your blank faces," Jesus cries, He as intense as they are banal. He has a screaming match with Judas, yet the followers keep checking in with their Howard Johnson's chorus.

Why *this* music? This rock with a symphony orchestra (scored by Lloyd Webber himself) that bedevils and worships the Passion? Why this retelling, with its odd omissions and emphases? Barabbas, freed in Jesus' place despite being not only a criminal but a subversive, never appears. Pilate, who turns up quite late in each of the Gospels, is given a solo in

Act One adapted from his wife's dream in Matthew 27:19: "Have thou nothing to do with that just man." "Pilate's Dream," to a string choir over acoustic guitar and eerily incorporating music already associated with Jesus, establishes the provincial governor as unwilling to kill. But he must, because He wills it.

And why this show at this time? Did it fulfill demands for a pop sound on Broadway?

In fact, those who were calling for New Music failed to respond to the show. What did they think a pop musical of the early 1970s would be like if not this? Rice's lyrics lack sophistication, but he's smart. He knows that Mary admires Jesus, Judas mistrusts Him, and Pilate wishes he were in Indianapolis. Rice also knows enough to keep Jesus enigmatic, a dramatic figure but also hieratic and sacrificial. How else to characterize the Son of God?

The popularity of single numbers in the show, such as Mary's "I Don't Know How To Love Him" and "Everything's Alright," obscures the superior quality of the ensembles, when music and lyrics must spur themselves to keep up with the fast-moving story. The popular solos have an easy appeal, but they don't really go anywhere. "Herod's Song" always rouses the audience, as a set piece in which a grotesque humiliates himself with androgynous caperings. Of course, O'Horgan's production was replete with androgynous caperings; but the number sticks out stylistically as a vaudeville strut. It doesn't match the rest of the music. (It was composed earlier, for an unfinished show about the Lionheart called *Come Back, Richard, Your Country Needs You*.)

No, the best of the score comes after Herod's one scene, after Mary's healing "Could We Start Again Please" (the sole piece written separately for the staging) and "Judas's Death," almost a *Gypsy*-style "Judas's Turn," recapitulating themes to sum up the show's argument. The best begins with the climax of the central relationship, that of Jesus and Judas. In the Gospels, Judas is dismissed virtually in passing. (Matthew 27:5: "And he cast down the pieces of silver in the temple, and departed, and went and hanged himself.") Here, he is given his own Passion, screaming, "You have murdered me!" to God: but which One?

Then comes the climax of the physical action, the trial leading up to the Deicide. It is as well the climax of the music, though anticipated in the overture: for here Lloyd Webber and Rice put aside Top 40 for a driving terror of a scene, as Pilate desperately tries to save Jesus and the mob furiously demands His execution. But is He not the King of the Jews? "We have no king but Caesar!" the chorus insists, in a line straight out of John 19:15. Rice tops it with an invention of his own, Pilate's frantic "You Jews produce messiahs by the sackful!," a reference to the proliferation of heresies and schisms in the Mediterranean world, when life consisted exclusively of subsistence and religion.

The churning music is a violence itself, though we are not spared the sight of Jesus being whipped. O'Horgan had Pilate so outraged by Jesus' refusal to defend Himself that he fiercely counted out the thirty-nine blows through an ugly mask with a great protruding tongue. Then, in a turnabout into an appalling humility, he tenderly cradled the fallen Jesus in his arms.

What followed can only be called blasphemy: a resurrection of *Judas*, with a backing girls' trio, on a butterfly float to sing that "Superstar" single. This was followed by the elevation of Jesus in the giant robe (and the crown of thorns), a Resurrection before Its time, for *this* was followed by the Crucifixion, on a gold triangle against a blackened stage area. O'Horgan's finale was clumsy: the crowd ran onstage in an uproar and gleefully hurtled down through a trapdoor as the orchestra played the B side of the single and the lights slowly faded.

After a year of sold-out-or-nearly houses, *Jesus Christ Superstar* began to run down. It never reached a second anniversary, though London's simpler and more honest staging, by Jim Sharman, saw the work to an eight-year run at the Palace Theatre, at the time a West End record for a musical. New York revivals, in yet other stagings, have failed. Europe still likes it, but no one has attempted to bring back O'Horgan's frivolous Golgotha.

There was yet another putative redemption of the traditional Broadway sound, the classical solution, merged with avant-garde theatre. In some ways, this was comparable to what Kurt Weill was doing with Bertolt Brecht in Berlin during the final years of the Weimar Republic: composer Stanley Silverman and writer, director, and designer Richard Foreman's *Elephant Steps* (1970), *Doctor Selavy's Magic Theatre* (1972), and *Hotel For Criminals* (1974). These are not musicals per se, but "theatre pieces," as much of Weill-Brecht was. And note that Silverman and Foreman collaborated on a production of *The Threepenny Opera*, as we'll see in a few chapters.

To appreciate Silverman-Foreman, one should know that there were great stirrings in the classical world at about this time, just like the one on Broadway. It's bad enough if the American theatre "needs" New Music. What if Western music as a whole needs New Music? True, for about two generations, symphony, opera, and such had lost the ability to interest the bulk of the public in new work, as much of this was twelve-tone composition. By 1970, twelve-tone was half a century old, but audiences still hadn't accepted it. Twelve-tone isn't the classical world's rock. Twelve-tone is difficult; rock is easy. (Rock also has a place in the world, just maybe not on Broadway.) But now that twelve-tone had produced all its masterpieces decades earlier, its place seemed to be in academia or at emperor's-new-clothes concerts, where fashion outlawed honesty.

This belief in the avant-garde *because* it is avant-garde rather than because it has merit is what I call "revolutionism." And, indeed, there was a leftist political edge to all this. The composer and conductor Pierre Boulez made this clear in an interview with the German magazine *Der Spiegel*, reprinted in translation in other Western countries. Was Boulez being facetious when he advocated blowing up opera houses, when he fancied writing an opera to a libretto by Jean Genet, when he suggested that artists had more freedom in Castro's Cuba than in Europe?* Not surprisingly, Boulez was another of those twelve-tone composers nobody wants to hear. Even as a conductor, he is not universally admired.

Now, why have we to ponder all this? Because the 1970s is when the musical starts to figure in highbrow considerations. It will become less easy for the intellectual to scorn that part of Broadway—or, at least, he'll have to scorn it more discerningly.

Did he take to Silverman-Foreman? Their works claimed good venue credentials, mounted not on The Street but at the Lenox Arts Center in Massachusetts, near Tanglewood, and then moved to non-Broadway places. *Elephant Steps*, billed as "a fearful radio show," is a loony opera about loons, first performed in 1968 and then at Hunter College in 1970. *Doctor Selavy's Magic Theatre*, with lyrics by Tom Hendry, and also about loons (but this time there's therapy), was seen at the Mercer-O'Casey Theatre. *Hotel For Criminals*, for which Foreman once again served as librettist, was performed in a "space" in Westbeth.

---

* The Swiss police took Boulez literally. Though the interview appeared in 1967, somewhere, somehow, it was sitting in an active file, and after the attacks on America on September 11, 2001, Boulez was arrested in Bern. Unfortunately, he was later released.

Revolutionists prefer off-Broadway to Broadway and spaces to proscenium stages—but isn't Silverman-Foreman too genially avant-garde to satisfy the radical? There is too much art here, and no politics. *Hotel For Criminals* even dares elitism in its celebration of Louis Feuillade's silent-movie serials of the underworld, a corner of film history known to few. At least the heroes are murderers and thieves, exactly what Pierre Boulez looks for in an opera librettist. Here are Fantomas, Irma Vep, Judex, and others right off Feuillade's screen in the mysterious Paris of secret doors and false panels, where villains drive silver sedans and promenade in slow-motion conga lines. Feuillade was phenomenally popular and subversive; *Hotel For Criminals* is neither. Worse, it is entertaining, as Silverman browses through café-conc' and Kurt Weill for atmosphere.

This is revolution? With so much of the old blended into the new? And yet isn't that how all art forms evolve? Even cinema, the twentieth century's foremost new art, spent its first few years largely imitating the stage. And lo, our favorite sansculotte, Pierre Boulez, not only enjoyed *Dr. Selavy* but blessed the production with a blurb to flourish in the ads: "A most enjoyable evening of fun and craziness."

Silverman is elegant in pastiche. *Dr. Selavy* (note the pun on "C'est la vie") contains whole resuscitations of the thirties dance number, with tap breaks, in "Swinging at the Stock Exchange"; of opera in varying styles, in which electric guitar meets the baroque, all in "Three Menu Songs"; of radio-crooner cheer-up ditty, with skating-rink organ and girl-group doo-wah, in "Every New Beginning"; of rock-and-roll $\frac{6}{8}$ shuffle in "He Lived By His Wits"; even of the punctuational woodblocks of Kabuki theatre.

Silverman is diverse in pastiche. *Elephant Steps* seems to be made almost entirely of the noises of modern opera and the sights of modern theatre, with its atonal expressionism and non sequitur libretto, its Rock Singer and Ragtime Lady characters, its stage directions such as "Max and his henchman, Otto, lure Hartman to a radio station where they hope to force him to make damaging statements about Reinhardt, who is, perhaps, a mysterious magician."

There is a problem here. A little pastiche is good musical-comedy thinking; the practice goes back at least as far as Offenbach. Some works absolutely demand it. When George S. Kaufman and Marc Connelly's *Beggar on Horseback* was revived at Lincoln Center in 1970, Silverman (with lyricist John Lahr) constructed an elaborate revival of twenties show biz for the play's dream sequence. It was not only entertaining, but correct.

However, a load of pastiche, spread throughout a work, puts one's show in a special category. It works for *Chicago* because *Chicago* is a satire that spoofs its own characters. It works for *On the Twentieth Century* because its cartoon operetta helps us relate to the larger-than-life subject matter, with its Svengali director, clown soprano, and camp-ups of bygone theatre forms.

Actually, the Silverman-Foreman works are already in a special category, because they correspond to no living genre. *Chicago* is recognizable fare: a big dirty funny Fosse show. But *Dr. Selavy* is . . . what? A madhouse. Every Fosse musical is a Fosse musical. Every Richard Foreman piece is something new.

In a few cases, the musical stayed Broadway by adopting its own version of pop. In other words, by not turning into rock musical, rock opera, or theatre piece. *Georgy* (1970) is an example, albeit a 4-performance disaster that nobody liked. Based on the English film *Georgy Girl*, with a book by Tom Mankiewicz and a score by George Fischoff and Carole Bayer (who later added on Sager), *Georgy* might have made it with stronger ingredients.

The cast, for instance. The movie offered Lynn Redgrave as the ugly-duckling heroine, Charlotte Rampling as her solipsistic roommate, Alan Bates as the boy-friend figure, and James Mason as the older man who cares for Georgy. It's a tight quartet of major people. The musical's roommate, boy friend, and older man were the capable Melissa Hart, John Castle, and Stephen Elliott—not imposing enough—and Georgy was Dilys Watling, too pretty and not imposing at all. This role needs a breakout début, the sort that finds the actress playing a bit of "who, me?" wonder as they cheer her curtain call. It may seem paradoxical to demand dazzle from a character without glamour, but many musicals are about the triumph of riffraff—*Flora, the Red Menace* and *Funny Girl*, to name two *Georgy*s of the 1960s.

Georgy's score, too, lacked interest. Mainly character numbers—the chorus is simply extraneous fill—the songs work best for the two women, quite different in their natures:

GEORGY: (with her usual friendliness) Hullo, Meredith. Where've you been?
MEREDITH: (with her usual self-satisfaction) Out shoplifting.

The Heroine's Wanting Song, "Make It Happen Now," is actually swinging rather than wistful; and Meredith's establishing number, "Just For the Ride," enjoyed orchestrator Eddie Sauter's electric keyboards and guitar, squealing brass, and rock drumming. It jumped into a dance section like a whirling dervish's bossa nova.

It's all very contempo—as one might expect of the musical version of a film released just four years before. Still, three of the songs are traditional fare—the tender title number (for Elliott), nicely scored for just keyboard and voice; "Half of Me," the typical Heroine's Second-Act Quandary Song; and the score's highlight, "Sweet Memory," one of those irresistible tunes reiterated in ever higher keys, a slow strut building to the chorus' *sell-it!* climax, then fading out on one solo voice.

The underpowered casting and so-so score made *Georgy* not a bad show, simply a lackluster one. Another title with a pop sound shows us exactly why *Georgy* failed: *Purlie*'s spirited cast and *Purlie*'s high-energy score.

An adaptation of Ossie Davis' 1961 comedy *Purlie Victorious*, *Purlie* (1970) was in fact an unnecessary musical: because there was no adaptation. Philip Rose produced both works. Apparently believing that the original play deserved a run longer than its 261 performances, he put on what was in effect a revival of the play with the score of a musical.

The story—about a southern black preacher who defeats a white racist landlord known as Ol' Cap'n—was not opened up in the slightest. The *Purlie* book, by Davis, Rose, and lyricist Peter Udell, not only does not add any roles but omits two. Rose even retained the original play's set and costume designers, as if protecting its look along with its text.

But he did allow Udell and his composer, Gary Geld, to write a vibrant and role-specific score, for a big singing-dancing chorus as well as for the principals. Admittedly, the chorus is there simply for atmosphere—in the opening and closing frame of a joyous funeral (Ol' Cap'n dies) called "Walk Him Up the Stairs"; in an ironic salute to Ol' Cap'n, "Great White Father"; in the usual second-act opener, "First Thing Monday Mornin'"; and in the happy-ending celebration, "The World Is Comin' To a Start."

But the character numbers have point and style: one after another, these people really land. Purlie (Cleavon Little) has the jaunty but determined "New Fangled Preacher Man." His love interest, Lutiebelle (Melba Moore), takes the adoring title song, very unlike the production-number title songs of the 1960s in that it is written from her intimate perspective and for her alone to sing. Later, she got the driving, soaring "I Got Love," which propelled Moore to stardom and a Tony and reminds us once more exactly what *Georgy* didn't have.

The comedy spots, too, fit perfectly. Purlie's Uncle-Tomming Uncle Gitlow (Sherman Hemsley) offers his credo in "Skinnin' a Cat," and Geld and Udell even found something for Ol' Cap'n (John Heffernan) in his Darwinian rationale for exploiting his black employees, "Big Fish, Little Fish." Best of all is a running gag: Ol' Cap'n's nice-guy liberal son (C. David Colson) is eternally trying out his own socially conscious ditties on Idella, the cook (Helen Martin, another holdover from *Purlie Victorious*, though in a different role than in 1961). The songs are hideous to a fault, one might say. Yet each time Colson offers to sing one, Martin patiently says, "All-righty," as the audience braces itself. "That ain't it, honey," she tells him after it's over. The joke climaxes when the son joins the blacks in defying his father, whereupon Ol' Cap'n drops dead of shock—standing up. This is what sets off Charlie's "The World Is Comin' To a Start," as Idella cries, "That's it, Charlie, that's it!"

Purlie's pop sound works well because the numbers were not inserted into the story but rather discovered there. It sings so naturally that one wonders why it wasn't a musical in the first place. One never felt that about *Georgy*; and *Dude*'s pop seemed to draw its energy not from the story but from itself.

Then, too, for all *Purlie*'s racial battle cry—and this is deeply felt throughout the script—it really is a universal story about the oppressed taking control. Much of the fun is just fun:

OL' CAP'N: You, got anything to do with what my boy's been thinking lately?
IDELLA: I didn't know he had been thinking lately.

Some of it has a political edge:

OL' CAP'N: Just this morning, the boys was telling me, this son of mine was performin' . . . all kinds revolutionary songs 'bout integration of Negras—*Negroes* he called 'em. Four years of college and he still can't say the word right.

Nevertheless, all of it belongs to that musical-comedy tradition that expects the good guys to triumph on stage if not in life. In fact, it's because the good guys don't win out in life that they have to on stage.

Purlie, which seemed so effortlessly entertaining, was something unusual: an old-fashioned structure of show with New Music and a "relevant" outlook. At 688 performances, it was one of those "hits" that lost a bit of money because of having to move halfway through its run. It went out of the red, however, on the national tour, headed by Robert Guillaume and Patti Jo (who had succeeded Melba Moore on Broadway). The tour dropped in on Broadway for a two-week New Year's bash at the end of 1972, and we'll no doubt be hearing from it again.

All the same, *Purlie*'s use of pop did not alter the belief of theatre people in traditional theatre music. *Purlie* could contribute to the history, not change it. It was Stephen Sondheim who changed it, in *Company* (1970).

Some breakaway shows have been all but unappreciated when new. One thinks of *Porgy and Bess* and *Candide*; and *Allegro*, *Love Life*, and *The Golden Apple* remain unappreciated, though the last tantalizes the aficionado. But no show was as misunderstood as *Company*.

This is odd, because its theme is very clearly stated: the absolute intimacy of marriage is very difficult but very necessary. The piece takes place in modern-day middle-class Manhattan. Designer Boris Aronson stylized this in a unit set: a steel-and-Plexiglas jungle gym of open cubes, connected by elevators and ladders, with a big playing area downstage and projections upstage.

The protagonist is Robert, a thirty-five-year-old bachelor, and the ensemble comprises five married couples and Robert's three girl friends. The book, by George Furth, examines Robert's social dates with each of the couples and romantic dates with the women, framed at each end of the two acts by Robert's surprise birthday party.

The score is made of character and situation songs that support the theme, developing Robert to a crucial moment of self-discovery. The actors, in 1970, are Broadway veterans or promising newcomers, with a real brand name in Elaine Stritch and a Novelty Star in the Robert, Dean Jones, a leading man in Hollywood who had done Broadway but never a musical.

And the staging team was Hal Prince and Michael Bennett. It doesn't sound like a revolution, does it? *Company* isn't the first Broadway pop opera, like *Porgy and Bess*. It isn't from a presumably unadaptable source, like *Candide*. It isn't a parable, like *Allegro*, or a vaudeville, like *Love Life*, or a revival of nineteenth-century burlesque in "ballet ballad" format, like *The Golden Apple*.

Let us try to see why *Company* is as difficult as it is easy. First, the theme of Robert's ambivalence about—as they now term it—Commitment confused people. Even the unit set confused people, though each of the five couples had its own "cube" in the construction, as an abstraction of the couple's living quarters or simply of their place in Robert's life. But what *was* that set? An apartment building? Are these people all neighbors? "Everywhere I walk in New York," Aronson later said, "I see my set." It's the city itself, exciting and hard, like love.

The subject of *Company* is marriage, and the subject of marriage is romance; but this is not a romantic show. Does Robert really like these friends of his? Does he even know them?—because he often seems taken aback, as if by strangers. Asked how many Puerto Ricans and blacks he knows, Robert answers, "I seem to meet people only like myself." But they're not like him: they're married. And how did he meet the older Larry and Joanne, for instance? What do *Company*'s people, Robert included, do for a living? Why don't we see any kids?—because at least David and Jenny mention having some.

And what about the sheer lingo of *Company*, the rat-a-tat New York not-always-witty-but-if-nothing-else-fast repartee that we hear? To pick but one example: in a bar, Larry excuses himself, leaving Joanne and Robert alone at the table. Joanne, drink in one hand and smoke in the other, freezes Robert in her headlights. So he goes into a rambling tirade that is part social improvisation and part nervous breakdown. And when he finishes, she says:

JOANNE: When are we going to make it?

which is the most unnerving moment in the whole decade, and, besides, does she mean it or is she making a point? Why do we not know for certain what people are really thinking in this show? Because that's also true in life, or because George Furth is arch?

Worse: why is Robert apparently the most forthcoming of all the characters in his speech while always holding *something* back? As one of the company tells him, "You always make me feel like I got the next line." We know Harold Hill, King Arthur, Amalia Balash. Heck, we even know Panama Hattie. We don't know Robert.

His friends think they do. Yet they, too, are a problem for some of the show's public—naggy Sarah and competitive Harry, for instance. Or doting Paul and unwilling Amy, who in her bridal dress sings the famous motorized patter section in "Getting Married Today," refusing to go through with it. Robert may be closer to her than to the others; in a cut number, "Multitudes of Amys," he revels in an obsession with her and ends determined to marry her. But the line "Seems there are more of her every day" evades commitment by expanding it beyond reach.

Company constantly veers from the affirmative to the elusive. Like some people we know, it's in denial. The score reflects this, moving from the celebratory title number through the ironic "The Little Things You Do Together" and "Side by Side by Side" (which even has an ironic staging when each male in turn indicates his partner and Robert is forced to indicate no one) to the celebratory "Being Alive." But note that the first celebration is of threesome *social* company, the latter of one-on-one *romantic* company.

Still, like the actors running all over the set, the score doesn't just collaborate with the narrative. It horns in on it. "The Little Things You Do Together" isn't a song as much as a bunch of commentaries interlaced into Robert's scene with Sarah and Harry. These three go into freeze-frame while Elaine Stritch looks down on them from above with the usual Stritchian derision: as if she were a theatregoer tonight, too. Comparably, the acerbic sophisticate Marta punctuates the park scenes between Robert and each of his girls. April is first, Kathy second, and when it's Marta's turn she simply finishes off the song and goes right into dialogue with Robert:

MARTA: You wanna know why I came to New York? I came because New York is the center of the world and that's where I want to be. You know what the pulse of this city is?
ROBERT: A busy signal?
MARTA: The pulse of this city, kiddo, is *me*.

It's the edgy, self-absorbed, but also creative city, completely unlike the edgy, self-absorbed, but also creative city that we learned in *On the Town*. The two scores are also completely different. The older show really contains *two* scores, one serving Jerome Robbins classical dance theatre and the other serving George Abbott musical comedy. *Company*'s music is so taut that its darkness glitters. The harmony seems to bite at the melody yet the melody prevails, till a line such as "Everybody dies!" comes off as a triumph. Here is that rarest of things in the musical: an *accurate* score. It sounds like the people in the show, just as the choreography looked like the people in the show. Only Donna McKechnie was a genuine dancer; Michael Bennett had everyone else dance the way the characters would if they had been forced onstage one night to perform in a musical. This one.

The cast as a whole was an odd bunch, an ensemble of Stritch, McKechnie, Barbara Barrie, Charles Kimbrough, and some other perhaps not entirely brilliant performers, all carrying the show together. But, remember, this is the difficult *Company*, so the Novelty Star needs to be replaced two weeks after the opening.

Apparently, Dean Jones was simply uncomfortable playing Robert, and it was announced that he was too ill to continue. But in fact he was superb at laying out Robert's many paradoxes. Jones' replacement, Larry Kert, poured out the voice but made no attempt to play anything but his own amusement at being the center of a crazy concept musical.* One wonders if *Company* would have outrun its 690 performances if Jones had stayed with it. But then—the difficult *Company* again—Jones' richly troubled Robert only gave the public more to worry about.

I think *Company*'s public was worried because this was the first more or less naturalistic musical. Beyond the visual stylizations, the authors capture something like real life in New York. We don't hear about jobs or kids because the action is cut to its essentials. There is no exposition, no backstory, no data. The piece is made entirely of how people express themselves and how they feel, so the surface matter so common to other musicals keeps breaking apart like thin ice in this one. There's danger below: the truth.

This is no doubt why the original final number, "Happily Ever After," was cut in Boston, to be replaced by "Being Alive." They are two versions of the show's theme: intimacy is difficult but necessary. However,

---

* This is probably the best place for the Larry Kert Birthday Party Story, which takes us back to when *Company* was still playing and may not be true. Kert was about to blow out the cake candles when someone urged him to make a wish. With a smirk, Kert said, "Who do you have to fuck to get out of *Company*?" Sondheim replied, "The same people you fucked to get in it. Happy birthday, Larry." And left.

"Happily Ever After" is half-empty and "Being Alive" is half-full. They both spell out what Robert most fears doing: giving himself away. But "Happily Ever After" is brutal. If this is the truth, Robert is still resisting and the show lacks conclusion. "Being Alive," expansive and decisive, has traction. Robert is being *drawn* to the end of his journey.

In fact, "Being Alive" is one of the show's few moments in which Prince, Bennett, and Aronson stop showing us so that Sondheim can tell us. It's "I Get a Kick Out of You," "Soliloquy," "Something's Coming": the singer alone with the audience. The rest of the show is all Presentation. When Robert asks Harry, "You ever sorry you got married?," Robert is no longer physically present in Harry's apartment. The *show* asks the question. When Stritch got to "The Ladies Who Lunch," a spotlight took her out of the action, and she addressed the cue line, "I'd like to propose a toast," to the audience. Or consider the four surprise-party scenes, each written in a different style, to bring out various aspects of the company that Robert keeps.

Let me gloss this oddest of classics with two personal stories. The first time I saw *Company* was during previews, which are generally attended by theatre enthusiasts, who don't wait for critics to tell them which titles to collect. They are curious. This show and its audience were getting along quite well till the three girl friends joined forces at a mike, as if they were a vocal group, for "You Could Drive a Person Crazy." Suddenly, at this combination of spoof and point number with such careful cultural observations as the colloquial grammar error in "Which it only makes a person gladly," the audience started leaning forward to catch the wordplay in real time. We wanted to see the music, come closer to the delight. It was contagious; we were grinning at one another. It was something that theatregoing too seldom delivers: a discovery.

Not all audiences are curious. My second tale takes us out to Westbury Music Fair, for *Company* in the round with a cast headed by George Maharis and Vivian Blaine. By the time Blaine got to "The Ladies Who Lunch," the public was departing in great numbers. They had had enough of being mystified, and of suspecting that if they *did* get the show, they would resent what it was saying. Mass walkouts in arena theatre are very demoralizing to the actors, because they can't avert their eyes: there's rejection no matter which way they turn. Perhaps Westbury Music Fair is the wrong venue for the truth.

There's also the gay thing. Because a thirty-five-year-old straight bachelor is rare, because some of the creative team were perceived to be gay, and because the sheer flash and dazzle of the staging is something not generally associated with heterosexual art, some assume that Robert is simply closeted. (Less well known, but also pertinent, is the fact that Robert was originally to have been played by Anthony Perkins, the very model of a closeted gay man even after he took a wife and sired children; and Larry Kert, for that matter, was the least closeted man in New York.)

However. Robert does and says nothing that a gay man would. We see him seducing a stewardess; a gay man wouldn't. At one point, all the chorus men say they hate opera, so Robert apparently doesn't even know anybody gay. Revivals in New York and London in the 1990s shaded a bit of gay into one scene; but this seems mere social renovation, comparable to the London staging's casting Robert as black.

Here's a third personal story. A successful producer and his actress wife liked to give theatrical parties in which performers would improvisationally entertain at the grand piano. Dorothy Loudon would recall her cabaret act; Russell Nype, back from a tour of *The Music Man*, would create a Harold Hill medley; Dolores Gray would sing "Here's That Rainy Day"—"in," as she barked at the pianist, "A Flat." I was at one such party when the guests included an operetta duo. The soprano was nice and the baritone testy, perhaps because he had made it to Broadway as a leading man but once, at that in a bomb.

The party occurred just after *A Little Night Music* had opened; the sheet music was on the piano. Trying to interest the baritone in a duet, the hostess held up "You Must Meet My Wife."

"I don't know it," said the testy baritone, testily.

"Oh, let's wing our way through it," she suggested. We're all troupers here.

"I *don't like* that man's music," said the baritone, now openly hostile. "He writes for *himself* and his *friends!*"

What did he mean by that? Was "friends" a euphemism? The New Music is gay? Were there equivalent complaints back in the 1920s, when the New Music was Jewish? Sondheim spent the 1970s producing five consecutive masterpieces—*Company, Follies, A Little Night Music, Pacific Overtures,* and *Sweeney Todd*—yet was, at that time but not after, the most contested major talent in the musical's history. Those five shows are rivaled only by Rodgers and Hammerstein's first five stage works—*Oklahoma!*, *Carousel*, *Allegro*, *South Pacific*, and *The King and I*. But Rodgers and Hammerstein were accepted masters at that time and after—taken, even, for granted. Sondheim was *argued*.

What happened, really, is that the New Music was too dense and restless for some listeners. Not everyone gets "difficult" music; some can't hear music at all. One critic called Sondheim's music "slick, clever, and eclectic." "Slick" is just wrong, "clever" is condescending, and to call the most original of composers "eclectic" is simply deaf.

The safety line adopted by doubters was that Sondheim's lyrics are fine but his music lacks melody. A problem arose: smart people were getting this music, making the doubters look inadequate. Sometime in the 1970s, the slower listeners caught up with Sondheim, mainly through repeated hearings; by then, to denigrate the music was cultural suicide.

By now, Sondheim is master without equal. Not if one reads his reviews, no: but in general. The retrospectives, the catalogue's eminence in cabaret and recordings, the references throughout the culture. Sally Field can tell moviegoers who she and Burt Reynolds are in *Smokey and the Bandit* just by expressing admiration for Sondheim and getting no response from Reynolds: she's got culture, and he's white trash. Performer Rick Crom does an act at the piano made of the *Oklahoma!* score in the Sondheim version—the style is that special, that verifiable. A young meister of the next generation, Jonathan Larson, invents a Sunday-brunch replica of the near-title number from *Sunday in the Park With George* in *Tick, tick . . . Boom!* with the expectation that all in the house will get it. And Alan Chapman writes "Everybody Wants To Be Sondheim (but me)," a captivating spoof whose music is meant to sound pre-Sondheim but is in fact just as liberated by the little night music as everything else. Chapman wants to write for "the ghost of Ethel Merman"; and, yes, Cole Porter is wonderful. But Cole Porter is over. This is the Age of Sondheim.

Interestingly, only once before has one musician so dominated the Broadway scene: Victor Herbert, in the Second Age. The great Third Age barons such as Kern, Rodgers, and Gershwin knew no king; there was too much talent floating around for any one man to take top title.

However, in Herbert's day, the musical had the status of the theatre's poor relation. There was simply no notion of the master score that needs to be heard multiple times, whenever possible onstage in full-scale performance. Illustratively, the two biggest hit musicals of the first decade of the twentieth century were *The Merry Widow*—a European import, as all the classy titles were—and, home-grown, *The Wizard of Oz*, a book show with a revue's miscellany of numbers by a coven of writers. In the Third Age, however, America's greatest songs came from Broadway: "Ol' Man River," "Night and Day," "Falling in Love With Love." When Victor Herbert arrived in America, there were no great songs, only popular ones. Herbert invented the Great American Song.

He was ubiquitous in the culture, in summer band concerts in the local park, in medleys sawed out by restaurant chamber groups, on recordings, in specially commissioned accompaniments to silent movies, on ceremonial occasions (an Inauguration March, for example, in President William McKinley's honor in 1897), and of course at the family piano.

Above all, Herbert was Classical. A cellist and conductor (of the Pittsburgh Symphony), he married an opera singer and composed one work for each of New York's two major opera companies. But Herbert was Popular as well, composing for Paul Whiteman's band. By bridging the genre gap, Herbert created the idea that all music was equal—or, at least, that pop had an education, too.

So he gave the musical respectability. And—unlike all his coevals cited earlier, in the Conclusion—Herbert was prolific, contributing forty-three complete scores. He was famous for making his own orchestrations; this is the least of it. What he did was to separate for potential development or retirement the constituent forms of the musical—fairy-tale extravaganza (in *Babes in Toyland* and *Little Nemo*), which died out; "comic opera" (i.e., operetta, in *Naughty Marietta*, *Mlle. Modiste*, *Sweethearts*), which turned into *Rose-Marie* and, later, sort of, *Camelot*; musical comedy (*The Red Mill*, *Miss Dolly Dollars*), which, as *Annie Get Your Gun* or *The Pajama Game*, is not as emancipated from Herbert's day as one might think; the revue (*The Century Girl*, *Miss 1917*); and burlesque (*The Magic Knight*, a spoof of *Lohengrin*) another dead form. Herbert even tried out a form that hardly existed at the time, the intimate "play with songs," in *The Only Girl*, the smash hit of 1914 that led directly to the Princess Theatre shows of Jerome Kern, P. G. Wodehouse, and Guy Bolton.

Why all this about Victor Herbert when discussing Stephen Sondheim? Because Herbert is the creator who gave the musical a reason for being and a need to perfect itself: a destiny. But Sondheim wasn't that destiny. Sondheim's revolution changed the musical's destiny, which was still on Herbert's track as late as the 1950s as a kind of balancing act—so much song, dance, comedy, sometimes more soprano, sometimes less star clown, and always an unfinished melody of some kind. This is *Naughty Marietta*: less star clown. It is also *The Pajama Game*: more star clown, and the melody is the seven-and-a-half-cent pay raise.

Obviously, that isn't *Company*. Such earlier Sondheim shows as *West Side Story* and *Gypsy* anticipate the purging of Victor Herbert, but it is *Company* that achieves it. *Company* purges the musical, period. Before *Company*, one could speak of "musical comedy" and the "musical play." No more. Herbert defined the forms by segregating them. Sondheim defines through integration.

Or are we putting too much emphasis on the musical's origins? If one goes back too far into history, doesn't one get nothing but silly and inchoate? Herbert always seemed the bandmaster, as at the start of the overture, when the drum would spank out the rhythm as the woodwinds danced and the brass went marching. And those chatty syncopations! The going-native ragtime numbers! Okay, Herbert wrote wonderful ragtime. But nobody wanted him to.

Origins matter. Offenbach is the inventor and Herbert the alchemist: and next comes Sondheim, throwing out the soprano and the star clown and even the unfinished melody. True, Robert learns to sing it (in "Being Alive"). But *Company* abounds with questions even so. If Victor Herbert is right, we need to hear Robert's melody in its finished form: Kathy, Marta, April, which is she? If Sondheim is right, we need only see that Robert now knows that his melody *may be finishable*: which is not at all the same thing.

The similarities that unite Herbert and Sondheim as they frame the Golden Age tell us about time. The dissimilarities tell us about music. When the form's composer-in-chief is nationally popular, he and Broadway are in sync with a public. When he is controversial, however much eventually accepted, Broadway is losing its public. It is the difference between an innocent and a disillusioned time—and this brings us to the second Sondheim-Prince-Bennett-Aronson collaboration. In its book, its score, and its original staging, it is arguably the greatest of all musicals. Yes, I said in its book.

2

ALL THOSE GLITTERING YEARS

FOLLIES

Some mistake *Follies*' strength for a weakness, assuming that it is literally a reunion of old show-biz folk in a theatre on the eve of demolition and that the characters are physically speaking their lines to one another as we look on.

No. Rather, try to imagine a theatre that once hosted glamorous and essential entertainment. As its art lost power, it fell into mean use, and is now to be torn down. You walk past it one evening with the uncanny feeling that, behind the boarded-up windows and the scaffolding, something is going on inside, some magical retrospective. It's a dream: a reunion of the shadows and echoes of the old show biz that once defined America. No one human is inside the building, yet something is *there*, saying goodbye. All the fairies are singing to the moon.

A photograph of Gloria Swanson in the rubble of the Roxy Theatre helps fix the event for us. One of the great movie palaces, the Roxy was being demolished in 1960 when Swanson posed for photographer Eliot Elisofon amid the wreckage, dressed in a décolleté black gown and feather boa, her black-gloved arms outflung in what must be ecstatic survival amid the makings of requiem. She looks exactly like someone "doing" an entrance into the party that *Follies* is presumably hosting.

The picture might have inspired Sondheim and his librettist, James Goldman, but in fact the photo came into play somewhat late in the composition. Just as *Company* began as eleven one-acters about marriage, all to feature Kim Stanley dashing off to her next wig change, so *Follies* began in greatly different form. It was a murder mystery entitled *The Girls Upstairs*. Yes, it took place at a reunion of showgirls and their husbands, but there were no younger players reenacting old loves and revealing old mistakes, no ghosts haunting the theatre. Gradually, the past seeped into the plan, turning the place of action into Roxy rubble and the cast into Gloria Swanson.

So, on April 4, 1971, after a drum roll and four ominous chords, the Winter Garden's curtain rose on the most famous of the *Follies* images: a towering showgirl alone at stage center, a vision so white that one might almost see through her, and so very still. It was the first of the *Follies* ghosts: and it was that photograph, too, wasn't it? Only Swanson was reaching for heaven and this model's arms were merely extended. Swanson *needed* something; this showgirl seemed complete in herself. To music of an eerie beauty, she began to move very slowly across the stage, highlighted by the baby-pink teasing of the celesta. Ghost music. Now another showgirl appeared. Then musical-comedy types: a line of high-kickers waving hats, a pair of ballroom dancers, singers, all white against the darkness and each set moving to its own rhythm in its own style, a silent cacophony of music and time.

The *Follies* ghosts. Today, they are a part of the musical's history, as famous an invention as *Lady in the Dark*'s opera dreams or *Cabaret*'s Emcee. *Follies* was stuffed with them, not only as extras but for the principals and minor characters as well, some with important bits and four with considerable roles. But that first image, of the theatre (= American life) aware of the death of its past (= old show-biz formulas), prepared one for the show's highly stylized realism. It was realism in the abstract, with characters blurting out things they are actually only thinking; with the past almost pleading with the present and the present berating the past; and with entire numbers serving metaphorically rather than naturalistically.

The show's last image, too, told one that *Follies* is a dream: as the four leads prepared to depart, one noticed that the reunion party had completely vanished—waiters, tables, orchestra, guests. Had any of it *really* been there at all? Moreover, part of the theatre's back wall was gone, as if the demolition of the building had already begun. What, with people still inside? Like *Company*, but much more so, *Follies* was not a show to be taken literally.

The show's four leads are grandees Ben and Phyllis and losers Buddy and Sally. They were a quartet in youth: Buddy thought Ben was his best friend, and roommates Phyllis and Sally shared the merry complications of dating and cheating and hoping. When the boys and girls get together, they greet each other with lines important enough to be repeated throughout the show. Sally says, "Hi." Ben says, "Girls." Phyllis says, "Ben." Buddy says, "Sally." Because Phyllis loves Ben and Buddy loves Sally. *Really* loves, for life. But Sally doesn't know whom she loves yet—or is she too shy to admit that it's Ben? She just says, "Hi." And Ben doesn't love. He says, "Girls," because either will do.

That is, provided she can move up with him to fulfill his social and professional ambitions: legal bar, bestseller list, foundation presidency. Phyllis can. She's smart; Sally is a dope. By the time Sally can admit that she wants Ben, too, he's with Phyllis. But there's something about Sally; there always will be. She's lovely and simple and easy, something genuine in Ben's world of obligations and fixes. And Phyllis is dimly aware of Sally's power over him. She thinks everybody wants Ben: power. Ben thinks everybody wants Sally: youth. They're both right.

That is the core of *Follies*. It all occurred before the show starts, some thirty years back; and it occurs again during the show, as we watch. The conflict between this quartet in the present (John McMartin, Alexis Smith, Gene Nelson, Dorothy Collins) and their younger selves (Kurt Peterson, Virginia Sandifur, Harvey Evans, Marti Rolph) is played out against the present-past of the old show folks' party staffed by young people (who seem to have no idea what's going on, including the waiter with whom Phyllis trysts) and the present-past of Sondheim's version of the Golden Age songbook. Add to this Sally's belief that the quartet can be reconfigured to suit a dream she has never renounced: Ben and Sally, starting tonight. Then set all this inside a doomed theatre and one has the impression that *Follies'* authors are among those who believe that the Golden Age is over. As Harvard student Frank Rich noted in his now-famous *Crimson* review of *Follies* during its Boston tryout, "Its creators are in essence presenting their own funeral."

This is that "disconnect" in American culture that happened somewhere between *Gone With the Wind* and *Bonnie and Clyde*; or between bestselling novelists with three names and William Burroughs; or between Milton Cross and Milton Berle; or simply during Elvis Presley. *Follies* was not your father's musical, but it was about him.

Oddly, *Follies* has the makings of a work of decadence. When art is fresh, it is vigorous, uncluttered, and direct, like *King Dodo*. Or *Show Boat* or *Street Scene*. When art is moribund, it is dispirited, fastidious, and symbolic; but *Follies* isn't. On the contrary, Sondheim seems literally to revive the old song forms, as if not examining so much as authorizing them. They may take some getting used to, but then all of Sondheim from *Company* on does, because, *one*, the musical structures are larger—more eventful—than show writing had been; and, *two*, the lyrics plow so deeply into the action that it's difficult at the first hearing to enjoy the melody while concentrating on the words.

So Sondheim launched the line of our modern "two-listen" writers such as William Finn and Michael John LaChiusa, two other composer-lyricists whose complex constructions need a bit of break-in to be appreciated. And of course these nuanced scores are ideal for repeated hearing. Have you noticed how the swirling little vamp that introduces both Sally's "Don't Look at Me" (on harp, viola, and piano) and Ben's "The Road You Didn't Take" (now on the more élite harpsichord, as befits the suave magnifico) is never given to Buddy or Phyllis? It bonds Ben and Sally in their secret romance of old—and in the dire little notion, alive in both their minds, that they might yet make the dream come true.

Or have you noticed that "Losing My Mind" records a slow-motion *folle journée*, from dawn to lights-out? Have you heard Jonathan Tunick's stepwise celesta scale beginning on "I dim the lights" and ascending just over two octaves to rest perfectly on the third of the D Flat Major seventh chord to which the harmony has moved at that moment?

It's a huge score, more music than book in a show so tight that there seemed no place for an intermission. "Too Many Mornings" offered the least unlikely punctuation point, and was used later in the original run; but I saw also an intermission curtain at the end of "Who's That Woman?"

Many *Follies* buffs call that their favorite *Follies* number; I wonder if they realize how essential it is, quite aside from its merit as sheer entertainment. It's a great campy thing, with an excellent dance arrangement (by John Berkman) that calls up a few old styles in soft-shoe and Dixieland variations of the tune. It also serves a tablespoon of realism in this potion of fantasy, in its straight-on look at six former showgirls backing up a vocalist (Mary McCarty) in an impromptu re-creation of their old specialty, the Mirror Number. Phyllis and Sally are among the group, who sloppily recall the original steps and the hand gestures of a woman quizzing the looking-glass.

Exactly! That's *Follies*' abiding image: the observation of self (or the failure to observe), the pose (or the dispelling honesty), the scary mirror on the wall that tells. Who's that Ben, that Sally, the one so sure that his life is a sham and the other so apparently the happy homemaker, except for the suicide attempts? *Follies* itself is posing in its poster art, but a crack of doom breaks the face of beauty: everybody dies. Remember?

So when Mary McCarty finishes her vocal on "That woman is me" and slithers offstage to let the dancing take over, the six *Follies* ladies go through the old motions. But now comes a trick from co-director and choreographer Michael Bennett and lighting designer Tharon Musser. Throughout the show, the ghosts have been *materializing*, just like real ghosts. They don't enter. They don't even try to slip on unobserved during some distraction. Musser created a code of lighting pools so strictly defined that *Follies* players could be invisible in blackness and, after one step forward, *appear*.

The trick was most effective in "Who's That Woman?" As the six old dames modeled and pranced, their younger selves popped into view to dance a real Mirror Number, in costume (short skirts all a-beam with tiny mirrors) and with the gala energy of innocent youth that deserves a mirror and doesn't need one.

But hold. The taps on the girls' shoes would have given them away in the darkness and thus compromised their magical entrance. Instead of coming back from the past, they would have been walking on from upstage. So they were outfitted with rubber soles, the tapping supplied by chorus boys performing a secret Mirror Number in the Winter Garden basement, their sound effects piped upward into the auditorium.

"Who's That Woman?" centers *Follies* in many ways. The pastiche is superbly turned, not least because it doesn't rehabilitate an old genre. "Beautiful Girls" suggests the "Pretty Girl Is Like a Melody" anthems that John Steel sang in Ziegfeld's revues; "Losing My Mind" is pure torch song; "The Story of Lucy and Jessie" recalls the "Eadie Was a Lady" or "Saga of Jenny" number. However, nothing like "Who's That Woman?" existed before *Follies*; but something like it *could* have existed. It's the kind of song they used to write: they just didn't think of it, particularly not with a refrain that starts on the tonic major seventh and reaches the dominant with a flatted third just four seconds later.

"Who's That Woman?" also marked one of the several *Follies* moments in which the writing and the staging reached a level of clarity not heretofore known in musicals. Even those who found the show baffling could see the bright-eyed, paying-no-price damsels of old Broadway dancing not only behind and around but right in the middle of the panting old gals of the present. There had been showstopping numbers before; this was a showstopping *perception*.

Indeed, what Prince, Bennett, Aronson, Musser, and costume designer Florence Klotz created in that original *Follies* was at once astonishing and heartbreaking: the perfect production, never to be duplicated and thus, after the original run ends, a reproach to any future staging attempts. At $800,000, it was the second most expensive musical to that time (after *Coco*). No question, producer Prince gave director Prince all the room in the world. But what makes the staging live in memory is not Ziegfeldian décor—that came along quite late in the evening, in any case, when *Follies* presented its own personal *Follies* revue. No, again, it was the perceptions turned into visual hooks.

Here's another: during "Waiting for the Girls Upstairs," after the flashback, when the youngsters go off to dance at Tony's, their four seniors seemed to glance at one another, then suddenly move bleakly away, even flee. Another: when the quarrels among the four broke into Loveland, the climactic revue, and a series of drops came flooding down on the Roxy rubble while figures out of Fragonard came preciously forth, one saw a kind of "Who's That Woman?" set change: the elegant old style correcting the vulgar present. Another: when Ben broke up in his folly, "Live, Laugh, Love," conductor Harold Hastings called out lyrics to him and rapped his baton to bring the number to order. Most *Follies* buffs recall a kickline of robots at this point, but I remember a few of the dancers glaring at Ben—for lousing up the routine, or for losing faith with this style of show biz and the America that so to say lived, laughed, and loved through it?

Much of this concerns Hal Prince's vision of the show, for it was he who originated the concept of the ghosts. Some of this also concerns Michael Bennett, who by then had danced and choreographed on Broadway but was now headed for the extraordinary parade of *A Chorus Line*, *Ballroom*, and *Dreamgirls*. *Follies* was the perfect Bennett show in its jagged crosscutting of energies, for his was a contentious personality and a contentious talent.* Bennett himself thought *Follies* not Bennett enough, not with that dangerous book. A Bennett musical does not provoke. It dazzles. Someone once told Bennett that he should direct a revival of *The Mikado*, probably imagining another thrilling crash-up of ancient art and youthful power. And Bennett replied, "What's *The Mikado*?" He was an ignorant genius.

Follies got vastly mixed reviews, from "utterly magnificent" to "ingenuity without inspiration." Nevertheless, it ran for fifteen months despite very heavy running expenses (including, at first, a cast of fifty-one). Further, *Follies* won the Drama Critics Circle Award and received Tonys for score, direction, choreography, and for the three designers and Alexis Smith. The production lost its entire investment and the tour collapsed on its second date, in Los Angeles. Some call that a failure.

However, by 1971 the very notion of "hit" and "flop" is becoming useless except in the strictly commercial sense—and isn't a producer's bookkeeping the least interesting aspect of the chronicle? The implication of "hit" is that a show pleased people strongly enough to leave something behind, whether a song or two, a cast album, a movie version, or simply the potential of being revived someday. A "flop" was a show that vanished. Obviously, in days of lower costs, a hit made money and a flop lost money. But by 1971, hits lost money. No show that wins *Follies'* awards and runs over a year and eventually gets four major recordings, all the while becoming a classic by any standard of measurement, can be called a failure.

There's something else worth mentioning: the intense loyalty of all the communicants to that original production. Theatre folk don't usually regard a failure as one of the great experiences of their lives.

Oddly, it started badly for Alexis Smith, the one cast member who won universal acclaim. Though she and her husband, actor Craig Stevens, had toured as the two New Yorkers in Amish country in *Plain and Fancy*, Smith more or less talked her way through her three numbers. Her *Follies* audition, in Los Angeles, was terrible, but then she coached with David Craig, in not only how to vocalize but how to present herself in every

---

* You know who Bennett is in *A Chorus Line*? Not director Zach, but Sheila, the angry grown-up among the kids.

moment of an audition—chitchatting with the team, relating to the accompanist, how to stand, eyes and teeth, the whole sequence placed and timed to demonstrate the senior Phyllis' ruthless self-confidence, yet with a feeling of spontaneity.

Fine... but. "What if they ask me to sing the song a second time?" Smith asked David Craig. "I can't do all the gestures and things all over again, can I?"

"That'll never happen," said Craig.

So Smith sang for *Follies* once more, the team fell in love with her, and Sondheim called out, "Take it down a half-tone and sing it again."

A smallish company toured the country in the wake of the original, with Robert Alda, Vivian Blaine, Jane Kean, and Don Liberto in the leads and a host of twilight celebrities such as Hildegarde and Lynn Bari in the cameo roles. On Broadway, only the "I'm Still Here" cameo had gone to a star, Yvonne De Carlo. The others were such genuinely obsolete names as Fifi D'Orsay, Ethel Shutta, Justine Johnston, and Michael Bartlett. But the tour's casting of names that some theatregoers actually could place added something to the experience. Cabaret diva Hildegarde's "Ah, Paris!" authenticated *Follies*' nostalgia in a way that the obscure-to-the-point-of-mystery Fifi D'Orsay could not have. True, the French-Canadian D'Orsay would seem to hold genetic entitlement over Hildegarde, raised in the German city of Milwaukee. And D'Orsay's almost clownish vivacity aligned more correctly with the kind of singer who would have relished an "Ah, Paris!"—Gaby Deslys or Mistinguett, say—than did Hildegarde's insinuating smoochy-koo.

Nevertheless, there is something documentary about letting old glamour embody old glamour in a work party about the death of old glamour. The 1990 Long Beach, California *Follies* that starred Ed Evanko, Juliet Prowse, Harvey Evans (graduated from Young to Old Buddy), and Shani Wallis assigned the cameos to performers arguably more famous than some of the leads: Yma Sumac, Dorothy Lamour, Susan Johnson, and Denise Darcel. And at the triumphant, or perhaps simply vindicating, *Follies* at a New York Philharmonic concert in 1985, the cameo players included Elaine Stritch, Licia Albanese, Liliane Montevecchi (a very Gallic "Ah, Paris!"), Phyllis Newman, and Betty Comden and Adolph Green.

London did not see *Follies* till Cameron Mackintosh produced it in 1987 at the Shaftesbury Theatre with Daniel Massey, Diana Rigg, David

Healy, and Julia McKenzie (who played a fascinating but ultimately too intelligent Sally). Our own Dolores Gray, a London favorite ever since she starred there in *Annie Get Your Gun* in 1947, sang "I'm Still Here." But the lesser cameos went to people like Maria Charles (the original Dulcie in *The Boy Friend*) and operetta soprano Adele Leigh (for "One More Kiss"), somewhere between Fifi D'Orsay and Yma Sumac in show-biz eminence.

So far, so good. London's director, Mike Ockrent, and choreographer, Bob Avian, put the complex machine together beautifully. (Was it Ockrent who asked one of the parading Beautiful Girls in the first number to plant a sentimental finger-kiss on the stage-right proscenium as she passed?) And designer Maria Björnson created a particular look for Loveland, with a fake-perspective apartment building in "You're Gonna Love Tomorrow" and a vast piano for Ben's Folly—so grand that the chorus came dancing out of it.

But Mackintosh wanted to find more warmth and less regret in *Follies*, and James Goldman unfortunately obliged, with a new book that dropped many key lines. For instance:

> CHRISTINE: You're Phyllis, aren't you? I'm Christine. I had the dressing table next to yours. (No reaction from Phyllis) Don't you remember me at all?
> PHYLLIS: You never liked me.
> CHRISTINE: What a thing to say.
> PHYLLIS: I never liked you, either.

Probably it was feared that this makes Phyllis look hard and unforgiving. In fact, she is both soft and forgiving with those who matter to her. What this exchange shows us is that Phyllis is fearless. Her independence consists of not caring what anyone thinks of her—except Ben, of course, and as he has never figured this out, he is afraid of her, because she is the only person who sees through his imitation of a philosopher-king. What he also doesn't know is that *his* Mirror Number doesn't matter to her. She loves the man, not the image.

Moreover, if one cuts even the few lines quoted above, one removes an essential piece from the puzzle that is *Follies*. Everything is made clear—but only in this diffuse, almost improvisational way. Something in one scene extrapolates something from an earlier scene that someone will substantiate *in a lie* in a later scene. The truth is even worse. Try this shocker from the last scene:

SALLY: I can't stand up.
BUDDY: I'll help you.
SALLY: I should of died the first time.
BUDDY: Cut that out.
SALLY: I should of been dead all these years.

You thought I was making that up about Sally's suicide attempts earlier, didn't you? That's because people seem to know the *Follies* they last saw; and lately each *Follies* has been pruning and rearranging the book as drastically as Goldman did for London. Yes, he did think of some arresting new touches. At one point the ghost of Young Phyllis impulsively kissed Buddy on the cheek and he put his hand to it, crying, "What was that?"

But, in all, Goldman got it right in 1971. One reason that the book was blamed for *Follies*' controversial reputation was that the show as a whole is packed with *fleeting* images. It can be difficult to absorb the action while enjoying the magic. Another reason is that Goldman wrote a kind of libretto that had never before existed: two hours of real time in which messages of falsehood and honesty vie with each other to solve the eternal mystery, which is "What happened and what can we do about it now?"

The third reason is that the songs are about feelings and the book is about doom. It is not even an O'Neillian doom, an artistic doom looking back to the Greeks. It's a *doom* doom, yours and mine, and that's hard to enjoy. True, easing up the tension gave Mackintosh a longer run for his *Follies*; and the show did play beautifully in London. But it wasn't as interesting as the first *Follies*, even with four new songs.

Follies boasts a cornucopia of a score, what with such cut numbers as "All Things Bright and Beautiful," a duet for Ben and Sally, now the substance of the show's invocational prelude; "Bring on the Girls," which preceded "Beautiful Girls" in the same spot on the same idea, later reclaimed for the *Stavisky* soundtrack; "Can That Boy Fox-Trot!," replaced by "I'm Still Here" to expand the show's past-versus-present theme; and "Uptown/Downtown," the first version of Phyllis' Folly, replaced by "The Story of Lucy and Jessie."

Even so, the show opened in New York with the sheer volume of an operetta. There were twenty-one separate numbers (and the "Bolero d'Amour," for the typical ballroom couple popular in shows of the 1920s and 1930s, composed by John Berkman). Adding new numbers for London inevitably meant losing some, including—and this is amazing—"The Road You Didn't Take," with its quintessential line, "The Ben I'll never be, who remembers him?"

Of course, more Sondheim is always welcome, even the lackluster "Country House." Designed, apparently, to domesticate Ben and Phyllis' feral relationship, it doesn't sound like the rest of the score. Yet another "Uptown/Downtown," called "Ah, But Underneath," allowed Diana Rigg to take a bath onstage; and Ben's new Folly, "Make the Most of Your Music," a well-nigh symphonic item to match that grand piano the chorus came out of, is even friskier than "Live, Laugh, Love." But Ben didn't have his breakdown during the number in this *Follies Lite*, losing one of the work's most telling effects. Newcomers don't know what's happening. It's more of that real time, the "performer" rejecting his "role" while the curtain is up. Is *Follies* the problem, or is *Follies* the solution?

Definitely not the solution are Goldman's relentless revisions—yet another set for a 1996 BBC radio performance from Drury Lane, with Denis Quilley, Donna McKechnie, Ron Moody, and Julia McKenzie again. (At least the entire 1971 score was reinstated, complete with the "Bolero.") Goldman might well add lines to clarify the action for radio listeners—"sighting" the ghosts, and inventing a framing airwave personality supposedly reporting on the reunion. Even so, 1971's ingenious riddling of past and present was once again replaced by paragraphs of the obvious, even the banal.

Here's another great *Follies* moment, and another instance of composition and staging indissolubly mated: in 1971, in the show's first minutes, the "haunting" was intruded upon and thus dissolved by the reunion-party staff. Into this nexus of then and now came—actually *ran*—Dorothy Collins, greatest of all Sallys. Of course, she would be the first to arrive. She has come to rid herself of Buddy and redeem her pipe-dream coupons for the Ben who, she thinks, belongs to her. Collins made a breathless speech to one of the staff, tight and quick and all the exposition that Goldman allowed, except for Dimitri Weismann's eulogy just before "Beautiful Girls." Inside of twenty seconds, Sally hit about seven character points, and here's the moment now—one of six chorus-girl ghosts broke out of line and came over to stare at Collins: herself, thirty years later. It was a flash of lightning, our realization that the ghosts are not decoration but the very stuff of the story.

Granted, the BBC performance didn't need the exposition (which was covered in preperformance talks and by the new announcer character) and obviously couldn't have shown Young Sally's ghost. But if one keeps cutting away at an already lean book, one is left with a score and cue lines.

Each book revision, though always credited to Goldman, takes away content and adds debris. At the Paper Mill Playhouse in New Jersey in 1998, the reunion party was literalized so fully that we saw guests departing just before the last scene, heard them chattering and jesting. But, again, this is less a party than an exorcism. By the end, we should be left with not Merry Villagers but with just our four leads and the present time: for the past is finally over.

The Paper Mill staging, at least, was lavish. Even a throwaway like "Rain on the Roof" enjoyed its ghostly cohort miming the original number upstage in yellow slickers; Ann Miller, Kaye Ballard, and, once again, Phyllis Newman and Liliane Montevecchi contributed cameos. Donna McKechnie moved over to Sally, ceding her BBC Phyllis to Dee Hoty, and many were they who loved this *Follies*. However, production values do not make up for a vitiated scenario. The more party, the less *Follies*.

There was talk of moving the Paper Mill show to Broadway, but in the end New York saw its *Follies* revival under the auspices of the Roundabout Theatre at the Belasco in 2001, almost exactly thirty years after the original. The theatre was perfect, built (in 1907) by a showman not unlike Dimitri Weismann, for while David Belasco didn't produce musicals, he was noted for spectacle. The auditorium, good-sized for its day, seats only 1,008. But the stage is surprisingly deep; and the place has its own ghost.

Directed by Matthew Warchus and choreographed by Kathleen Marshall (and with the usual destructive script changes), this latest *Follies* made do with an orchestra of fourteen and a bargain-basement Loveland. This sabotages the conjuring up of the spendthrift Golden Age show biz that lives at the show's heart. Also, not all of the cameos worked well. It was a treat to see *Oklahoma!*'s original Laurey, Joan Roberts, for "One More Kiss," and Jane White's "Ah, Paris!" was sensational, put over not as a genre piece but as her personal character song. Polly Bergen's

"I'm Still Here," presented as if she were entertaining at the party tables and then trimmed to a powerful soliloquy, won universal acclaim. But Marge Champion and Donald Saddler's bolero, retitled "Danse d'Amour," was embarrassingly feeble, cut down during previews to little more than a bit. (Champion couldn't get her few spoken lines down, either. When she was on, it was Samuel Beckett's *Follies*.)

Some also scorned the casting of Gregory Harrison, Blythe Danner, Treat Williams, and Judith Ivey in the leads. This quartet has an "actory" sound, fit for *A Streetcar Named Desire* or David Mamet. In fact, both men had sung on Broadway, and Blythe Danner would have if *Mata Hari* (1967) had come in. True, she was only in the chorus; but Alexis Smith proved that the right non-singer can sound wonderful in this part. It was really Judith Ivey's Sally that raised the eyebrow, at least the eyebrow of those who see this as the Barbara Cook role.*

Still, *Follies* is one of those musicals that need very strong acting from the lead players, and director Warchus was able to give the work its most significant *Personenregie* since 1971. One truly understood what was happening among these four people—what had drawn them together and then blown them apart. Ivey especially helped us comprehend how one crazy dream could stay vital all those years despite its being a dream of youth, ineluctably extinguished by age. Her "Losing My Mind" was not Barbara Cook's, no; but it was well sung and brilliantly acted, becoming almost savage at the end.

Truth to tell, and despite some flaws, this was a superb revival. Wonderfuly quirky touches stay in the memory—how, as a photographer was about to shoot the party guests, their ghosts turned to the camera and struck poses as well; how, just after that, Betty Garrett (the "Broadway Baby" cameo) went into a nostalgic trance, staring out at the auditorium; how Gregory Harrison's Ben froze, with who knew how many contradictory thoughts, when he first saw Sally again; or how the "Who's That Woman?" ghosts slyly blew into the number on a trapdoor in the deck. If one blinked, one missed it.

---

* Ivey spelled Jane Lapotaire on Wednesday matinees in the title role of *Piaf* (1981), a big singing role, and was to have sung again as Adelaide in a cancelled *Guys and Dolls* revival with Ron Silver, Patti Cohenour, and Tom Selleck under director-choreographer Michael Kidd.

The Roundabout *Follies* did not succeed, but then *Follies* does not succeed, not in the conventional sense. The work is simply too smart for its good. While praising the Roundabout production in *The New Yorker*, Nancy Franklin wrote, "It's possible to think that *Follies* is a great show and yet not entirely love it; to think that it's invaluable and yet not feel embraced by it. You may walk out of the theatre feeling a little mixed up inside, as though you had just received the most unforgettable parting kiss of your life."

3

IF EVERYONE GOT WHAT THEY WANTED

MUSICAL COMEDY I

Musical plays generally differ from one another; it's musical comedy that has to learn new ways of doing the same things again and again. An unusual setting, a new plot twist . . . or a Novelty Star. The 1969–70 season was especially rich in these: six book shows were built around performers not known for song and dance or even for stage work. *Jimmy*, the first musical of the season, in late October, offered "the other side" of *Fiorello!* in the adventures of James J. Walker, the corrupt mayor whom La Guardia defeated.

Frank Gorshin, most famous as The Riddler on television's *Batman*, seemed a not unlikely choice. He could sing, more or less, and had flair for comedy. Moreover, he bore quite some physical resemblance to the subject, to be presented as one of those lovable rogues. Certainly, everyone in the show dotes on him; one song title was "The Darlin' of New York."

However, Gorshin had nothing to play but that darlin', as he kept asking for a divorce from his estranged wife (Julie Wilson) and scandalized the town in adultery with a showgirl (Anita Gillette). There was some political background as well. Still, the show lacked *Fiorello!*'s historical detail, not to mention its more genuinely darlin' protagonist.

Melville Shavelson, who co-wrote and directed the Bob Hope film *Beau James*, from Gene Fowler's Walker biography, wrote *Jimmy*'s book, and Bill and Patti Jacob wrote the score. All three did terrible work—not inept, just boring. The cliché historical drop-ins: Al Smith, Texas Guinan, Eddie Dowling, even Prohibition enforcers Izzy and Moe, who had had their own flop musical in 1962, *Nowhere To Go But Up*. The cliché numbers: Gillette's twenties pastiche "Oh, Gee!"; the loving salute to a locale that in real life no one thinks twice about, "Riverside Drive"; Wilson's ironic torch number, "I Only Wanna Laugh"; Gorshin's confused-hero solo, "What's Out There For Me?," and, later, defiant-hero solo, "Life Is a One Way Street." The cliché plot troubles, cliché set-change music, cliché usherettes.

Yet, again, there was nothing floppo about *Jimmy*. It wasn't laughable. Hollywood's Jack L. Warner produced it, so everyone wanted it to be. But Warner hired Joseph Anthony to direct, Peter Gennaro for choreography, and Oliver Smith for the scenery. That's not laughable: that's sound Broadway showmanship. With his Hollywood millions, Warner kept *Jimmy* running into the new year, though no one knew anyone who saw it.

Next came *Buck White*, which played for a week in December. Oscar Brown Jr. wrote the book and score, adapting Joseph Dolan Tuotti's play *Big Time Buck White*. This was the most aggressive of the black racist harangues that proliferated at this time, running on critics' intimidated indulgence and foundation money. The latter was given in the belief that these events are somehow "well-meant." How can anything that furthers racism be well-meant?

And why make it a musical? *Big Time Buck White* treats a black political meeting awaiting the arrival of the title character, a rabble-rouser. If the piece has any validity, it lies in the improvisational nature of the event, the feeling that one really is at a political meeting and that powerful resentments will be aroused. But musicals by their nature cannot absorb the aleatory, so the premise becomes fake.

The only reason *Buck White* got on in the first place was the Novelty Star, boxing champ Muhammad Ali, in the title role. Ali managed to keep his dignity, but he was neither actor nor singer, reminding some of turn-of-the-century vaudeville, when athletes and other celebrities were put on bills not for any talent but simply to be shown. Hadn't television made this unnecessary?

If Gorshin lacked box-office pull and Ali was simply out of his element, Katharine Hepburn in the name role of *Coco* was a Broadway Christmas present in mid-December: a star with giant appeal, set off so well that the song and dance would work around her—literally, on a vast revolving set—while she did what she did best: defy the conformists and sneaks with her New England grit and directness.

She was playing Parisian dress designer Coco Chanel, without the slightest attempt to seem or sound French. No, this was Kate the Absolute, a Broadway regular between movie jobs all her life but now, at the age of sixty, making her musical debut. Alan Jay Lerner and André Previn wrote it, Michael Benthall and Michael Bennett staged it, Cecil Beaton designed it, and film sequences supplied the distant men in Coco's life, lovers and neglectful Papa. The cost was $900,000: the most expensive show to that time.

One reason was the wardrobe, a riot of colors and styles—all reds, for example, in evening wear, bikini top and flowing skirt, *King and I* cut, tartan; or blue and white in sailor suit, *pour le sport*, slinky party, mandarin; whole dances of them pouring down a great staircase or going into model freeze, all wrist and waist. They'd prink about in the changing room, and then the revolve would kick in and a whole new crowd of them went on parade as Bennett's routines amazed the eye.

Some thought it a fashion show disguised as a musical, but there was more to it than that. Lerner's book was quite funny, giving Hepburn plenty of aphorisms and judgments to snap off with her characteristic rueful clarity. When a male columnist was scathing about Coco's determination to end her retirement and restorm the fashion world, Hepburn commented, "There's no bitch like a man, is there?" And when her new collection failed, who strode onstage at the start of Act Two, fixed the audience with a look, and said—this word, from her, was quite shocking at the time—"*Shit!*"?

True, Hepburn's vocal limitations stuck Previn with a few tuneless marches that she could chant, caw, and even rap her way through. But a star show needs an eleven o'clock number with some ring, and Hepburn managed somehow or other to sing—or at any rate to justify in her unique way—"Always Mademoiselle." Her regretful-triumphant credo and the score's highlight, the song was powered out by the orchestra alone as the set revolved once more, Bennett's mannequins thrilled the house, and Hepburn was uplifted, redeemed, starred.

There actually were some good things in the music, especially the two numbers for David Holliday as a reporter in love with Coco's protégée, Gale Dixon. "Let's Go Home" is pure romance, but "A Woman Is How She Loves" is hot-tempered, a jazz waltz on a new idea. It refutes Cole

Porter's suggestion—in "Is It the Girl (Or Is It the Gown?)," from *Seven Lively Arts*—that clothes make the girl. "You dress for yourselves, not for us!" Holliday sang. It's a clever premise, and very right for this impatient, intelligent character.

There was a gay figure, too, a new-wave designer (René Auberjonois) who loathes Coco. He had the show's floppo number, "Fiasco," a buxom tango staged for Auberjonois to sing to an utterly silent and gloating Charlene Ryan. Shouldn't she have sung, too, or simply made herself scarce? It looked strange. George Rose, as Coco's lawyer, came off only a bit smarter in Lerner's favorite type of solo, a wry conundrum on the ways of *l'amour*. This was the jaunty "When Your Lover Says Goodbye," the kind of song nobody writes anymore. It's half character number and half revue spot: what they used to call a "specialty."

The critics dismissed *Coco*, and the public enjoyed it for nine months. Hepburn's contract up, she left the show. As we know from the trouble that followed when Nathan Lane and Matthew Broderick left *The Producers*, one cannot replace the irreplaceable. Then someone had a brainstorm. Don't recast Hepburn: recast Coco Chanel. So they brought in one of the few performers whose charm can fairly be called "ineffable"—Danielle Darrieux. She's a beauty, she's French, and, lo, she can sing! The voice was thin but exquisite, and the show turned into something it hadn't been yet, a vehicle for the character. Now that they were actually being sung, the protagonist's numbers didn't sound any more melodic. But at least now they were songs. However, Darrieux lacked box-office magnetism, and *Coco* had to shut down till Hepburn came back for the tour. In the end, that great white elephant turned a profit.

Gantry, which takes us past the New Year into 1970, closed on opening night. This suggests a real disaster. But it had much more to work with than *Coco*'s bio fluff, in Sinclair Lewis' 1927 novel *Elmer Gantry*, one of the first works to note how show biz infects every aspect of American life, including religion. Here the Novelty Star was Robert Shaw, who brought a stinging intensity to the role of the corrupt preacher. His was another of those "Yes, I can't" singing voices, with a gruesome vibrato. But where Hepburn hiked through her numbers, Shaw pounced on his. His co-star, Rita Moreno, actually could sing; and of course the tent-revival setting allowed for hand-clapping gospel, with the infectious rhythm and the high-flying soprano soloist (Gloria Hodes). A couple of these choruses, "Show Him the Way" and "He's Never Too Busy," suggested what *Gantry* might have been, as did Shaw's ballad "(I'm looking for) Someone I've Already Found" and a comic quartet for the typical Sinclair Lewis hypocrites in suits, "Foresight."

Moreover, where *Coco* was almost entirely panned, *Gantry* got mixed notices, though none was genuinely favorable. It was not a good show—and not remotely the dandy piece of entertainment that *Coco* was. Too much of Lewis' novel was missing from Peter Bellwood's lumpy book, and when Stanley Lebowsky and Fred Tobias' songs weren't almost okay, they were terrible. *Gantry*'s failure sent its director-choreographer, Onna White, back to choreographing only, a sad loss. Even the George Abbott Theatre was punished, by being turned into a parking lot.

Six weeks after *Gantry* came *Minnie's Boys*, with Novelty Star Shelley Winters as Minnie Marx, the mother of all stage mothers, coaxing and nagging the eventual Groucho, Chico, Harpo, and Zeppo to show-biz triumph. Shelley Winters as the star of a musical might sound like a stretch, but she had some experience: Katisha in a high-school *Mikado* and small roles in: a Civic Light Opera *Rio Rita* starring Joe E. Brown, the pre-Broadway tour of *Meet the People*, and, in New York, *Rosalinda*. After some movie work, she played Ado Annie late in *Oklahoma!*'s original New York run; and she looked great in *Minnie's Boys*' twenties clothes.

But something definitely went wrong. None of our previous four Novelty Stars had more entitlement than Winters, yet it was she who had the very public disaster, greatly irritating some of the show's staff, making an entrance at a preview loudly complaining about her costume, and at one point huffing out of the theatre shortly before curtain time.

The problem may have been a typical tryout hell—two delirious months of it, and not out of town but at the Imperial Theatre, for all New York to see. Scenes and songs and even personnel were thrown in and out, not wisely. Minnie's most intimate moment with her boys, "They Give Me Love," was good enough to include on the cast album but cut from the show in all the destructive excitement. It may be that audiences at the first rough preview saw a better show than the critics did.

Winters, a brilliant actress but, in preparation, a plodding Actors Studio arguer, could not work in chaos. Parts of her performance implied that she might have been quite winning under different management.

It was a funny show, as when Winters' Jewish Mother tries to create guilt with phony sacrifices:

> MINNIE: (To all four) I'll tell you how important I think this opportunity is for you boys—I'll cut off my beautiful hair and I'll sell it for a wig.
>
> ADOLPH [HARPO]: Mama, that *is* a wig.

And it was a touching show, especially in "Be Happy," a minor-key song ironically meant to cheer us. Orchestrator Ralph Burns brought in an accordion for an almost European feeling, emphasizing the number's plaintiveness. We expect celebration from a song of this title; instead, it's gushingly sentimental, a cliché: exactly the terms in which this mother thinks. She consoles with sadness. In most of the show, Winters was tentative, without star sparkle, as if she had no idea why people write, appear in, or attend musicals. Suddenly, in "Be Happy," she opened up and was quite moving.

Minnie's Boys in general was rather enjoyable, though it lasted but 76 performances. The book, by Groucho's son, Arthur Marx, and Robert Fisher, does one thing well, very gradually bringing the quartet to the zany guises they became famous for. But Larry Grossman and Hal Hackady's score is rather better, announcing the twenties setting in the first number, "Five Growing Boys," a charleston, and constantly incorporating the brothers' anarchic comedy, in ad-libs as well as lyrics. A vaudeville drag queen (Richard B. Shull) saw his act demolished by the Marxes in "Underneath It All." "You Remind Me of You" gave Groucho a chance to give a lovesick landlady (Julie Kurnitz) the Margaret Dumont treatment. And "The Act" brought down the curtain as the four finalized their shtick.

The actors were Lewis J. Stadlen (Groucho), Daniel Fortus (Harpo), Irwin Pearl (Chico), and Alvin Kupperman (Zeppo), making up for Winters' vacant spells with superb "you are there" backstory. Stadlen was to go on to play Groucho in other venues; and Fortus enjoyed a wonderful solo in "Mama, a Rainbow," building the melody in intensity and then topping it off pianissimo. The four together took stage in the show's best five minutes, the first-act finale, "Where Was I When They Passed Out Luck?" Marked in the score as a "funky gospel waltz," it's a situation number of a classic kind, utterly in character but swinging with good sound.

Does the proliferation of Novelty Stars mean that birthright headliners are becoming scarce? The last Novelty Star of the 1969–70 season came on like a Broadway veteran. She couldn't really sing, but she could put a number over, and she had the tang, the flair, the "I know why I'm here" that Shelley Winters lacked. And she was playing an actress. What more do you want, in *Applause*, than Lauren Bacall?

The producers wanted Rita Hayworth, who at least had starred in film musicals (though her singing was always dubbed). The onset of Alzheimer's forced Hayworth into sudden retirement; but was this shimmering goddess right for Margo Channing in the first place? *Applause* is, of course, the musicalization of *All About Eve*, which brings us to the Bette Davis kind of star: flamboyant of gesture and diction, Baby Jane and Queen Elizabeth I, a woman that never existed except in Bette Davis movies. It isn't Rita Hayworth. It isn't Lauren Bacall, either; but the Betty Comden–Adolph Green book managed to respect the movie while scaling down its freaky bits. In fact, one doesn't realize how bizarre *All About Eve* is till one looks at *Applause*.

For instance, *All About Eve* opens with an awards ceremony, to prepare a flashback narrative. The film's writer-director, Joseph L. Mankiewicz, invented the Sarah Siddons Award, and the event looks like a slightly grand dinner party. *Applause* takes place in real life, so it opens at the Tony Awards, with comic Alan King presenting. Of *course* it does. *All About Eve*'s theatre world promises topmost stardom to the ruthless. That's fame! riches!! glamour!!! That's a Tony, not a rubber-chicken dinner and a prize named for a forgotten eighteenth-century tragedy queen.

Or take the producer in the story. The movie's Gregory Ratoff is one of those fat Europeans with an accent, Hollywood's idea of a Broadway producer. (Of course, Hollywood's idea of a Hollywood producer is suave Adolphe Menjou; the nerve.) In *Applause*, the producer is Robert Mandan, a trim, serious guy in a suit. A *human* guy, even. His (cut) establishing song, "The Loneliest Man in Town," is a cri de coeur, not some gleeful dream of crushing actors and humiliating writers.

Nor is *All About Eve*'s lesbian subtext even hinted at; and George Sanders' creepy–crawly–minty critic is deleted entirely. *Applause* did have Lee Roy Reams as Bacall's hairdresser, Duane. When Bacall asked Reams along on a jaunt and he begged off with "I've got a date," Bacall replied, "Bring him along!" It was a surprise laugh, and a hint of how hip this

Margo Channing is, very 1971 where the movie's Margo is trapped in the social cautions of the 1950s.

Indeed, the show even had a bit of male nudity (backal, not frontal) from some Joe Allen's waiters spoofing *Oh! Calcutta!*. But in all important things, *Applause* was mainstream musical comedy, a director-choreographer project (for Ron Field) with an unexpectedly able star and a perfectly placed Charles Strouse–Lee Adams score. Donald Pippin's vocal arrangements pulled the higher chorus voices way up for that *fill-the-house!* excitement that had been in style for twenty years; Robert Randolph's sets kept the story moving from place to place without pause, as designers now could; and Philip J. Lang requisitioned an electric guitar for the pit, as this ultra-contemporary sound was in fact more than a decade old by then.*

The best song in *Applause* was "'Smashing'—New York Times," a haunting ballad that turns critics' blurbs into love talk. The number was cut, but then *Applause* is filled with cut numbers, from a jittery tryout that saw much finessing and even the loss of the Eve, Diana McAfee. She was not devious enough, it seems. Penny Fuller, her replacement, filled the bill with sweet danger: one had the feeling that she, too, would be playing Queen Elizabeth I one day. She had only two numbers—perforce, as songs tend to reveal characters and this character wanted no one knowing her.

Bacall was in eight numbers, quite a feat for someone who supposedly can't sing. And, true, the long-lined "Something Greater" extends her overmuch. But "Who's That Girl (in the permanent wave)?," a self-deprecating period piece as she watches herself on television in an old movie, is a no-fail charm song, not least because Bacall herself *was* the girl she's mocking. "But Alive" is musical comedy's favorite thing, a Big Lady having Big Fun (in a Village bar, with the native boys ecstatically crying "Margo!" as if she were

---

* The guitar was useful in establishing a country-western tone for scores that otherwise sang in pure Broadway, such as *Li'l Abner* in 1956 and *Destry Rides Again* three years later. The bohemian atmosphere of *The Nervous Set*, also in 1959, would want a guitar for that beat-folky Village air. *Bye Bye Birdie*, in 1960, emphasized a souped-up, all-out electrical instrument in the music of Birdie and the kids only. But later that year, *Do Re Mi* included an electric guitar not only for the pop numbers but even in, for instance, "Asking For You," a ballad for the operetta hunk in the love plot. This was real integration—and remember that guitars in musicals go back at least to *Show Boat* in 1927, when Magnolia accompanies her reprise of "Can't Help Lovin' Dat Man" thus.

Judy Garland). "Welcome To the Theatre" is an ironic anthem, a warning more than a welcome. "One of a Kind," a duet with Bacall's vis-à-vis, Len Cariou, amusingly gives the pair no breathing spots in their run-on lyrics. But the best number in the final score is "Backstage Babble," after one of Margo's premieres, in which bromidic compliments are rendered in nonsense syllables and even nonsense melody lines.

Applause ran twenty-six months in New York and sent out two touring companies, with Bacall and also another Novelty Star, Patrice Munsel: a solid hit. There were even hit musicals with the *usual* stars. However, there was also unusual fumbling by writers who should Know By Now. For instance, why did Richard Rodgers want to make a musical out of Clifford Odets' *The Flowering Peach*? A comedy about Noah and the Flood in Odets' unique New York Jewish dialect is just novelty enough as a play. As a musical, it will lack the singing-dancing chorus, the eye-filling designs, the crazy jokes that we love about musicals. True, *Coco* also lacked the traditional chorus, *Applause* was too contemporary for amazing visuals, and *Gantry*, aside from "Foresight," hadn't a joke in it. But *Two By Two* (1970) was going to be awfully Old Testament. I don't want to go.

At least Peter Stone's book shaved down the abrasive nature of Odets' dialogue. (Noah's family members in the play, like the Bergers in Odets' best work, *Awake and Sing!*, treat one another with astonishing rudeness.) Lyricist Martin Charnin gave Rodgers verses for the kinds of songs that Rodgers had written with Hammerstein—Noah's temporizing waltz "Why Me?," the contentious "You Have Got To Have a Rudder on the Ark" (Japheth, the youngest of the sons, is the rebellious one), the wistfully rueful "Something Doesn't Happen" (for a daughter-in-law in love with Japheth but married to his brother Ham). This was Rodgers' first show since *Do I Hear a Waltz?* in 1965, when lyricist Stephen Sondheim stretched him with more unusual song premises—not completely out-of-the-way ideas, just ideas that Rodgers had never got before. Charnin brought Rodgers back to home territory.

This is not necessarily a good thing. *Do I Hear a Waltz?* is lovely, but some of *Two By Two* sounds like a drudgefest, including the hoedown that opens the second act, "When It Dries"; and Madeline Kahn's raucous solo, "The Golden Ram," which did at least close with her enviable high C; and even the main ballad, "I Do Not Know a Day I Did Not Love You." Yes, it soars: but laboriously.

Nor was the cast anything special, except Walter Willison's impassioned Japheth and Tricia O'Neil's unhappy young wife, who gets what may be the world's first divorce to marry Willison. Of course, the Noah was a headliner, Danny Kaye, returning to Broadway for his first book show since *Let's Face It!*, in 1941. Raging and clowning, decreeing and prancing, Kaye seemed determined not simply to center the show but to overpower it. Piling shtick upon shtick, Kaye went out of control after he suffered a leg injury, returning to careen about the stage on his wheelchair like a Marx Brother and, later, to tease the other actors with one or the other of his crutches. Please don't make me go. One day, Kaye let out a hideous snarl at Willison, apparently because Willison got a Tony nomination and Kaye didn't. Do I hear Pearl Schmuck?

Two By Two was a modest hit, while the vastly superior *70, Girls, 70* (1971) closed in a month. What, a John Kander–Fred Ebb show based more or less on the British movie farce *Make Mine Mink* doesn't work? But there is some fumbling in the very idea of the piece. Was it wise to build a musical comedy around a cast that had mostly come out of the graveyard (or at least retirement), playing pensioners stealing fur in order to fix up and finally buy their decrepit residential hotel? *Make Mine Mink* offered not oldsters but a group variously aged. Isn't musical comedy as a form devoted to the longings of youth?

A lively dance break in the opening number, "Old Folks," suggests the secret vitality of the long-lived. But in real life, old folks do not dance and delight. They babble incoherently and ploddingly block your way in the aisles of D'Agostino and have no friends but stewed prunes and then they completely die. One recalls how Florenz Ziegfeld explained his casting, in the Marilyn Miller musical *Sally* (1920), of a dowager character with the twentysomething showgirl Dolores: "Nobody wants to look at an old woman." Or an old man, except in *King Lear*.

The project did at first hope to cast very special old people—Lotte Lenya, Martha Raye, others. Making do with, for the most part, people even more obscure than *Follies'* Michael Bartlett and Justine Johnston was not great showmanship. Nor was it wise to veil the plot in a confusing show-within-a-show setup. Some of the songs had no connection to the action, sung not by characters in the story but by performers in *70, Girls, 70*. Some of the scenes were announced as taking place in the Broadhurst Theatre, where *70, Girls, 70* was playing. *What?*

Beyond this, however, *70, Girls, 70* is enjoyable, especially for its tuneful score. There is one floppo number, "The Caper," in which Hans Conried outlined tactics for a heist. (Perhaps the entire role should have been cut when David Burns dropped dead playing it during the Philadelphia tryout.) There are also too many of those contextless numbers, making *70, Girls, 70* something like a book musical with the score of a revue. Mildred Natwick, one of the few actresses who made aging seem glamorous, had mostly book numbers: her gala return to her extended family in "Home"; her delicate introduction into the action of the notion of death in "The Elephant Song"; and the quietly jubilant Affirmation Number that musical comedy dotes on, "Yes."

The show's best number was Lillian Roth's "See the Light," on a woman whose larceny takes her from furs to men to religious redemption, the whole supported by garrulous abba-dabba vocal backup. But Ebb sneaked in a wicked lyric in "Do We?," in which Lucie Lancaster and Gil Lamb addressed the audience's putative question: do these geezers ever go the beast? Modesty forbade a direct answer. But in the season of the *No, No, Nanette* revival and *Follies*—both of which also cast ancient performers—it was fun to hear the question asked.

Over Here! (1974) was another entry in what critics were now viewing as a Nostalgia Cycle. Its authors, book writer Will Holt and tunesmiths Richard M. Sherman and Robert B. Sherman, were not in the veteran class of Richard Rodgers and Kander and Ebb. Nevertheless, they should have done better; for here was more fumbling.

Not that "America's Big Band Musical" was misconceived. A re-creation of Hollywood's wartime musicals, it brought back the two surviving Andrews Sisters, Patty and Maxene. (LaVerne had died in 1967.) The setting, realized as a kind of art-deco Norman Rockwell, was a cross-country train trip of draftees and kibitzers. The cast took in such future stars as John Travolta, Marilu Henner, Treat Williams, and Ann Reinking; and director Tom Moore and choreographer Patricia Birch reveled in the attitudes of swing. The Andrewses are aboard the train as entertainers, looking for a voice to fill out their trio. They do—but she's a Nazi spy (Janie Sell) complete with lipstick transmitter and camera-in-a-compact. The spy is unmasked, however, when it turns out that she knows all the verses to "The Star Spangled Banner."

It sounds like fun—the hot-spot dance-up in "Charlie's Place"; the novelty polka in "The Good Time Girl" (her loose morals transmit venereal disease); the World War I veterans' march, "Hey, Yvette," with its middle-section threnody for fallen comrades, "The Grass Grows Green"; the black porter's view of things, "Don't Shoot the Hooey To Me, Louie"; the Marlene Dietrich send-up for the spy, "Wait For Me, Marlena." There was very little spin and absolutely no camping. The era was lovingly revived, from the opening photographs of the personalities and headlines to the after-the-bows encore by the Sisters of "Beer Barrel Polka," "Boogie Woogie Bugle Boy," and their other hits.

"Slick and cheerfully witless," said *Time*. It's an encomium, in a way. Hollywood's wartime musicals were witless. I think *Over Here!* could have used more slick. The source material was so well observed that the soldiers' names took in Misfit, Utah, and Lucky, right off the forties screen; and the Andrewses made their entrance on a jeep to go into the title song with "The bugle boy blew his rat-ta-tat-too"; and a dream sequence incorporated Sonja Henie skating, James Cagney shouting, Esther Williams stroking, and Marilu Henner smiling back at us in Betty Grable's white swimsuit pose.

In fact, *Over Here!* was so authentic that it almost wasn't pastiche: it was an Andrews Sisters show staged thirty years later. Again, there was nothing wrong with it. But maybe its book was more functional than amusing. Maybe the Sherman Brothers' relentlessly diatonic harmony wants some altered chords. Or maybe *Over Here!* needed an Ella Fitzgerald, even a Joan Davis: people who actually did something during the 1940s besides being sisters. At 341 performances, the show could be termed a near hit, and it certainly launched a few careers. But all the Knowing Innocence ought to *go* somewhere: or what does it know?

Even sure-thing properties could flop badly. Kaye Ballard as Molly Goldberg is excellent casting—but is it a sure thing? Wasn't Molly Goldberg, with her folkways-of-the-Bronx saga, another *Over Here!*: a call from some other place and time? The Goldbergs, a Jewish couple with two kids and an allegedly lovable Uncle David, succeeded on radio, Broadway, and television, but there never was any plot. All depended on the charm of Gertrude Berg as a Miss Fix-it matriarch and head writer of the scripts.

Berg died in 1966, so the creative team of *Molly* (1973) was on its own. They were inexperienced in the Broadway musical—book writers Louis

Garfinkle and Leonard Adelson, with Adelson writing lyrics to Jerry Livingston's music, all under the direction of Paul Aaron. Adelson died and Aaron was replaced; but that didn't help. The new lyricist, Mack David (aided, it was rumored, by others), and the new director, Alan Arkin, were also unfamiliar with musicals. Arkin had directed a Neil Simon hit, *The Sunshine Boys*, the previous season. Take notice: a comedy about two retired Jewish vaudevillians who would have been more or less of musical-comedy age in 1933, when *Molly* takes place. The connection, at least to *Molly*'s producers, was obvious: Alan Arkin does good thirties Jewish.

What *Molly* needed was not *The Sunshine Boys*' Alan Arkin but *The Sunshine Boys*' Neil Simon, doctoring the script. (It got Murray Schisgal, at any rate.) And what *Molly* especially needed was George Abbott, for *Molly* was the perfect Abbott musical comedy—no complex musical structures to puzzle the Abbott ear, and no Grand Themes. Just the desire to entertain and, perhaps, dilate momentarily about such musical-comedy verities as happy families and optimism in hard times.

In other words, *Molly* had potential, as long as every show needn't be *Follies*. Many people thought Gertrude Berg inimitable, irreplaceable; but Ballard has a nice way with urban ethnic projection. The character is one of those "managers," urging on the plotlines, fond of children, humoring villains; and the star was eager to swell that big Ballard voice through the score, through individual lines, even through individual notes. It's a singing style unlike any other, and was at its best here, in eleven numbers. Merman would have balked, but Ballard must have seen *Molly* as Her Big Show.*

It was certainly Her Big Part, as she led the women's chorus in a touch of front-stoop philosophy, "If Everyone Got What They Wanted (after a while, it's no longer a treat)"; seizing the day in the Big Belt number, "A Piece of the Rainbow"; going sly with local entrepreneur Swen Swenson in "Cahoots"; trying an imitation of *Company*'s hell-for-leather patter number, "Getting Married Today," in "So I'll Tell Him"; musing nostalgically with her husband in "I Was There," the opposite of *Fiddler on the*

---

* Her commitment was such that she consulted a numerologist, who suggested that she drop a letter of her name. I still say that the show needed George Abbott rather than a numerologist, but "Kay Ballard" dominated the posters along with a Hirschfeld of the star in Gertrude Berg attire, an accolade. Even more interesting is the billing of the Uncle David: "'also' starring Eli Mintz." "'Also'"?

Roof's "Do You Love Me?" in that these two have always adored each other and have no qualms about saying so; trying out a comic solo, "I See a Man," that was a flash point for the aforementioned rumors about the doctoring of the score; and closing in a surging anthem, "Go in the Best of Health."

It's not a brilliant score, but some of it is tuneful in an old-fashioned way. And that was *Molly*'s downfall. The *Daily News*' Douglas Watt called the show "a warmed-over corpse," because it was a time-capsule piece, fifties in its structure, its conventions, its use and kind of songs. And, of course, had it been done then, Gertrude Berg could have played Molly after all.

But it wouldn't have been a musical with Berg, would it? It would have been a musical *around* her. One can visualize it in the rest of *Molly*'s score, as when Daniel Fortus, a boy with a crush on a haughty girl, sang "In Your Eyes" on the same emotional crescendo he had used in his *Minnie's Boys* solo. Or when Swen Swenson led the sort of vocals that invariably freak into big pointless dance numbers. The thinking behind *Molly* assumed that all musicals bring the second-act curtain up on musical revelry of some kind. Yes, in the 1950s: "Hand Me Down That Can O' Beans" or "A New-Fangled Tango" or even the more pointed "You Did It." Molly's equivalent was "The Mandarin Palace on the Grand Concourse," which turns out to be nothing more than a Chinese restaurant. Why sing about that? In the 1950s, one could get away with it. By the 1970s, it seemed to be trying to deny *Company*.

Even so, something about this bomb of bombs lingers in one's recollections. Is it the effortless cheer of "If Everyone Got What They Wanted," with half the women holding to the melody while the others sing decoration? Is it the haunting ethnic melody in "I Was There" when Ballard sings to her husband, "I believed in you then and I believe in you now," so confident of her trust? Or is it simply that Ballard was entitled to star in a hit Broadway musical?

At least her show was produced. Here's another sure thing: *Bus Stop: The Musical* (   ). As *Cherry*, it was announced for an opening on October 5, 1970 at the Winter Garden, with David Cryer and Paula Wayne as the cowboy and the small-time singer he chases, Art Lund as Cryer's older friend, and Vivian Blaine as the owner of the eatery where the original play took place. Now, that's an Elaine Stritch role—she played *Bus Stop* between the *On Your Toes* revival and *Goldilocks*. Stritch was busy with *Company* at the time of *Cherry*; all the same, a Stritch role in a straight play about to be opened up for music makes this a promising project. And Cryer, Wayne, Lund, and Blaine were all fine singers. As with *Molly*, there's a scarcity of expertise on the creative team: composer Tom Baird and lyricist Ron Miller and book writers William Inge and Gerry Raad. Inge wrote *Bus Stop*, of course, and he was an expert writer: just not of musicals. Tom Panko was to be the director-choreographer, and, as my parentheses imply, *Cherry* never materialized.

This was happening more and more. Shows would be announced, sometimes even with theatre and date—yet it was all wishful thinking. Worse, some of these announcements would periodically reappear, often with personnel changes as various participants became exasperated at the sluggish development. One almost has the feeling that Broadway is running out of material and is thus reluctant to give up on anything with potential. This is not a sign of an art in bloom.

Worst of all were the shows touring minor auditoriums "prior to Broadway," generally with work of such poor quality that they didn't deserve even to bomb on The Street. Usually, the writers would be unknown but the players prominent, as with W.C. (1971), on certain aspects of the life of W. C. Fields. Mickey Rooney and Bernadette Peters starred, but who were book writers Milton Sperling and Sam Locke?* Al Carmines wrote the score; but he was never as adept when doing his own lyrics as when collaborating with others, such as Gertrude Stein or Maria Irene Fornes. Playing what remained of the fifties summer-music-tent circuit, *W.C.* offered a somewhat original concept in the biographical musical, avoiding the fall-and-rise plots of *Gypsy*, *Fiorello!*, *Funny Girl*, and such to imagine the filming of a Fields bio punctuated by reminiscence and commentary. Still: Mickey Rooney as W. C. Fields? Maybe the role is uncastable, except with some nobody who could fold himself into a Fields imitation. And how does one produce a star show without a star?

W.C. never really had a shot at Broadway. But that mainstream sixties invention the David Merrick–Gower Champion super-musical very

---

* Aficionados will fall on the name of Locke with a glad cry, as he was the co-author, with John Latouche, of *The Vamp*, the show that almost ended Carol Channing's career, in 1955.

nearly suffered an out-of-town closing in *Sugar* (1972). Now, *this* is fumbling: Merrick and Champion can't make a smash out of one of the funniest films of all time, with a Jule Styne–Bob Merrill score, Jo Mielziner sets, and Robert Morse in drag?

The film, as all must know, is *Some Like It Hot*, Billy Wilder's twenties spoof, based on a German film of 1953, *Fanfaren der Liebe* (Fanfares of Love). But hold. What if Merrick can get the rights to the original but not to Wilder's remake? The German movie is simply about two musicians wearing disguises to get jobs in bands. It was Wilder who added in all the good stuff—the St. Valentine's Day Massacre, the gangsters after the two heroes, Tony Curtis' Cary Grant imitation, Jack Lemmon's dalliance with eccentric millionaire Joe E. Brown, and Marilyn Monroe. None of this is even hinted at in the German film. But why do *Some Like It Hot* without its contents?

Merrick went ahead anyway, initially with Jerry Herman and Michael Stewart writing a swing-era version of the tale. This did allow them to devise new troubles for the leads to get into—and note that the show, *One of the Girls*, would have been the first Herman-Stewart-Champion work since *Hello, Dolly!*, the biggest musical-comedy hit of all time.

There's no fumbling yet. Merrick finally got hold of the rights to *Some Like It Hot*, but Herman and Stewart were too involved with their concept to jump to Merrick's snapping fingers. So he turned to book writer George Axelrod, along with Styne and Merrill, for *Doing It For Sugar*.

There's still no fumbling, though Merrick replaced Axelrod with Peter Stone a few weeks before rehearsals were to start. Merrick replaced others, starting with Johnny Desmond as the head gangster, Spats Palazzo. Tap dancer Steve Condos took over, turning it from a singing to a dancing role. But Merrick also replaced Jo Mielziner, something that simply never happens. This came about when Merrick and Champion saw Mielziner's set installed at the Kennedy Center before Mielziner had a chance to light it. The deep red of the auditorium seemed to drain the color out of Mielziner's brown color scheme, and Merrick's treatment of this dean of designers was . . . well, the best one can call it is "trademark Merrick."

Robin Wagner redesigned the show in no-fail pastels while everything was changed in a mad spree of changings. Morse survived, along with partner Tony Roberts, Cyril Ritchard (in the Joe E. Brown role), and

Elaine Joyce. But Merrick brought in a very parade of fixers to improve upon Stone and Champion while putting off the premiere with extra tryout stops to absorb the revisions.

Merrick was haggling with a flop, trying to bargain its defects down to where the show's high points would overwhelm them. One can do this. But the show had few high points in the first place. The music was good second-rate Styne, the book a taut reduction of the screenplay, and Morse a treat. Still, *Sugar* was a terrible idea, because the material was completed when Billy Wilder made *Some Like It Hot*. How is one to find a place "past" that film, how to flip it into music and dance? One loses the menace of the gangsters, the Chicago winter into Florida sun, the Monroe, Curtis, and Lemmon of it. Then, too, doesn't drag lose all *its* menace onstage? Drag is performance; stage is performance. But film is "reality," and men in drag in a movie aren't being silly—they're being women, a truly subversive concept.

One can flip *Green Grow the Lilacs* into *Oklahoma!* because the play so wanted to be a musical that it was tailored for Broadway with a lining of folk songs. One can flip *Don Quixote* into *Man of La Mancha* because the Cervantes is a romantic work, and music is romance. One can even flip $8\frac{1}{2}$ into *Nine*, though it is shocking how well that bizarre masterpiece played. There are secrets in these sources; genius sniffs them out.

Sugar was no work of genius. It ended up as enjoyable, at least. But pedestrian. "Penniless Bums" turned a line of unemployed musicians into a quodlibet, one theme sung against another. This is cute. "The Beauty That Drives Men Mad" found dragsters Morse and Roberts tossing their pocketbooks into the house while spouting smutty puns (including one that Frank Loesser had already used in "A Secretary Is Not a Toy" eleven years before, in another Robert Morse show). This is cheesy. "Hey, Why Not!" conjured up a Hollywood fantasy dance for Sugar and a row of Fred Astaires. This is dandy. "Tear the Town Apart," for Steve Condos and his gang, brought out dance arranger John Berkman's dire side with curious high-hat cymbals and nosy bongo drums, then snarling brass and roving piano, as if even the instruments of the orchestra were looking for Morse and Roberts, the witnesses to a gangland slaying. Though it was danced and chanted and not sung, it is possibly *Sugar*'s best number—the one moment when *Sugar* found something in the story that *Some Like It Hot* didn't already have.

A just-made-it hit at 505 performances, *Sugar* did not get to London till Tommy Steele staged it as his own vehicle, in 1992. There was tampering—bandleader Sweet Sue's floor number, "When You Meet a Man in Chicago," was reassigned to Sugar and moved up to become her establishing song. Three numbers were dropped. Scott Joplin's "Maple Leaf Rag" was sung, to new lyrics, and two earlier numbers were recycled. One, from the Styne–Merrill–Liza Minnelli television musical *The Dangerous Christmas of Red Riding Hood*, gave Sugar yet another establishing song, "I'm Naïve." The other is Merrill's alone, *Breakfast at Tiffany*'s "Lament For Ten Men" (now called "Dirty Old Men" and replacing "November Song," for the Miami millionaires). It does *Sugar* no good at all. It's a stupid little piece, suggesting a child getting a rise out of the grown-ups with a no-no word. Of course, *Sugar* was created by tampering, so it's difficult to know where to call a halt. However, recent revivals in Europe have been restoring the original tunestack while retaining "When You Meet a Man in Chicago" as Sugar's first vocal.

So what was *Sugar* in all? A Good Idea musical that wasn't such a good idea after all. The following Merrick-Champion show, *Mack & Mabel* (1974), really *was* a good idea: the professional and romantic adventures of director Mack Sennett and star Mabel Normand in the silent-film days of antic cops, bathing beauties, and pie throwing. *Sugar*'s problem was that it had already been done, and done better; *Mack & Mabel* was something new with a dynamite title and two wonderful stars perfectly cast. And, just to pile it on, *Sugar*'s score is of the functional type, good enough at the time, while *Mack & Mabel*'s score has made the show buff's shortlist of permanent achievements. It's Herman's own favorite of his scores.

Mack & Mabel lasted only 65 performances: so what went wrong? It wasn't Robert Preston as surly, no-frills Mack or Bernadette Peters as feisty yet wistful Mabel. Yes, those are character stereotypes. But Preston and Peters will put an individual spin on everything they do. Lisa Kirk and Jerry Dodge headed the support, and Michael Stewart wrote something new in the Merrick-Champion genre: a sad story about comics. *He's* undemonstrative, obsessively distracted by work, while *she* wants not to be too terribly disappointed by him over and over again. But she always is. Worse, she dies.

This is only ten years but a great deal of history after the central Merrick-Champion piece, *Hello, Dolly!*. That show is a timeless tale filled with lovable eccentrics. *Mack & Mabel* is a two-person story set in an era when certain things were happening that could never happen again: an art was invented and developed by folk who were not artists. But this only illustrates for us a difference between *Dolly!*'s 1960s and *Mack & Mabel*'s 1970s—carefree musical comedy's absorption of the serious musical play's aesthetics.

As it happens, *Mack & Mabel* scants its subject matter somewhat. Though Sennett liked to claim that he was imitating French innovators, he did introduce tricks into comic cinema, as when Fatty Arbuckle, changing his shorts, gestures to the camera to stay above the waist. Sennett also directed America's first six-reel comedy, *Tillie's Punctured Romance*, in 1914, when one reel was the norm in this genre and two reels rare.

We get none of this in *Mack & Mabel*, and nothing of Arbuckle, Charlie Chaplin, Ben Turpin, Marie Dressler, Gloria Swanson, Harry Langdon, and gag man Frank Capra, all of whom worked for Sennett. At that, the show has Mack discovering Mabel when she gets into a fight on his set trying to claim payment for a take-out deli order. In reality, Normand had already been at Vitagraph when she was promoted to lead at Biograph under Sennett (and D. W. Griffith).

True, *Mack & Mabel* is entertainment, not academic revelation. Still, there is no sense that something marvelous and American is undergoing its formative evolution virtually from one day to the next. Where is the sheer awe at film's power that Peter Bogdanovich gave us when the leads of *Nickelodeon* attend *The Birth of a Nation*?

Mack & Mabel began well, with a kind of jump cut into Chase Music that was a full orchestra's equivalent of silent-movie piano: the Overture. Then, after a book scene of Mack ruminating in his studio on the eve of losing everything to the overwhelming talkies, he went into "Movies Were Movies," a very generic yet at the same time extremely characterful number, a Jerry Herman specialty. He's working at the center of musical comedy: first vocal, big star, time, place, action. But he's also putting his protagonist into evidence: bravado and bluster, minimizing his life's work as a mere livelihood while glowing pridefully in the history that his business made. It's devious and brilliant, like the best of Herman: enjoy yourselves but listen to what these people say. Herman uses the familiar to lure us into the specific.

Champion used "Movies Were Movies" to launch the story. As Preston sang, players came out of the darkness of present-day 1938 to engender the 1911 of Sennett's beginnings, with the actors, the grips, the cameraman, the piano lady. As the song ended, we were suddenly at the first day of the history: movies were *movies*, something happening in every frame. It was a handsome start-up. However, later numbers featuring the Keystone Kops at a hospital fire and bathing beauties shooting down a curvy slide bordered on the floppo.

My guess is that Champion had no sympathy for this antique art. What's *silent* film to the master of the musical? *Mack & Mabel* isn't a romance or a satire, Champion's natural forms. It's a cultural study containing a romance. And it has a dark side; dark shows need book room or an operatic score. Champion's shows got only song-and-dance room.

What are we to make of Jerry Dodge's final exit, when a narrating Preston says, "Hey, you know a funny thing about Frank? I think that bastard was in love with Mabel all those years. He never said it, but I'll bet he was, just the same." There has been no hint of this for the previous two and a half hours. It is simply thrown at us. Is this clumsy writing by Michael Stewart, or Champion filleting a libretto out of fear of spoken drama?

It may be that *Mack & Mabel* was the wrong subject for the Merrick-Champion musical. How would Hal Prince have treated it? He would have loved the way Mabel's phonograph supplies the vamp for the first ballad, Mack's "I Won't Send Roses." Prince would not have loved "When Mabel Comes in the Room," and Champion didn't love it, either. This is titlesongitis without a title song. Unfortunately, the 1960s promoted—in such shows as *Camelot, Hello, Dolly!, Mame, Cabaret*, and *Promises, Promises*—the notion that smash hit shows had title numbers, or at least Big Lady salutes. The producers thought so, anyway. It was Alexander Cohen, not Jerry Herman, who wanted a "Dear World" for *Dear World*; and David Merrick's musical taste matched that of a baseball-field hot-dog vendor. So Mabel comes in the room, and rides a camera crane out over the public, and dances with the most uncharacterized chorus since the 1920s.

Other numbers upheld Herman's use of genre to specify his people. For instance: the Heroine's Self-Esteem Number: "Look What Happened To Mabel," a gleeful strut that suggests an unworldly young woman admiring herself, visibly tickled at her own talent. (Champion staged it as Mabel's first look at the rushes, facing the audience in the projector light.) The "Gangway, World!" galop: "(This time it's the) Big Time," which functioned as a Travel Number to get Mack's New York crew onto a train for California. The Heroine's I Hate Him Number: "Wherever He Ain't." And of course the Torch Number: "Time Heals Everything."

Genre is upended, however, in "Tap Your Troubles Away," musical comedy's venerable solution to problems but this time performed alongside scenes of Mabel's degradation as a drug addict and even murder suspect. And one odd number, "Hit 'Em on the Head," explains Mack's physical comedy in music that actually sounds like a guffaw. Champion made Herman replace it during tryout fever with "My Heart Leaps Up," an inferior piece; the earlier number has been restored in revivals.

A flawed but always interesting show with two of the most engaging stars of all time, *Mack & Mabel* got horrible reviews. One wondered if the critics had tired of the whole Merrick-Champion thing and wanted it over. The Tony people, astonishingly, wanted Jerry Herman over. They nominated the two stars, Champion (twice) and Stewart, designers Robin Wagner and Patricia Zipprodt, and the show itself. The nominees for Best Score were: two popular shows (*Shenandoah* and *The Wiz*, which won), one show that ran 9 performances (*The Lieutenant*), and one show that wasn't a musical (Robert Wilson's *A Letter For Queen Victoria*, billed as an "opera" because of Wilson's love of flamboyance and spectacle). Of course, the Tony people routinely mortify themselves with outlandish propositions, such as the failure to comprehend the meaning of such words as "book" and "musical," and omissions so bizarre that one thinks of them as the oversights of the blind. The truth of it is that the Tonys need Jerry Herman more than Jerry Herman needs Tonys.

Generally, a failure like *Mack & Mabel*'s means sudden death, at least on all main stages. But *Mack & Mabel*'s cast album collected a following, and a beloved score gets its show revived. Book alterations tried to soften the hard edges or combine the Lisa Kirk and Jerry Dodge characters. The show's fortunes really changed when Olympic ice skaters Torvill and Dean used the show's overture for a routine on television. This led to a London concert in 1988, then a staging there in 1995, with Howard McGillin, Caroline O'Connor, and Kathryn Evans. McGillin sang the heck out of the music, giving the story more life than ever. Yet it remains a dark show in its essence and cannot be lightened. Mabel keeps trying to draw out Mack's sensitive side, but he doesn't have one. On Broadway, originally, he finally gave in with an "I love you, Mabel Normand"—the curtain line. It seems too little too late. But the "imaginary" Mabel Normand movie-comeback finale used in London is fraudulent, a happy ending for a story that ends sadly.

The very sound of a Merrick-Champion-Herman *Mack & Mabel* is Easy Smash; the title itself should run for years. In fact, this was a Tricky Idea musical, an ever more common form from this decade on. Now I've got two for you whose combined runs total 24 performances, though one had a superb score and the other was extremely entertaining. And each of the two centered on a great star of the postwar American musical. One was Barbara Cook. The other was Don Murray.

Cook's show, *The Grass Harp* (1971), was billed as "a musical play," not necessarily because it had not a single laugh and contained very little dancing. It even lost the Merry Villagers that had been included in its source, Truman Capote's 1952 play of the same title, from his novel. Eighteen actors gave the straight play; the musical used but nine (and five little kids). But then, Capote's tale of a dysfunctional family whose more wistful members flee real life in a symbolic tree house is not proper material for a musical comedy. There's not much humor in the play, either, though it delights in the sound of Capote's Southern Gothic Genteel. Here's the play's first speech, spoken by the black maid to fifteen-year-old Collin:

> CATHERINE: It's a good thing you got your growth, because now you'd stunt it for sure; smoking and dancing and floozies—those are among the several things that will stunt a boy's growth and drive him crazy.

That line reappears almost verbatim in Kenward Elmslie's book of the musical, and in general the adaptation is astonishingly tight. Much of Capote—and certainly all his most important thoughts—resounds through the musical, now in the script and now in Claibe Richardson and Elmslie's score.

This can't have been easy, for unlike the people in *Applause* or *Mack & Mabel*, Capote's folk are genuine eccentrics. You call it Southern Gothic: they call it Southern Life. The musical deleted their worst habits, such as the heroine's wearing vanilla extract as cologne. Still, we have the two Talbo sisters, the bossy yet vulnerable Verena (Ruth Ford) and the primly loony Dolly (Barbara Cook); the maid (Carol Brice) so loyal to Dolly that she calls Verena "that one"; the Talbo cousin Collin (Russ Thacker) and Dolly's beau, Judge Cool (John Baragrey); and the con man (Max Showalter) who wants to market Dolly's tonic recipe. A cosmetics saleswomen in the play called Miss Baby Love Dallas became Babylove the faith healer (Karen Morrow), with a brood of chicks. This was a smart move for the musical version, because faith healers belt out revivalist rave-ups, here backed up by the kid chorus. In fact, the show gave Morrow one of the great tours de force in "The Babylove Miracle Show," a thirteen-minute sequence of ten musical numbers that tore the Martin Beck apart from roof to pit.

What other musical combined three such great voices? Cook was an anointed diva and Morrow was on the rise, but Brice had had bad luck. She was the black classical diva whose prime fell between the eras of Marian Anderson and of Leontyne Price, Martina Arroyo, Camilla Williams, Mattiwilda Dobbs, and Grace Bumbry. So at first she was overshadowed and later she was crowded. Like Anderson a contralto, Brice was major enough to make the first studio recording of Gustav Mahler's *Songs of a Wayfarer*, with Fritz Reiner and the Pittsburgh Symphony, but was too often in the wrong place, such as that bomb of bombs *Saratoga* (1959). Here she was perfectly cast and set off with the richly harmonized "If There's Love Enough," the devilish "Marry With Me"—plucked right out of a paragraph of Capote—and "Indian Blues," a jazzy complaint with, the score reads, "tom-tom beat."

The aficionados among my readers will already be at one with my invocations, for *The Grass Harp* stands among the most cherished of Broadway scores, so eloquent in Richardson's major seventh and flatted ninth chords, so personalized in Elmslie's understanding of the sense in Capote's sensibility. Is Dolly's confessional "Chain of Love"—another song pulled right off Capote's page—the single greatest soprano solo of the decade? The *era*? The television critics on NBC and ABC so responded to the music that one likened the show "to an opera, but a fun one," and the other called it "a highly sophisticated fairy tale."

Then why did the show collapse after a single week? Here's the Tricky Idea factor: a more or less plotless straight play can charm on atmosphere and Capote poetry and tinkly Virgil Thomson accompaniments, not to mention the Dolly of Mildred Natwick (and a house favorite, Johnny Stewart, as Collin). However, the structure of a musical is based on the constant heightening of communication by the songs (and dances, if any). Something must be *accomplished* within each number. The plot must move, a character must land, a joke must play. A spoken play (or a film) can drift a bit. A musical must deliver *and* it must do so appropriately. A good number for the wrong character can throw an entire evening off course. *The Grass Harp* has very little action, so its numbers treat character or incidentals. There are no plot numbers, no *Carousel* Bench Scene or *Company* "Barcelona." There's no stretch, no getting there, and the piece becomes a beautiful concert, as frustrating as it is meaningful.

The other Tricky Idea musical is *Smith* (1973). Yes, I was joking about Don Murray's being a musical star. But that is more truly *Smith*'s joke: Murray, as a funless botanist, found himself trapped in a fun-filled musical comedy. So it *has* to be Murray. It couldn't be Robert Preston or Danny Fortus, because they loved to be in musicals. Murray's botanist, Walter Smith, doesn't believe in them.

Technically an off-Broadway entry, *Smith* played at the Eden Theatre, the full-sized house on Second Avenue at Twelfth Street where the Phoenix Theatre introduced *The Golden Apple* (1954) before its move uptown and where, as we'll see, two major Broadway hits of the 1970s began their runs. *Smith* had to receive its public in a house of Broadway proportions because there is no jest in being trapped in a little bitty show with bitty attitudes. He's trapped in Rodgers and Hammerstein, in Kurt Weill, in Jerry Herman, with a real orchestra and dogmatically pastel sets and "Wear me!" costumes. Yet the plot suggests Maria Montez. Murray must travel to tropical Balinasia to seek out a plant whose juice serves either as a miracle diet or an aphrodisiac.

But which? As Dean Fuller, Tony Hendra, and Matt Dubey's book and Dubey and Fuller's score had it, it doesn't matter, because musicals aren't about plants. They're about Boy Gets Girl (Virginia Sandifur). The joy of the evening is that the musical's conventions aren't helping Smith at all. They bewilder and hinder him. People keep singing at him (even his mother), phones lack wires, candle flame can be unscrewed from the candle, stagehands give advice. The native chief of Balinasia is a senile thespian who can't remember lines and finally just bursts into a helping of

The Tempest. A comical Irish maid, doubling in a second role, retains her Irish accent though it makes no sense anymore. A Frenchman living on Balinasia turns out to be—no, not Ezio Pinza: Maurice Chevalier, in the usual "Enjoy life" waltz, "Onh-Honh-Honh!" Even when Murray starts to fall for Sandifur, she drifts offstage so that an Agnes de Mille–style dancing counterpart can glide in to drag Murray into an irritatingly athletic Dream Ballet.

You would have loved it, if you were already an expert in musicals. If not, at least some of *Smith* might have perplexed you. The thing about Tricky Idea shows is that when they work, they're *The King and I* or *West Side Story*. When they don't, they're a cult show with a cast album; or they vanish, like *Smith*.

If the growing lack of birthright stars and the fumbling of such pros as Richard Rodgers and Gower Champion seem to cast a shadow on the 1970s, at least the black show was tooting along in a kind of second youth. Its first youth was way back at the start of the century; but early success did not ultimately create a full-scale flowering. *That* came in the 1920s, most famously with *Shuffle Along* (1921) and *Blackbirds of 1928*, but counting a number of black shows each season.

Now, in the 1970s, blacks were again creating, as well as performing, black shows. Melvin Van Peebles wrote all of *Aint Supposed To Die a Natural Death* (1971) and also produced and directed *Dont Play Us Cheap!* (1972). The first, an enraged racist mishmash subtitled "Tunes From Blackness," was staged (by Gilbert Moses) well enough to get respectful and even very impressed notices; white-guilt foundation money helped keep it going for 325 performances. Set in present-day Harlem, it was a musical in only the fringe sense, for Van Peebles wanted his lyrics chanted or declaimed rather than sung, and the only dancing arrived when later *Saturday Night Live* comic Garrett Morris offered "Lily Done the Zampoughi Every Time I Pulled Her Coattail." Lily (Barbara Alston) accordingly adduced the zampoughi on a platform overhead. The author's context, however, was that Morris was in prison for Lily's murder. And the final number, "Put a Curse On You," had Minnie Gentry, as a trash-can scavenger, hurling abuse at the audience.

Dont Play Us Cheap! was less alienating, a book show where *Aint* was virtually a revue; funny where *Aint* was humorless; and a saucy chaos. *Dont* recalls the aforementioned *Cabin in the Sky* formula of angels and devils fighting for control of human souls—a continuation of sketches popularized in the twenties black revues and apparently a trope with its source deep in the minstrel show and antebellum plantation culture. For all we know, it may date back to prehistoric African myth.

In the typical twenties sketch, a devil and an angel vie for influence over a male; the customary temptations are a jug of corn liquor and a high-yaller beauty. Van Peebles' spin presented two devils (young Joe Keyes Jr. and veteran Avon Long) dispatched by Satan to disrupt a Harlem party. It seems a modest assault, but the joke (as in *Finian's Rainbow*) lay in the humanizing of the pair, tempted themselves. *Dont* held out exactly half as long as *Aint*, probably because Van Peebles' staging lacked the professionalism that held *Aint* together.

Two black woman put together a show of more general appeal in *Don't Bother Me, I Can't Cope* (1972), whose success encouraged it to move from the fringey Playhouse down to the Edison. Vinnette Carroll conceived and staged and Micki Grant wrote (and led the company of twelve in) what they teamed "a musical entertainment" because of its loose structure. A revue made entirely of song and dance (with some rhymed dialogue here and there), *Don't Bother Me* challenged Van Peebles' cynicism with a sometimes critical but genuinely joyous outlook.

It was a celebration, from the vibrant opening, "I Gotta Keep Movin'," through the naming of black luminaries but also of John and Bobby Kennedy in "They Keep Coming," to the finale of the well-wishing "Good Vibrations." Typical of Carroll and Grant's program was the first line of "So Little Time": "I've got no time for hating."

The design was perhaps the simplest in musical history: a bare stage adorned with two gray ladders. The men wore comfortable clothes and the women mild dress-up. The show had the air of a church variety night performed by Broadway-level talent. "Two Black women," Carroll wrote, "wanted young Black artists to have material on which to sharpen their instruments and watch as their grandparents sit in the audience and say 'Amen.'"

The Wiz (1975) was a different matter altogether, a traditional big book musical put on by blacks. Not only the writers and cast but even most of the production team was black. Even the content was black, though based on L. Frank Baum's classic children's book that informed the MGM film with Judy Garland. Baum himself had written the book for the first musical version, *The Wizard of Oz*, way back at the start of the Second Age; it veers considerably from the original. The film is more faithful and *The Wiz* most faithful yet, correcting the film's revisions of Baum, such as replacing the silver slippers with ruby ones because red basks in Technicolor, and pretending the whole Oz adventure was a dream.

What gave *The Wiz* its jazz was an evening-long joke that never staled: the music, performing style, and dialogue all went black without putting any ethnic strain on the story. Dorothy still started from Kansas, not Detroit, still picked up the Scarecrow, Tin Woodman, and Cowardly Lion, not the Will Mastin Trio. Yet the entire show gamed with the material—a stunt possible only because the audience knows the story from the film. Here's a taste of Dorothy's encounter with the good witch, whose magic never works. She's going to read Dorothy's name off her magic slate:

ADDAPERLE: Shirley!
DOROTHY: No.
ADDAPERLE: (faltering) Denise!
DOROTHY: No.
ADDAPERLE: (desperate) Starletta?

Finally, the witch asks Dorothy simply to write her name on the slate.

ADDAPERLE: (reading the slate triumphantly) Dorothy!
DOROTHY: You call that magic?

But the quest awaits, so Addaperle and a handful of Munchkins sing "He's the Wizard," a swing-easy plot number with wild vocal punctuation from the Munchkins, now sudden cries and now chromatic glissandos. After the number, the witch warns Dorothy to avoid the poppies:

ADDAPERLE: This kind will put you to sleep for a hundred years. It's terrible, wakin' up and your clothes are all outta style.

She then tries to disappear, but her magic wand turns into handkerchiefs.

ADDAPERLE: Trouble is, honey, I ain't been disappearin' much lately. I been takin' the bus.

A lot of *The Wiz*'s power derived from Geoffrey Holder's elaborate costume plot, especially dazzling against Tom H. John's simple sets. But it was a smartly written show to begin with, the book by William F. Brown and the score by Charlie Smalls. Holder also directed (after Gilbert Moses left during the tryout), George Faison choreographed, and the cast was solid. Hinton Battle, Tiger Haynes, and Ted Ross played the three companions, Clarice Taylor and Mabel King were the two witches, and Andre De Shields took the title role. Above all was the Dorothy of Stephanie Mills, a cute little bit who rooted the daffy black talent show in reality. Everything else was Apollo Theatre specialty shtick; Mills was playing the story.

More than *Georgy* and *Purlie*, *The Wiz* showed the American book musical absorbing the pop sound. Smalls' lyrics deal heavily in the assonance that pop ignorantly takes for rhyme ("crazy" and "baby") and lack the craftsman's niceties. Nevertheless, he marries R&B and gospel to the needs of a theatre score. It's a far jump from "We're Off To See the Wizard" to "Ease On Down the Road," but the latter asserts with sly charm the black feeling of the whole show. And note that while the MGM movie stingily assigns one melody to all three companions' establishing songs, Smalls dignifies them with unique turns. The Scarecrow's "I Was Born On the Day Before Yesterday," with the cleverest lyrics in the show, sounds like the autobiography of an innocent kid hired as a supermodel and pushed out onto the runway. The respelled Tinman, patched together of old parts with a garbage-can torso and a Budweiser can as his left calf, has the piano-driven "Slide Some Oil To Me." As Tiger Haynes likes his tap, the music goes into vaudeville hoofing noises for a Haynes solo. The Lion's "I'm a Mean Old Lion" is of course all vamp and no tune: a front of a number, cowardly music.

The Wiz ended up a Tony festival, claiming seven awards, including Best Musical. It ran four years, too. But a 1984 revival with Stephanie Mills attracted no interest. Was the show a one-off, like *Of Thee I Sing*, *Follow the Girls*, and *Can-Can* a big hit of its moment that may never sustain a revival? Or did *The Wiz*'s sluggish film version harm the firm? It seemed a smart idea—to reset the action in a fantasy New York. And the cast includes Diana Ross, Michael Jackson, Nipsey Russell, Ted Ross and Mabel King from Broadway, Richard Pryor as the Wiz, and Lena Horne. But Sidney Lumet's direction has no pace, no jump. The last shot typifies the film's lack of fizz: back from Oz, schoolteacher Ross heads for her brownstone apartment. As she nears the stoop, we look for some punctuational visual—an extra glimmer from an Ozzy streetlamp, say. Something smiling somewhere. We get nothing: Ross reaches her door and walks in. This movie doesn't finish. It stops.

For all the titles in this chapter, then, we have but a single classic, *Grease* (1972). Jim Jacobs and Warren Casey's spoof of fifties teen culture is another show that opened at the Eden, then moved to Broaday. It launched the careers of Carole Demas (Sandy, the heroine), Barry Bostwick (Danny, the hero), Timothy Meyers (Kenickie, the toughest of the boys), Adrienne Barbeau (Rizzo, the toughest of the girls), Walter Bobbie (Roger), and Kathi Moss (Cha-Cha Di Gregorio). But its most immediate effect was the promotion of director Tom Moore and choreographer Patricia Birch as experts in period pastiche, which led them to the stylish resuscitations of *Over Here!*.

Grease is eternally revivable because it isn't about the 1950s. It *uses* the 1950s—the attitudes, the music, the brand names. (The kids attend Rydell High School, a reference to pop singer Bobby Rydell.) What *Grease* is about is cliques and dating and cars and fitting in, a euphemism for the crushing of the individualist spirit in a fascism of conformity.

That may read a bit heavy for a piece that is almost entirely a put-on. Almost entirely: for in five minutes near the end, the authors move out of their comical mode into something substantial. It's a jarring and wonderful moment, and I'll get to it presently. For now, we should emphasize the fun of *Grease*, for its central joke travels through not only the dialogue but the score.

Much of the spoken humor deals in stereotype, as in this encounter of the square and the cynic:

EUGENE: It's been very nice talking to you, Betty.
RIZZO: Yeah, see ya around the Bookmobile.

But the score plays games as well, making character numbers out of antique rock and roll in "Freddy, My Love," "Greased Lightnin'," and "It's Raining on Prom Night."

"Summer Nights" is actually *two* character numbers, for while Sandy tells the girls about the boy she met at the beach, Danny tells the boys about *his* romance. Of course, she met Danny and he met Sandy, and they have no idea that they'll be attending school together—that in fact the girls are in the cafeteria and the boys are on the school steps just outside (though we see the two groups a few feet apart in the by-now customary unit set). It's a little like a rock-and-roll "And This Is My Beloved."

A high point of the score, "Summer Nights" reveals something arresting about the two leads. She wistfully recounts what we believe really happened; he reinvents their virginal courtship as his erotic exploit. For Sandy, the utmost of their abandon was to stay out till ten o'clock. In Danny's version, he scored a home run.

On one level, this is fifties teen practice: the girls are chaste and the boys are men. But only Kenickie is experienced. The others are children enjoying *The Mickey Mouse Club*. Danny is a conformist, an adherent of cool. Sandy is pure in the cultural sense: unformed, even somewhat independent. It is *Grease*'s sad parable that social success and independence are mutually exclusive. Sandy will have to conform—to swear off chastity, at least in look and manner—or she cannot have Danny.

So *Grease* is not just a spoof; some real life hides behind the dance numbers "Shakin' at the High School Hop" and "Born To Hand-Jive" and the comic waltz "Look at Me, I'm Sandra Dee." But for the high spirits of "All Choked Up," the ending could be called unhappy: Sandy ultimately conforms, calling up one of the other girls to help her with a wild-kid makeover in black leather jacket, tight slacks, cigarette, and chewing gum. Worst of all, she has had to make the ultimate sacrifice in honesty: stuffing tissues under her bra cups.

The event that pushes Sandy over the edge is the dark five minutes I spoke of earlier, a confrontation between Rizzo and Sandy. Rizzo fears that she is pregnant (by Kenickie), which in fifties blue-collar America was tragedy indeed. Sandy offers sympathy, which Rizzo brutally rejects. Yes, Rizzo is in big trouble. And even if she weren't facing unmarried pregnancy, her future has no promise. But the conformism that she adheres to does at least give her self-belief. That's *her* independence. And she lets Sandy have it with the score's best number, "There Are Worse Things I Could Do." This keening torch song is a war cry. "I could hurt someone like me" is its second best line. The best is the contemptuous "But to cry in front of you." Technically the show's second couple, Kenickie and (especially) Rizzo hold the show's center, as the exponents of the social code that the show examines. Danny is the cynosure and Sandy the sweetheart—but the code is not about appeal. The code is about survival.

Even as the work was pursuing its eight-year run, the film appeared, like *Cabaret* one of the few phenomenally successful movie musicals after *The Sound of Music*. And as with *Cabaret*, songs written for the film (variously by John Farrar, Barry Gibb, and, together, Louis St. Louis and Scott Simon) have dogged stage revivals. "You're the One That I Want" places itself easily right where "All Choked Up" was, and the new number improves upon it, though we do lose the show's one reference to Elvis (through his "All Shook Up"). Sandy's "Hopelessly Devoted To You" and Danny's "Sandy" are useful ballads that fit almost anywhere in the action.

But where to put the title song? Introduced over the film's cartoon credits by Frankie Valli, "Grease" is theme and credo—but it's Barry Gibb's hindsighted abstraction, not something that the kids would articulate themselves. A production in Vienna in 1994 solved the problem by starting the show with both "Sandy" (as the main couple's duet) and "Grease" (for the ensemble) as out-of-time scene-setters. This Vienna production, spoken in German but sung in the original, found other expedients in taming this now oversized score. "It's Raining on Prom Night" became Cha-Cha's party piece at the prom (as Sandy "duets" with her in inset). And, because this is Europe, Rizzo finished off "Sandra Dee" with a coloratura cadenza rising to a high B flat.

One odd thing about *Grease* is the way that its many scenes—in and around the school, at kids' houses, the Burger Palace, and a drive-in—were all played in that unit set. Perhaps a full-scale staging with drops and wagons would have been prohibitive for an untried idea by and with unknowns. Money is the problem, so much so that shows can't even afford to go to Boston for a tryout. Now they go to London.

4

DECCA BROADWAY

AMERICANS IN LONDON

Another of the many factors that altered the musical's history in the 1970s was the loss of pre-Broadway tinkering time, more important than many might suppose. The tryout is where chaos is moderated, where gaffes are silenced and tired moments invigorated.

Can't they reckon what's wrong in rehearsals? No. Only an audience can tell them. As we noticed with *The Grass Harp*, musical numbers tend to emphasize points of character, plot, atmosphere, and so on. If one is singing the wrong number, one may not discover it till it starts flopping in front of the public.

So the tryout is sine qua non. Such out-and-out hits as *The King and I*, *Hello, Dolly!*, and *Funny Girl* were near misses saved out of town; but countless other shows underwent the Cinderella tryout, from nothing doing to hit of the ball.

However, it must happen out of New York, away from the chattering public. A work in tribulation in some other place creates gossip, but it's filtered and contradictory. Inconclusive. It is also in short supply—how many who saw *Hello, Dolly!* in Detroit could tell New Yorkers in those years before the Internet? This was hiding in plain sight. A show struggling to right itself in front of eight audiences of New Yorkers a week, however, is inviting a scandal.

Once again, the money crush led to an unsatisfactory solution. Because most shows lose money on the road, the New York preview system was adopted, which meant playing your weakest performances before your worst enemies, the usual disaster fans, and idiots who think that technical problems with the set mark an aesthetic flaw in composition. *Merrily We Roll Along* (1981) and *Titanic* (1997) underwent extensive revisions during previews. But they had started badly, and word of mouth so tricked the town that critics ignored the finished show to review the first preview.

But here's another road. With English production costs so low, why not perfect one's show in an English tryout, then let it run in London? If it works, it can come home, set to go.

It's not that strange a notion, for American writers created shows for England in the 1920s and early 1930s. Jerome Kern contributed to English productions but composed four on his own. George and Ira Gershwin, Rodgers and Hart, Schwartz and Dietz, and Cole Porter all wrote for the West End—all more or less in imitation of the West End style. The Gershwins' *Primrose* (1924) observed such English character types as the top-hatted "dude" and the rambunctious shopgirl, and the score (written with English lyricist Desmond Carter) preferred to American jazz the typical English patter song in $\frac{6}{8}$ time. The eleven o'clocker, "I Make Hay When the Moon Shines," was modeled on Gertie Millar's "Moonstruck," in the beloved West End hit *Our Miss Gibbs* (1909). Of course, *Primrose* was not an audition for a Broadway hearing, but an autonomous project.

Ambassador was an audition. With a score by Don Gohman and Hal Hackady and a book by Don Ettlinger, this adaptation of Henry James' *The Ambassadors* played London in 1971 because the producers couldn't raise the money in dollars, even with two stars, Howard Keel and Danielle Darrieux. Some may be skeptical because of Keel's wooden performing style—but that's Henry James' point. *The Ambassadors* deals with a New England widower sent to Europe by the local beldame—pointedly named Mrs. Newsome—to rescue her son Chad from a liaison with a Frenchwoman. Of course, it's really the born-yesterday American's liaison with old Europe, the confirmed mercantilist falling in love with amour and esprit. We need the wooden Keel, to contrast with the mercurial Darrieux.

So this is a workable plot: Keel expects an adventuress and finds instead an education in womanhood. Chad will go home; yes: but Keel will remain, an American in Paris.* What chances for music! A soirée will make use of a quodlibet double chorus, "The Right Time, the Right

---

* I recall that MGM title because I think Keel wasn't at all wooden. Those *movies* were: *Show Boat*, *Kiss Me, Kate*, *Rose Marie*, *Kismet*. Such meager helpings of savory Broadway! A recently discovered secret document, *The Protocols of the Elders of the Freed Unit*, reveals that the purveyors of this enervating glop were trying to stupefy Americans into zombies and rule the world. Luckily, the release of the most evil of the titles, *The Band Wagon*, stirred the suspicions of J. Edgar Hoover. Though the Freed Unit pulled off an exculpatory ruse with the incomparable *Gigi*, Hoover's men closed the insidious project down.

Place." Keel will have doubting soliloquies, Darrieux the fun stuff—her credo, "Surprise"; her explanation of her affair with Chad, "Young with Him"; and the big second-act rouser, "That's What I Need Tonight." Besides the two stars, the entire cast was local, as was the creative team, except for Stone Widney, who directed, and Philip J. Lang, the orchestrator. It was all very Broadway, with the authentic sound, I'm sorry to say, of a fifties flop.

Yes, the score is smart and tuneful. It does most things right. For instance, the horrible comedy number for Chad's friend "Little Bilham" (as everybody calls him), "What Can You Do With a Nude?," which recalls such other horrible fifties comedy numbers as "A Headache and a Heartache" and "Never, Never Be an Artist." Or there is a nightclub singer's silly "You Can Tell a Lady By Her Hat," used as a foil to Darrieux's sorrow when she is confronted by Chad's awful mother. A flower girl can sing "Lilas" (Lilacs), which will be introduced when Keel arrives in Paris and later echoed for ironic emphasis in his deflated "What Happened To Paris?"

Like *Molly*, *Ambassador* was enjoyable but *outdated* work. True, *Molly* was a mess while *Ambassador* was orderly and sensitive. Also true, one can hardly encompass in any theatre piece the thrillingly lit photography of human nature taken by James' final novels; and *The Ambassadors* is one of these. Just to know that, like the Gospels, it has two significantly opposing Marys (Darrieux's role, Marie de Vionnet, and an expatriate American, Maria Gostrey) tells how ruthlessly dense James will be. Musicals cannot be dense—but did Keel's profession have to be standardized down to lawyer from his more Jamesian vocation in the novel, editor of a little magazine under the sponsorship of the overwhelming Mrs. Newsome?

Or consider Chad, so amazing in his European reincarnation that James spends many pages digesting the protagonist's impressions of him. Yet Chad is not entirely unwilling to go home. James classifies characters by who they are as intensely as a racist; but his races are Banker, Casually Envious Sidekick, Doomed Beauty, and such. The problem with *Ambassador* is that it classified characters by what they sang: operetta.

The show did not succeed in London. Still, it came to Broadway the following year, 1972, with a rewritten book (by Ettlinger and Anna Marie Barlow). Peter Rice's designs, Lang's instrumentation, and Widney's staging were maintained, along with Keel and Darrieux. Otherwise, the company was entirely new. Seven songs were added and seven dropped, including the old-fashioned "Nude" and "Hat" comedy songs. The opening sequence, in Massachusetts, was deleted; the work now began with Keel having just alighted from his train in the Gare Saint–Lazare. These were all improvements. Yet the work remained a lovely dinosaur. The critics gleefully savaged it, and composer Gohman took his life in despair.

Another London failure didn't try Broadway, though it boasted Charles Strouse and Lee Adams' most intriguing score: *I and Albert* (1972). There were a number of musicals about Queen Victoria in this time, off-Broadway and regionally, but this was the big one. With a book by Jay Allen and staging by the film director John Schlesinger, *I and Albert* was an imaginative and even crazy show. Polly James played Victoria and Sven-Bertil Taube her obsessively adored Albert; and there were tours de force by Aubrey Woods (as both the bellicose Palmerston and the liberal Gladstone) and Lewis Fiander (as the laissez-faire Melbourne and the interventionist Disraeli). One can gauge the inventiveness of the production in Fiander's two character numbers. In Act One, as Melbourne, his "Leave It Alone" expressed a kind of cynically Panglossian belief in a complete lack of governance, illustrated by a music-hall soft shoe. In Act Two, as Disraeli, his "When You Speak With a Lady" was, literally, a magician's act. He pulled India out of a hat.

How the authors of the *Golden Boy* and *Applause* songs turned into the makers of this almost bizarrely rich score is a wonder. *Golden Boy* is jazzy Broadway and *Applause* show-biz Broadway. *I and Albert* is not Broadway at all, and, beyond that, is indescribable, breaking all rules. The chorus, for instance, plays the English population—all of it, more or less—placing the personal story of Victoria, Albert, and their family within the frame of history. "It Has All Begun," at first a duet for Victoria and her confidante just before the coronation, opens up into a stirring ensemble, as if all the nation were hailing the queen. It's a logical way to start an evening that must cover a sixty-three-year reign. Similarly, "This Noble Land" is the obligatory patriotic anthem, and "Go It, Old Girl!," at Victoria's Diamond Jubilee, a sensible chronological marker. But a chorus of working-class folk, "I've 'Eard the Bloody 'Indoos 'As It Worse," balances the royal scenes with some real life; and "All Glass," sung before a view of the Crystal Palace at the Great Exhibition of 1851 in Hyde Park, brings in the towering scientific achievements by which Western Civilization identifies itself.

There were, of course, songs for the two leads, including a comic ballad, "Just You and Me," in which the queen and her consort try to rendezvous while their children keep interrupting with wishes and complaints. The second act emphasized how Albert's early death all but destroyed Victoria. Her keening "Draw the Blinds" is the most dramatic music in the score, a dark complement to the title number, which is a solo for the queen that builds from a fluty little strut to a gala parade of some giant marching band. But then, the score reflects the show's wish to present not only Victoria the person but Victoria the empress of the most powerful nation of the nineteenth century. Some felt that the book failed to pull all the parts together. But to hear the songs in story order is to sense the grasp that Strouse and Adams had on their subject.

The production, too, was dazzling. Schlesinger's handling of the many crowd scenes was widely praised, and his set designer, Luciana Arrighi, dressed the saga in projections and cutouts of antique children's-book illustrations. It's hard to know why the show did not succeed, and even harder with our next title. For this one *was* a hit in London. And unlike the austerely psychological Henry James and Queen Victoria, this one's topic was popular American subject matter—in fact, *the* American subject matter: *Gone with the Wind.*

It started in Japan, where the Toho Company presented it as *Scarlett* in 1970. Though the libretto was the work of Kazuo Kikuta and the cast Japanese, the company was otherwise Broadway all-stars: Harold Rome wrote the score, Joe Layton was the director-choreographer, David Hays and Patton Campbell designed, Lehman Engel (always Rome's first choice at home) conducted Meyer Kupferman's orchestrations, and Trude Rittmann composed the dance music.

The very idea of *Gone With the Wind: The Musical* thrills and vexes at once. All that emotion for music, those big characters! Even the pathetic Melanie and the uselessly romantic Ashley have possibilities, not to mention two of the grandest characters of all time, Scarlett and Rhett. But is it castable? And all that story, and the burning of Atlanta! In fact, *can it be done?*

The Japanese love American musicals, and Japanese musicals by Americans, and even Japanese musicals; so they had a great time. But in 1972, the show dared London, now under the familiar title. The book was by Horton Foote in the same Layton staging, one of the most elaborate of the time: the O'Hara plantation, dripping with wisteria; the Atlanta train station (with a real train); the famous ball at which Scarlett shocks the town by dancing while in mourning, played against a huge blowup of the Confederate flag; and, yes, the burning, too.

June Ritchie and Harve Presnell (of *The Unsinkable Molly Brown*) took the leads, she a more mature though no less charismatic Scarlett than Vivien Leigh and he rolling out that splendid high baritone in a musical equivalent of what Clark Gable used for confidence. The show ran a year in a huge theatre, so it seemed bound to come home, despite the ominous note of bad reviews from visiting American critics.

Indeed, this is the sort of show critics love to ghoul out on. It's so romantic, so twice-told, so . . . yes: so *corny*. That's the worst insult possible in a rock culture. The American *Gone With the Wind*, still in the Layton production but wholly recast with Lesley Ann Warren and Pernell Roberts in the leads, was to have opened in Los Angeles, toured for the better part of a year, then hit Broadway. But the California showing did not go over, and after San Francisco the show folded.

We are losing important history here. Harold Rome's career typifies the evolution of theatre music in the Golden Age, from hi-ho ditties to the dramatic sophistication of the "musical scene." An invention of twenties operetta but not popularized till Rodgers and Hammerstein, the musical scene is what gives modern shows their depth and point. Isolated song spots are mostly gone; now the music breathes with the story.

Harold Rome traveled with us, starting in the lowest of jobs as a specialist in revue. This is music without story or character. But by the 1950s, Rome had abandoned revue, and in *Fanny* in particular he exploited the musical scene—writing, in effect, partway to opera.

Now, in *Gone With the Wind*, Rome expanded into an intricate interlacing of speech and song—aided, I imagine, by the instincts of Joe Layton. Naturally, *he* would know enough to delay Rhett Butler's entrance till the Atlanta ball, have him defiantly escort the black-clad Scarlett onto the floor, and let him rip into an establishing song, "Two of a Kind." This better suited Presnell's sexy scooping up to high notes than Roberts' more limited instrument, but the climax really comes when the orchestra takes over as Rhett sweeps Scarlett around the stage and the good folk of Atlanta go off like astonished firecrackers.

This is fine old-fashioned showman thinking. But even a Christmas scene at Aunt Pittypat's was edited into a montage of big shots and close-ups, using music as a camera. The festive "Blissful Christmas" serves as a frame; then the holiday preparations feature Melanie's anticipation of Ashley's return in "Home Again." After underscored dialogue, the two numbers sang together, till more book led to a solo voice echoing the "Blissful Christmas" theme in a kind of fade-out as Scarlett pressed forward with her own anticipation, "Tomorrow Is Another Day."

Some of Rome's work here is, however, disappointing. True, what to do with Gerald O'Hara but give him an earnest and unbearable "Tara" anthem? Rome's is made of clichés—"proud and free," "wander this earth through." A charmer for young Bonnie Butler, "Little Wonders," is the opposite, too crazy and creative for such a little kid.

Still, doesn't it seem a folly for an all-American crew to have a hit with *Gone With the Wind* in foreign lands and not at home? And why are André Previn and Johnny Mercer collaborating with the English Ronald Harwood on a musical drawn from the English J. B. Priestley's novel *The Good Companions* (1974)? This one couldn't have been a tryout for a Broadway run, with its look at a minor-league "concert party" hooking up with three runaways, the whole gang then breaking through to success. First of all, Americans cannot fathom the concert party, with its idiotically monotonous Pierrot costumes and stupid jokes, as Harwood reveals:

JIMMY NUNN: I say, I say—whereabouts are the Andes?
MISS THONG: I don't know.
JIMMY NUNN: On the ends of the wristies!

Second, the novel (with its several movie versions, even the 1933 one with Jessie Matthews and John Gielgud) is generally unknown in the United States. The first English adaptation, by Priestley and Edward Knoblock, crashed on Broadway in 1931 despite a spectacular staging. Why would the musical appeal to Americans?

It didn't even appeal to the English, though the cast was headed by Judi Dench and the veteran juvenile John Mills, who hadn't done a musical in the West End in thirty-six years. (Mills got the star entrance, walking on hidden behind some luggage he was carrying. Luggage down. Loving ovation.) Dench played the old maid who suddenly takes off in her car, Mills the out-of-work prole who flees his horrible family. Christopher Gable (Tony in Ken Russell's cinematic deconstruction of

The Boy Friend) was the third of the runaways, a schoolteacher with a knack for writing catchy songs. Like the novel, the musical devoted a great deal of time to these characters' backstories. By the time they came together and joined up with the concert party, Act One was over and nothing had happened yet.

At that, Harwood's book is a cobble job, getting in all of the Priestley details and cuing up the numbers; one would not likely guess that this man wrote that superb character study *The Dresser*. It is the Previn-Mercer score that makes one wish that Americans were not giving their musicals to the English. Previn shames his *Coco* music with a real melodyfest: cheer-up songs such as "Slippin' Around the Corner" and "May I Have the Pleasure of Your Company?"; Gable's sprightly love song to his opposite, Marti Webb, "Susie For Everybody"; Webb's character song, "Stage Struck," and her serious ballad, "Stage Door John"; a showstopper for Mills, "Ta, Luv," with tap breaks at first and then a take-stage promenade as the brass instruments gorge heartily on the tune and the audience remembers why it likes going to musicals.

The Good Companions ran seven months, but not to a lot of full houses, and there were no plans to take it to Broadway; there never had been. Of the four shows discussed here, only *Ambassador* was specifically using London as a tryout, and only *Gone With the Wind* also had the potential to become repatriated. *I and Albert* and *The Good Companions* were American in authorship but English in subject matter, production style, and casting. Still, weren't they symptomatic of the disease called Money Problems? Worse, the failures of *Ambassador* and *Gone With the Wind* ended the contingency of the London tryout; the failures of *I and Albert* and *The Good Companions* discouraged Americans from pursuing work in London. One might read a stray credit here and there, as when London-born Jule Styne came home to compose the music of *Bar Mitzvah Boy* in 1978. But the cycle was over. As the flash success of *Jesus Christ Superstar* suggested, it was the English who would be using Broadway as an outpost from now on.

5

WHY CAN'T WE ALL BE NICE?

THE DARK MUSICAL

How about a musical in which a pedophile marries a woman to get to her twelve-year-old daughter? How about a Jewish banking dynasty fighting European anti-Semitism, Henry VIII killing his wives, Joan of Arc headed for the stake?

Remember when musicals were about how Adele Astaire couldn't get married till the stolen jewels were recovered? It's all *Oklahoma!*'s fault. Its discovery was that the best shows—and the biggest hits—often start with unlikely propositions. Unexpected characters, unmusical places.

Take *Cry For Us All* (1970), from William Alfred's 1965 play *Hogan's Goat*. Shouldn't this one be an opera? In late-nineteenth-century Brooklyn (a separate city then), a young man threatens to seize the mayoralty from the aged incumbent, who has no life but politics. The two men are rivals in the deepest sense, for both loved Agnes Hogan—dying as we speak, and supposedly because the younger man threw her over after he found her and the mayor in bed. To secure the election, the mayor exposes a secret that destroys his rival's marriage. In a rage, the younger man shoves his departing wife down a steep stairway, and she dies.

Building on foundations of immigrant Irish culture and intense religious feeling, Alfred narrated in blank verse of great beauty and power. It's a stunning play, with all the emotion and color that music needs. But for an open run on Broadway?

Won't Alfred's detailed social background get lost as the Big Scenes claim their Big Solos? Might the play's lack of comedy persuade the authors to slip in excrescent joke tunes? What if the composer is also the musical's producer, with the financial authority to stuff the piece with songs at the expense of Alfred's throughline of two men fighting over power as if it were a woman? Will the heroine, less important in the play than the dueling politicians, become a diva role, overpowering everyone else? What if the director is married to the diva and virtually makes the show on his wife?

It all happened. Alfred and the director, Albert Marre, collaborated on the book, and Alfred wrote, with Phyllis Robinson, the lyrics to the music of the producer, Mitch Leigh. Mrs. Marre, Joan Diener, played the lead role as *An Evening With Joan Diener*, with Robert Weede (the original Tony in *The Most Happy Fella*) as the mayor and Steve Arlen opposite Diener.

The support included Tommy Rall, Helen Gallagher, and Dolores Wilson in roles that were integral in the play and irrelevant in the musical. And, yes, Rall in "The Leg of the Duck" and Gallagher in "Swing Your Bag" had comedy numbers so floppo that Bhaskar had nightmares for two years. Producer Leigh stuffed *Cry For Us All* with eighteen separate songs while the book driveled away, and—icing on the cake—Howard Bay created a lumbering great set on a turntable that locked all the action into either the interior of the hero's house and the tavern below or the exterior of same. The rake of the all-important staircase was so steep that a stunt specialist warned that Diener might actually kill herself if she tried to fall down it at the play's climax. The entire cast immediately suggested that Diener take a practice tumble Just To See. Instead, the set was rebuilt.

Cry For Us All sounds like any number of failures that exist so that books like this one can make jokes about them. Thus it's interesting to be able to note that half of the score is very, very good, in that Mitch Leigh–*Man of La Mancha* way of the orchestra pounding out an ostinato while the voice rides above it on the melody. Neophyte lyricists Alfred and Robinson turned out to be quite accomplished—and they hewed more closely to Alfred's original material than the Alfred-Marre book did.

Some musical books are tedious and others incoherent, a mess of rewriting and insertions that circumnavigate without landing. *Cry For Us All*'s book was of the second kind, so much so that even critics who put in a mild word for Leigh's music now derided Alfred's original play. How could anything worthy have sired this chaos? Then, too, once a musical starts off wrong, all its unique inventions come off as worrisome rather than picturesque. For instance, Agnes Hogan's funeral, solemnized in the ferociously beautiful chorale of the title number, was to be heightened by an odd touch: Tommy Rall, an expert dancer, would present a solo during the music. It was to seem an impromptu thing, and not a stately keening but more of a dizzy jig. Had Cry For Us All been solid work, everyone would have loved Rall's dance as an expression of the moment—an abstraction of the entire work, even. Because the show was so *wrong* in general, the dance simply looked bizarre.

Joan Diener had the best numbers; maybe it was Mitch Leigh and not Albert Marre who pitched the show to her. Diener even jumped in on Gallagher's one solo, spicing the end of "Swing Your Bag" with three high notes culminating on a D. But some attention was won by three little boys who served as interlocutors. Apparently homeless, always running from truant officers, the trio seemed to know as much about the plot as William Alfred did. "See no evil," they sang, as the curtain went up. Later, they presented a pungent waltz on the moment when the young hero found the mayor with the woman they both loved.

In the mid-1960s, Cry For Us All's one-week run would have meant a loss of $500,000. By 1970, this size of flop meant a $750,000 loss. Even more expensive were two shows that didn't come in, Prettybelle and Lolita, My Love. Both were based on "difficult" novels, both were big productions drawing on major talents, and both died in the Shubert Theatre in Boston in early 1971, the latter right after the former. Let us get this straight: the lyricist and librettist of Brigadoon and My Fair Lady, and the composer and lyricist of Funny Girl, with the star of Mame and the director of Hello, Dolly!, close out of town?

Yes: and not because these two shows were Cry For Us All debauches. These two shows were too dark to live. As novels: fine. As movies: maybe, but that's pushing it. As musicals: no. Because there is still that Adele Astaire–and–the–stolen jewels thing in how most people think of the musical, especially those attending tryouts in Boston.

One has to ask why an old pro like Alan Jay Lerner thought he could get away with a musical of Lolita. Vladimir Nabokov's novel of a man's obsessive love for his stepdaughter so scared American publishers that he had to bring it out first in France; and discussion of possible censorship in England reached the highest levels of government. Nabokov's tale was, of course, literary gamesmanship, not smut. With his book-length puns and shadow figures and allusions-within-allusions, Nabokov was playing out the most elaborate cryptogram of his career.

A real-life staging of the material, however, must lose all that frivolous intellectual profundity. The play will *show* us Humbert Humbert lusting after young Dolores Haze, marrying her silly mother, reveling in the mother's death in a car accident, then driving his daughter-lover on a chase through the American outback of motels and fast food. The play will show and we will see. Worse, the music will humanize these people as Nabokov's pirouetting eructations do not. We will be faced with a tragic romance that is too sinful to be romance and too kinky to be tragic.

Jean Arnold's novel *Prettybelle: A Lively Tale of Rape and Resurrection*, is only a touch less strange. If *Lolita* is in part a European émigré's satire on American life in general, *Prettybelle* is regional, a look at southern racism. Its heroine, widow of the local sheriff, decides to redeem his murderous tenure by having sex with men of minority groups. She loses her mind, is institutionalized, and chooses writing as therapy. The novel is thus meta-fiction; Jean Arnold's version of what the fictional Prettybelle wrote.

There is nothing in Arnold as crazy as Nabokov's Clare Quilty, a Doppelgänger real enough to steal Lolita from Humbert but also a figment of Humbert's imagination. He is a reproach (= "clearly guilty") that Humbert kills as if killing the sin in himself. Still, Arnold's novel is, like *Lolita*, a challenge to the creative mind grown bored with the same old shows. A musical *Lolita*, a musical *Prettybelle*, will call up songs not yet heard. The librettos will invent new structural format. The stagings will be one-of-a-kind. One sees the attraction, but are Philadelphia (where *Lolita, My Love* opened) and Boston the right places for a preview? Their audiences are so conservative that, as late as the 1940s, shows in tryout had to make chaste modifications specifically for Boston or be closed. "Banned in Boston" was a running gag in American culture.

What if *Lolita, My Love* and *Prettybelle* had tried out in New York? Would they have run for at least some short while, leaving legends behind? Could Tonys have been won by the Humbert, John Neville, or the Prettybelle, Angela Lansbury—or Dorothy Loudon, stupendous as Lolita's mother? An audiotape of *Lolita* survives on disc and *Prettybelle* actually got a cast album, eleven years after it closed: so the two shows live in that twilight of being heard without having been properly seen.

Time was when shows closed out of town because they were—no other word will work here—terrible. The book was terrible, the score was terrible, the scenery was terrible, the actors were terrible. By the 1990s, shows can close out of town because the audience was terrible: shut of mind. Did Alan Jay Lerner expect Boston's matinée matrons to enjoy Humbert's song about his fantasies of killing his wife, "Farewell, Little Dream," capped, after she is run over in the street, by a gloating last chorus with a soft-shoe victory dance? Some plays hate the audience's values. This play hates the audience.

Did *Prettybelle*'s people look for good word of mouth after the lovable Angela Lansbury did such unlovable things as try to provoke a young black man to rape her? At least *Lolita, My Love* was easy to follow; *Prettybelle* unfolded according to its heroine's disorderly memory, and then leaped about in time, adding to the audience's discomfort.

Closed in Boston. Yet *Prettybelle* fascinates. Bob Merrill's book and lyrics, to Jule Styne's music, are not his best work. Gower Champion was even wronger here than he was for *Mack & Mabel*. The music lacks delight. Nevertheless, Lansbury's numbers can be quite touching. "To a Small Degree" is an impressive study of a marriage that works only because the wife won't tell the husband how unhappy she is. As Styne and Merrill delineate it, the bond was unclear, the love unstated, the life unworthy: but not enough to complain about. It's rare to find such everyday sorrow so cleanly set forth. We normally get the more colorful nervous-breakdown version, as in *Follies*' "Losing My Mind." In the end, *Prettybelle* is a bemusingly unpleasant show.

Lolita, My Love is a brilliantly unpleasant show. It got off to such a rocky start that after the Philadelphia premiere it abruptly closed to reappoint itself without the distractions of eight performances a week. So the show that arrived in Boston had been greatly overhauled. Lerner was one of the laziest writers in the musical's history, and one of the few Third Age names whose education did not protect him from constant errors of grammar and common knowledge—but he was very, very smart about people, so his best character songs are second to no one's. His composer, John Barry, was known for movie music, not least "Goldfinger." He was, however, a versatile talent, who could turn the pop on or off at will; and he had theatre experience.

John Neville's Humbert came off best, with ballads of irony and resignation, always in charge yet always the slave. "In the Broken Promise

Land of Fifteen" marries a folklike verse to a tango chorus, the whole melodically correct but for one unnerving "wrong" note—exactly the figure that Humbert cuts in the novel. In an ensemble for a party at Loudon's house to show off her new European lodger, Humbert, he lectures on great poets who loved young girls. "Dante, Petrarch and Poe," to a businesslike vamp, is Nabokovian to a fault, shockingly open about Humbert's cult of the "nymphet." (Nabokov defines her as "four foot ten in one sock.") As so often now, the orchestra alone continues the number but dialogue takes over temporarily, as Loudon greets Humbert's nemesis, Claire (respelled from the novel) Quilty (Leonard Frey):

> CHARLOTTE: I saw your play on tee vee a few weeks ago. I adored it. You know, the one about the two brothers in love with each other?
> QUILTY: . . . It was good, wasn't it? So much better than a brother and a sister. We had all that last year.

The problem with these dark shows is that, good or bad, they're *dark*. Not a lot of people are going to like them, unless they mitigate the darkness with humor and uplift such as we get in *Carousel* and *Man of La Mancha*. *Lolita, My Love*'s second-act opening, "At the Bed-D-By Motel," is a comic number (again, containing plot dialogue) dominated by a police convention: drunks, men goosing women, kazoos, and so on. The height of the fun is a voice-over paging a certain "Mr. Smith," followed by a stampede of every male present, ready to take the call. It's good old fun. But it's followed by Humbert's "Tell Me, Tell Me," an imploring love song to his impossible inamorata that is made, really, of Nabokov's amazed look at American youth culture. It's good and it's not fun.

Loudon, killed off halfway through the story, could not compete in vocal time. But she did have what might be the greatest number to be heard in a show that closed in tryout, "Sur les Quais (de Ramsdale, Vermont)." Composer Barry cleverly called upon the genre of *chanson* associated with Edith Piaf for a dream sequence in which Loudon saw herself as Mrs. Humbert. Vermont became Paris as she danced a cancan with the chorus men, thrilling us with show-biz excitement just before the authors kill her off.

Well, a crazy novel will give you a crazy musical. Too crazy and at times too true. One of those "concept show" numbers, in which much of the cast suddenly become commentators, brought Humbert to the climax of his journey. "How Far Is It To the Next Town" is the number, as Humbert chauffeurs Lolita in a mad dash from the rapacious Quilty. How far? "Too far," sings the helpless Humbert, who will lose Lolita, murder Quilty, and end in prison.

Some of the dark shows were more Tricky Idea shows with dark parts. *The Rothschilds* (1970) began in a ballroom set with a chorus called "Pleasure and Privilege," on life among Europe's aristocracy. It could almost have come from some old operetta, except for certain lyrics revealing how difficult life is for those without rank or power. As the number reached the expected tonic purity of the last note—the "resolution," so to say—the chord instead hit an eerie, altered harmony. The ballroom set moved off to reveal the entrance to Frankfurt's Judengasse: the crowded one-street ghetto. As the orchestra kept hitting away on that ominous chord, the city guard cried out the closing of the ghetto for the night, then harassed the show's protagonist, patriarch-to-be Mayer Rothschild (Hal Linden), late getting back from Hanover. After searching and taxing him, the guard looked on as mischievous children taunted Rothschild with "Jew, do your duty!," a demand for him to bow to Christians.

That sounds dark and it was dark, though directed and choreographed by Michael Kidd. He took over for director Derek Goldby and choreographer Eliot Feld after having made his name in saucy musical comedy—*Finian's Rainbow, Can-Can, Li'l Abner*. But musical comedy was starting to get scarce in this decade. The career of *The Rothschilds'* songwriters, Jerry Bock and Sheldon Harnick, is informative: as they move from pure fun in *The Body Beautiful* (1958) to fun about serious matters in *Fiorello!* (1959) and *Tenderloin* (1960). Then comes *She Loves Me* (1963), fun with a *but*; then *Fiddler on the Roof* (1964), a *but* with fun. Yes, *The Apple Tree* (1966) returns them to pure fun, but this is an interlude. If Bock and Harnick hadn't broken up after *The Rothschilds*, they would probably have gone on to make musicals out of Dostoyefsky and the Thirty Years' War.

With a script by Sherman Yellen drawn from Frederic Morton's bestselling book of the same title, *The Rothschilds* was a show about a historical development, a genuine breakaway. Yes, *1776* (1969) had been one such. Still, that show is small compared with this one, which covers the essential fifty years during which the European monarchies began their transformation into democracies.

Such grandiose subject matter can easily defeat the sharpest team; we'll presently see Leonard Bernstein and Alan Jay Lerner make a mess of comparable material. But *The Rothschilds*' authors created a structural binding device by developing Mayer's family as characters while uniting their enemies in actor Keene Curtis, playing four figures of the *ancien régime*. Presiding while never quite interacting, Curtis embodied an abstraction, a superb stroke.

The score is one of the most agile of the day, whipping about the map and taking in beggars and kings to sing of anything that the saga thinks is important: the serial births of Mayer's incipient banking house in "Sons"; Napoléon's capture of Frankfurt in "Allons"; an oppressed minority's wish for legal equality whose refrain takes off on a nagging flatted seventh tone, in "Everything"; one Rothschild son's profile at the London Stock Exchange in "They Say"; even the signing of a peace treaty in "Have You Ever Seen a Prettier Little Congress?"

A number one might have expected, from mother Gutele (Leila Martin) on the loss of her offspring as they disperse across the continent, went missing. This was the sentimental "Just a Map," originally the first-act finale as she released her boys to the needs of history. The scene was rewritten to feature a reprise of "Sons"—more dramatic. There's some humor even so. Solomon will go to Vienna, Amshel to Berlin, Jacob to Prague, Nathan to London. As for the youngest, Kalman:

MAYER: Kalman, you go to bed. It's late.

Kalman begs for an assignment, too.

MAYER: All right, go to Hamburg. It's as safe as going to bed.

Nevertheless, this is a solemn and even inspiring scene. For his farewell address to his sons, Mayer simply reaches back to the start of the act, to turn the Christian children's tormenting refrain into a war cry: "*Jew!*" Mayer exhorts his five boys. "*Do your duty!*" We see what a truly momentous undertaking is begun here. And the first-act curtain falls.

This is writing on the highest level, but it does deny us the salient Bock and Harnick charm, their "Where's My Shoe?" or "You Are Not Real" side. One of this team's great pleasures is the sly revelation of the Harnickian Jest, a lyric in which a character states something that is serious to him and funny to us. The connoisseur will recall *Fiorello!*'s "You remember him, he arrested you" and "I got a feeling it ain't democratic." In *Fiddler on the Roof*, Harnick redoubles the Jest with a lyric that is a pretense to a character but serious to the person he's addressing and funny to us: "She'll marry—what's his name?"

The Rothschilds develops too grand a theme to contain much comedy in the music. There is but one Harnickian Jest—"We're engaged!"—and very little dancing. When the movies first got into sound, it was feared that audiences would reject characters singing on screen except in a performing context, such as putting on shows or thrilling nightclubs. Now, in serious musicals, it is feared that Important Subject Matter precludes characters dancing except in ballrooms.

So Ann Reinking didn't dance in *Goodtime Charley* (1975), not really. Joan of Arc doesn't dance. King Charles VII of France did dance, but then he was Joel Grey and it was Grey's show. However, did we want a show whose protagonist is Charles VII of France? The leads were originally to have been Barbara Harris and Frank Langella, which might have thrown the top part spot to Joan and thus liberated the action. Charles VII was not an admirable or even interesting character—he lacked just about everything—whereas Joan was so amazing that if she lived today she'd still be ahead of her time.

Like *The Rothschilds*, *Goodtime Charley* treated important history, in this case the rise and fall of a village girl who, under saintly advice, broke the English conquest of France and helped lead Europe toward that nineteenth-century invention the nation-state. Also like *The Rothschilds*, *Goodtime Charley* adhered to chronicle with some fidelity. For instance, it made a Leitmotiv of the prophecy, known to everyone in Western Europe, that a virgin would save France. We even heard Charles' mother, Isabella of Bavaria, admit that he was conceived adulterously, which the real-life Isabella confessed—at least by implication.

True, the show did fudge its way around the real Charles' failure to save Joan from her show trial and incineration. It wouldn't do for Joel Grey to desert Ann Reinking after she got him crowned and, by inspiration, more or less created the entity of France. So, again, why write around a protagonist Charles when Joan is the true hero?

There was a lot of potential here, especially because *Goodtime Charley* broke away from *The Rothschilds*' style in an attempt to lock its history into a musical-comedy framework. Sidney Michaels' book, Larry Grossman's music, and Hal Hackady's lyrics tried to honor their subject while having fun with it. This can't be easy when your heroine is headed for the stake. Worse, much of the humor was off the rack, with the conniving Archbishop (Jay Garner) and General (Louis Zorich), the unloving royal relatives, the stereotyping of all kinds:

CHARLEY: My soldiers are worldly, rough men. What experience can you possibly have had to order them about?
JOAN: I've herded sheep. Men are easier.
[...]
CHARLEY: What if my men have other ideas, like living?
JOAN: Then I shall go forward alone. And when they see a young girl in such danger, they'll turn around and rush to my side.
CHARLEY: They're not heroes.
JOAN: They're Frenchmen!

Worst of all, while the authors struggled to figure out what Joan is, as warrior and saint, their Charles is the cliché wallflower learning confidence. He comes complete with an utterly incorrect character number, "Born Lover," in which he preens over his manly charisma while having none. It's someone else's song. So is his gently expanding "I Leave the World," giving eleven-o'clock-song dignity to a character deserving none. The song's title is a pun, for it is as much a farewell as a testament. But who cares what this ungrateful creep leaves?

Yet when the show wasn't making kowtow to its star, the score was unusually good. Another famous piece of the Joan myth found Reinking confronted by a bunch of courtiers, challenged to prove her godliness by picking Charles out of the throng. "Voices and Visions" suggests what this show might have been like had the authors rather picked Joan out. Her last number, "One Little Year," captures the tumult running through her mind in prison. These are not the strongest character songs ever written. But they *are* Joan songs.

Aficionados cite "Merci, Bon Dieu," a comedy song for court favorites Susan Browning and Richard B. Shull that grows strangely moving and lyrical, especially in Jonathan Tunick's aggrandizing orchestration. The regular choice of Sondheim, Tunick produced one of his best instrumentations for *Goodtime Charley*. The overture comes off as a tone poem announcing the mightiest of shows, starting with a little girl's voicing of the prophecy Leitmotiv. (It's supposed to suggest a medieval jump-rope nonsense chant.) Then the orchestra surges into a medley of themes as dramatic and idealistic as the subject demands. In fact, the overture has the character that the show itself lacks.

Except in the opening, "History." One of the cleverest of musical scenes, "History" brings the audience in on the situation facing France in the Hundred Years' War—the alliances, treaties, technical advances in war making. It is sung by statues of the historical figures surrounding the tale of Joan and Charles: his royal parents; Henry V of England; Philippe le Bon, who is the duke of Burgundy but no friend of the French; and a few others, including the Pope. Coming to life to argue and conspire, these eight characters, sung by performers with opera-weight voices, did something for history that your favorite teacher couldn't do: make it seem like Now. Lyricist Hackady was at his best here, showing us what Charles (or, really, Joan) was up against—not just the invading English but a Europe that put warlord power and politicking ahead of nationhood. Composer Grossman's contribution was a hopping little theme with a wily triplet, capable of growing in force till, at the close, orchestrator Tunick could sweep all up in a tiny cantata of power plays. Then a bed rose on an elevator in the stage floor, the eight statues slunk off, and Joel Grey made his star entrance awaking from that same number: his nightmare.

It was a smart staging (by Peter H. Hunt and Onna White, with some help from Bob Fosse), based on a unit set. Like the London tryout, this was another attempt to cut down the capitalizing budget. Instead of wholly different décor for each scene, the permanent setup (in this case a semi-circular colonnade) could be varied by this-and-thats dropped in or rolled up on the elevator. A great leafy tree for a riverbank scene actually seemed to sprout and spread; other expedients were less successful. Still, *Goodtime Charley* managed to suggest the fifteenth century without looking dowdy.

That's a problem with historical subjects: the clothes. If one's show is set so far back in the past that the men will be running around in pleated skirts and flowerpot hats, one will not be taken seriously. It worked for *Jesus Christ Superstar*, but that was a campy staging, however serious the work itself may be. *Nefertiti* (1977) was set in Egypt in the fourteenth century B.C., and that is *really* asking for trouble. That title! Those clothes! The names, such as Ipy and Horemhap! A piece like this doesn't need wags to jeer it down; it comes with jeers built in.

Nefertiti's story concerned two idealists who invent monotheism, only to be crushed by devious court factions. It sounds like *Goodtime Charley*'s "History." But *Nefertiti* lacked humor and the kind of verve that Joel Grey and Ann Reinking bring to everything they do. David Spangler's music and Christopher Gore's book and lyrics were not bad. Some of the songs had appeal, as well as such disarming titles as "Pardon Me a Minute" and "It Happens Very Softly," both for the title character, played by Andrea Marcovicci. In fact, the score was thought important enough to be recorded even though the show closed out of town.

Still, *Nefertiti* surely was what critic Ken Mandelbaum has termed a "don't" musical. You've heard of the "why?" musical. For instance: why turn the *Meet Me in St. Louis* movie into a musical when it already is one, and a perfect one at that? Besides, you can't possibly get anyone as good as Judy Garland and Margaret O'Brien. You might not even get anyone as good as Lucille Bremer.

Thus, *why* do it? As for *Nefertiti*, *don't* do it, because it will be silly. Scrolls, monster heads on poles, snake tiaras, invading Hittites—and not forgetting such other funny names as Tutmose and Tushratta. Don't do it.

And don't do *Rex* (1976), even if it has a Richard Rodgers–Sheldon Harnick score. Henry VIII is a fascinating figure, but he shouldn't sing in a musical. His daughter, Elizabeth I, is another matter. She sings very well indeed in one of Benjamin Britten's least appreciated but most inventive operas, *Gloriana*, because she is everything at once: king and woman, power and love. She turns men into bottoms; *that's* a show!

Elizabeth I is in *Rex*—I warned you that Penny Fuller was headed for this part—but the production was built around Novelty Star Nicol Williamson as Henry, so one couldn't easily change the show to *Regina*. Book writer Sherman Yellen could, at least, gentle the king down from the grandeur of his ruthlessness as he collects dead ex-wives while trying to sire a male heir. Again, it's not unlike the situation over at *Goodtime Charley*, where Joan was more interesting but the star had the story rights.

Williamson had perhaps too much story—twenty-seven years' worth, taking in the enmity of France, the Reformation, the various wives, the court minstrel, jester, and astrologer, and Penny Fuller's stage time, divided between two roles, first as Henry's great love Anne Boleyn, then as Boleyn's daughter, Elizabeth. One of *Rex*'s problems was that we never learned why the two roles were given to one actress.

We also never learned why producer Richard Adler hired Edwin Sherin to direct, as Sherin's only experience in musicals was getting fired from *Seesaw* in Detroit. Ironically, Adler had first offered *Rex* to Michael Bennett, who replaced Sherin on *Seesaw*, but Bennett was *Chorus Line*–hot just then and asked for too much money. Sherin's work on the straight play *The Great White Hope* made him a natural for *Rex*, Adler thought, as both had what Adler called "kaleidoscopic qualities." One knows what he means—the everything-happening-at-once vivacity of historical subject matter. Still, as the co-author of the scores to *The Pajama Game* and *Damn Yankees*, Adler should know that good play directors don't necessarily cross over into musicals.

Come to that, isn't the potential collaboration of grand master Richard Rodgers and arrogant upstart Michael Bennett a nightmarish idea? It was bad enough for Sheldon Harnick, already somewhat limited by the kaleidoscopic qualities of *The Rothschilds* and now utterly out of his element in a tale without charm. *Rex* hasn't a single Harnickian Jest. It even has a floppo number, a kind of jousting masque called "The Wee Golden Warrior."

Considering how goshdarn serious *Rex* is, it sang surprisingly well. Both Williamson and Fuller can project the insane aplomb of the Very Important Historical Personage; and some of the music is worthy of Rodgers' extraordinary career. We get the last Rodgers waltz in a duet for Henry and his minstrel (Ed Evanko), "No Song More Pleasing"; a duet for Williamson and Anne, "Away From You," that is classic Rodgers in melody, harmony, and structure; and the minstrel's lullaby for the new royal baby, "Elizabeth," brushed with feathery pianissimos. Williamson's soliloquies, however, are almost embarrassing, and the ticktocky "In Time" sounds like another of Rick Crom's spoofs.

Hal Prince dropped in to help Sherin before the opening; but *Rex* played out its advance and closed in six weeks. Its problem lay not in the staging, anyway. Its narrative was at once too expansive and not centered. Was Henry a villainous lust-glutton or a great leader who put his people's security above all else, even God? Then, too, there was that costume problem, with the tights and jerkins and flugelpants and Dolly Levi hats, even on the men. Barbara Andres, as Catherine of Aragon, Henry's first wife, had to wear close-fitting headgear that looked like the frame of a cuckoo clock. No doubt, designer John Conklin found it in a book of the period; but authenticity is no excuse.

After all the dire statesmanship of *The Rothschilds*, *Goodtime Charley*, and *Rex*—after, rather, the elegant slimebag courtiers, childishly gleeful war making, and homicidal monarchs—it's a relief to turn to *Shenandoah* (1975). Here we have only the Civil War to contend with, hot- and cold-blooded murder, even rape. Yet *Shenandoah* was thought of as a family show, which the other three certainly were not. Some even thought it vaguely in the Rodgers and Hammerstein line, if only because of its period Americana and the score's odd combination of the folksy and the passionate.

Shenandoah is based on the screenplay that James Lee Barrett wrote for the 1965 film of the same name, in which father James Stewart struggled to protect his Virginia farm and family from both Northern marauders and Southern draft officers. *Purlie*'s team of Gary Geld and Peter Udell wrote the songs, and, as with *Purlie*, producer Philip Rose and Udell co-wrote the book with the author of the source material. *Purlie*, however, is a highly consistent piece, its parts all of a match. *Shenandoah* is so diffuse that it is really two shows.

One is built around the titanic patriarch (John Cullum), exploring his humor, his morality, his still-vital love for his dead wife, his strangely placid ability to control five hotheaded sons of fighting age, plus a daughter, a daughter-in-law, and Boy, the twelve-year-old. *Shenandoah*'s father script is intelligent, and the father songs present a man in full true. "I've Heard It All Before," to rippling fury in the pit, gives us a man wise in his cynicism; "The Pickers Are Comin'" is tender with love for his barely nubile daughter; "Meditation" is autobiographical nostalgia rolled out at his wife's grave.

The other *Shenandoah* show is a trendy country-and-western vaudeville filling in when father Cullum is offstage. I don't mean to suggest a clever story-with-commentary, as in *Love Life* or *Cabaret*. No, *Shenandoah* thinks that it's all one show, a book musical. But the scenes without the father lost all the momentum and point that Cullum had so carefully built up. He had played leads in better shows than this, and could still collect Best Actor Tony nominations over a quarter of a century later. But this lead in *Shenandoah* may be the most interesting role he ever had. It's hard to imagine anyone else in it, though William Chapman spelled him during the original run and John Raitt took over for the tour. *Shenandoah* ran 1,050 perfomances in New York, and Cullum's towering (and Tony-taking) portrayal has much to do with that. At any rate, the featured cast, headed by Ted Agress, Joel Higgins, Donna Theodore, and Penelope Milford, had no more than functional roles.

In fact, they hardly had roles at all. The development of the father left little room for the second generation. They could obey (or defy) father, get married or killed, and search for Boy, kidnapped by the Blues because he was wearing a Gray cap. Their songs, too, did little or nothing to specify them: Boy (Joseph Shapiro) and his slave friend Gabriel (Chip Ford) asking meaningless ontological questions in "Why Am I Me?"; the two daughters duetting in country thirds in "We Make a Beautiful Pair," on the partnership of marriage; or Theodore and Ford kicking into a ragtime cakewalk in "Freedom," after Ford's manumission. The music is Top 40, enjoyable but completely devoid of the intensity of the songs in the "other" show.

One needs that intensity, because by Act Two the action has grown dire. The first scene ends with three scavengers pulling off that hateful con of befriending the character they're about to murder while the audience wants to shout a warning to him. Joel Higgins has mentioned that he and Donna Theodore are alone on the farm, and as he draws up the well bucket to give the strangers a drink, one of them stabs him to death. The killer wipes off the knife as he and his buddies glance at the house:

FIRST MARAUDER: A wife, he said.

And there it is. The dark musical, and we're stuck with it now. Couldn't they get another show out of the sharpshooting tomboy and the ego-sensitive matinée idol? Yes, it's *Annie Get Your Gun*, but it actually dates back as far as *Naughty Marietta* (sort of) and reaches up to *The Unsinkable Molly Brown*, *The Goodbye Girl*, *Crazy For You*, and so on. Actually, there have been dark musicals since the 1920s: such operettas as *Rose-Marie* and *The Vagabond King* have dark aspects, and *Deep River* is very serious indeed. But the dark shows weren't running the fun stuff out of town then.

In the 1970s, they start to. Stephen Sondheim, in his Age, even finds a way to darken a romantic comedy, in *A Little Night Music* (1973). He brings operetta back from the grave. But not for the murders shown onstage in the three twenties titles cited above. Not for *Show Boat*'s racial tragedy or *The New Moon*'s politics. Sondheim does it for naturalism, the one thing operetta never had.

A Little Night Music is deliberately studded with "wrong" notes—not in the music, but in the action, as when the teenage bride (Victoria Mallory) and the maid (D'Jamin Bartlett) get into an impromptu lesbian tussle, or when the pompous Count Carl-Magnus Malcolm (Laurence Guittard) pushes the lawyer Frederik Egerman (Len Cariou) into Russian roulette offstage and a shot rings out. They're *really* doing that? Can't someone get hurt?

The erotic in particular runs through this show, proving that earlier musicals had a love plot but not all that much sensuality. *A Little Night Music* is based on Ingmar Bergman's 1955 film *Smiles of a Summer Night*, but the movie merely informs rather than constitutes the musical's action, for Hugh Wheeler's book makes Bergman's love dance of changing partners less worldly and age-old, more hungry and immediate. It's like the difference between Europe and Broadway.

Bergman's film is one of those comedies that never laughs, while two of Wheeler's characters, old Madame Armfeldt (Hermione Gingold) and Countess Charlotte Malcolm (Patricia Elliott), deal respectively in Wildean aphorism:

> MADAME ARMFELDT: To lose a lover or even a husband during the course of one's life can be vexing. But to lose one's teeth is a catastrophe.

and bitchy putdown:

> CHARLOTTE: Oh damn that woman! May she rot forever in some infernal dressing room with lipstick of fire and scalding mascara! Let every billboard in hell eternally announce: Desiree Armfeldt in— in—in *The Wild Duck*!

Bergman fans felt that violence had been done to a masterpiece, not least by Patricia Elliott's *Sugar Babies–soigné* delivery. But the musical was simply another in the line of extremely faithful adaptations that completely reinvent the original material—*Carousel*, *The Most Happy Fella*, *Cabaret*.

The third of Sondheim's Hal Prince–Boris Aronson collaborations, *A Little Night Music* is famously the "waltz" musical, because all but a few measures are in $\frac{3}{4}$ or $\frac{6}{8}$ rhythm (though no musician would hear a waltz in $\frac{6}{8}$, which is duple- rather than triple-time). Perhaps the piece waltzes not literally but in its romantic glow: its period décor and regretful Scandinavian twilight, its quasi-Brahmsian Liebeslieder quintet and imagining of an antique French love comedy; its frame of dancing couples and deliberate quotation of *Der Rosenkavalier*;* even its use of an unusual number of legit voices, so many that, for once, the overture is not only played but sung; and especially its great welling up of "Send in the Clowns" when the central couple is at last united. It is one of the happiest consummations in the musical's long history of Boy Gets Girl.

The summer night, we learn, smiles three times—for the young, the fools, and the old. This notion binds the work, giving the sometimes amorphous pairing and parting of couples a throughline. All men and women are fools, the show observes, because sexual longing makes them so. The young are yet innocent, and the old are past their guilt. These two groups are exempt.

But lawyer and actress (Glynis Johns), count and countess, and seminarian son (Mark Lambert) and teenage stepmother know nothing and learn nothing, because they are self-absorbed. They are fools. The lawyer and the actress are the loves of each other's life, but he's still working out a whim for his virgin bride. The count is so obsessed with form that he has no feeling. The son and stepmother are in love with each other and don't know it:

ANNE: Dearest Fredrika, all you were witnessing was the latest crisis in [the seminarian's] love affair with God.
FREDRIKA: (one of the young, but smart) Not with God, Mrs. Egerman—with you!
ANNE: (totally surprised) Me!

In effect, Bergman's *marivaudage* has been cut up and stitched together again so that the action flows almost dizzily from surprise to surprise. Some scenes end before they are "finished," having been overtaken by the music. Some of the music is invaded by the story. And the Liebeslieder quintet come and go like the *Follies* ghosts.

For instance, when the lawyer and his young wife attend the theatre, the actress makes a star entrance, drops into a deep bow, and—says Wheeler—"old pro that she is, she cases the house." As she spots her old lover the lawyer, sitting at stage left, she freezes. So does the entire show—except for two of the Liebeslieder folk, sitting at stage right.

---

* It was orchestrator Jonathan Tunick's idea: the first seven notes of Richard Strauss' opera, played on the horns in "A Weekend in the Country" just before the "twice as upset as in" coda. Sondheim allowed it, but to him it's just high-class showboating.

"Remember?" they sing; and they come forward to launch a number that will, at intervals, pepper a great deal of the ensuing action. First, the lawyer gets his furiously suspicious wife home ("My, that was a short play," says the maid) in time to catch his son having just sampled a bit of original sin with the maid. (The lawyer approves.) Then, as the lawyer's household settles down for the night, he goes out for a walk. "Remember" has haunted this sequence, and its final chord of the tonic with a raised fifth—a perfectly unresolved resolution, which is what all these characters are living in—is repeated till the actress' rooms appear and the lawyer walks in, saying, "They told me where to find you at the theater."

A Little Night Music is loved primarily for the beauty of its music, its compelling look at how the hunger for physical ecstasy vexes the most orderly lives, and the great opportunities it offers both singing actors and acting singers. How many shows are magnificent enough to be, to a certain number of intelligent, stimulated, longtime theatregoers, their Favorite Musical? There's *Show Boat*, *Carousel*, *My Fair Lady*, *Follies*. And this one. But I think a goodly portion of its charm lies in its seamless integration. The book and music cohabit with the narrative as faithfully as young lovers who know of nothing in the world but each other. More than in the rest of the Favorite Musicals, the unity of arts is absolute.

This was certainly not the general state of integration at the time. In *Shenandoah*, for example, there is a powerful scene in which a recruiting sergeant tries to draft a few of John Cullum's sons and the family unites to run the soldiers off at rifle point. Cullum's lines here are laid out with the clarity of a politically minded personality who has been waiting for years to shred his opponents' worthless opinions. It's a tense and telling moment.

But no sooner have the soldiers and the older family members gone than the boys edge into a song cue:

JOHN: You know. . . something just occurred to me.
NATHAN: What's that?
JOHN: Well, I understand Pa and all that, but . . . but I'll bet if we did get into this war, we'd be hell.

and they're off into "Next To Lovin' (I Like Fightin')," which is there just to be there. Vaudeville.

In *A Little Night Music*, everything is there to worry the central theme and assist its forward motion. Why did the lawyer murmur the actress' name when napping? Why has he come to visit her after the play? Does he know that she has been waiting for his reappearance in her life for the last fourteen years? Does he miss her, too, or is he simply after a freebie? He gets one, and the show covers this all-important break in narrative continuity by celebrating their union with another number, Madame Armfeldt's "Liaisons."

It seems intrusive. In fact, it's her gloss on the love plot: mutual attraction is the worst reason to have sex. *She* thinks. In the view of this most fastidious of courtesans, sex must be a worldly, not a fleshly, transaction. It does not occur impulsively or just anywhere or without delicacy of introduction. Yet here are her daughter and the man the daughter loves establishing the central goal of the most romantic of musicals—the goal of bringing these two together permanently—by having sex for no purpose but the usual exaltation into the divine.

Later in the piece, on a visit to Madame Armfeldt's château, her servant (George Lee Andrews) and the Egermans' maid also have a cheap liaison. This originally gave rise to two numbers, his "Silly People" and her "The Miller's Son." His number restates the concept of the night's three smiles. Her number restates the relationship of romance and sex. Two numbers for the same "moment" slowed the action just when it must speed to resolution; and "Silly People," with its growling accompaniment and imagery of death, may have been too "wrong-note" even for this comedy of shadows. "Silly People" was cut, allowing the maid to make the show's most pungent statement—that whether one loves the spiritual man ("the miller's son" = the lawyer's seminarian offspring), the materialist ("the businessman" = the lawyer himself), or the aristocrat ("the Prince of Wales" = the count), life may never be complete without supplementary erotic information.

This time, a Sondheim show won not only the Drama Critics' Award but the Best Musical Tony that *Follies* had lost to *Two Gentlemen of Verona*. Book and score won as well, along with two performers and costumière Florence Klotz. (Boris Aronson lost to *Pippin*'s Tony Walton.) One understood also that ears were becoming accustomed to Sondheim's sound. The show ran 601 performances* and paid off.

---

* It is traditional though unprofessional to play a practical joke on the last performance. *A Little Night Music* closed on a Saturday night, and as William Daniels (who had replaced Len Cariou) bent over to crank his motorcar for its exit, mischievous stagehands yanked the car offstage, leaving Daniels looking wry. Still, the audience of well-wishers and friends of the production (and the usual schmudls who never get to anything till it's all but over) had their laugh. A pointless anecdote: but an authentic one.

The national tour, undertaken when the show was still playing New York, was headed by Jean Simmons, Margaret Hamilton, and George Lee Andrews; Simmons also played London, in 1975, with Hermione Gingold substituting for the originally cast Margaret Leighton. Prince directed the film version, which had trouble getting proper distribution till 1978, though Elizabeth Taylor and Diana Rigg headed the cast (with Cariou, Gingold, and Guittard). No one likes it, partly because much of the score is missing, and English accents abound, as if the setting were some town and manse out of Jane Austen. (Henrik, the seminarian, has become Eric.)

But there are compensations. More Sondheim: a lovely new version of "The Glamorous Life," new lyrics here and there, and a set of verses for the previously non-vocal "Night Waltz," under the title "Love Takes Time." Most important, the film incorporates footage of the Viennese *Night Music* playing at the Theater an der Wien. A replica of Broadway, it thus made possible the preservation of Aronson's traveling screens of birch trees and the way the musical began and ended.

One wishes that Prince had simply taped the show, period; but any movie must disappoint when the show is so good—darkness, wrong notes, and all.

6

NOBODY DOES IT LIKE ME

PIPPIN AND *SEESAW*

Here are two musical comedies that are not of the carefree sort of the old days. These two have dark edges: modern musical comedies, a very common form by the early-middle 1970s. Both are vehicles for not stars but director-choreographers, and each had at least one author who complained that his work had been defiled by show-shop gimmickry.

Otherwise, they are very different shows. *Pippin* (1972) is an original. A tight, smallish ensemble piece in which the featured players have specific and strictly limited roles in the action, it uses little scenery.

Seesaw (1973), an adaptation, is a big show filled with its Look and many extraneous characters, some of whom have no relation to the story. Also, unlike *Pippin*, *Seesaw* underwent such radical revision during tryouts that finally no one could say who was the author of its book.

There are more obvious differences. *Pippin* is eighth-century Europe and *Seesaw* contemporary New York. *Pippin* employed a Novelty Star (John Rubinstein, son of pianist Artur) along with a Novelty Cameo (Irene Ryan, Granny of television's *The Beverly Hillbillies*), while *Seesaw* starred a couple (Lainie Kazan, Ken Howard) that had come up the hard way, trouping and understudying. Or even: *Pippin* was a smash that many disdained, and *Seesaw* was a bomb with devotees.

What we need to emphasize in this pair is the new autocracy of the director-choreographer. The power that in about 1910 belonged to the producer, in about 1940 to the star, and after Rodgers and Hammerstein to the authors is now embodied in a Svengali to whom the absolute of libretto and score is just so much Trilby.

The trouble is that, in *Pippin*'s case, it's true. Who would have guessed that a Broadway hit would grow out of the amateurish little *Godspell** (1971), moved from La MaMa to the Cherry Lane and the Promenade (thence, in 1976, even to the Broadhurst)? With a book by John-Michael Tebelak that was actually his master's thesis at Carnegie Tech and with songs mainly by Stephen Schwartz, *Godspell* was the opposite of *Jesus Christ Superstar* in all respects. Small. Reverent. Idiotic. Jesus wears a Superman T-shirt, the girls look like Raggedy Ann, and the boys look like Stephen Schwartz. It's the joyous world-shout of "Hey, we're gentle clowns doing our comic yet so very touching little show!" Once, American girls dreamed of growing up to be Ziegfeld stars or, later, Julie Andrews. Now they dream of growing up to be *Godspell*'s "Day by Day" Clown.

This international hit was apparently Schwartz's idea of what a musical is supposed to be: stupid hippies singing sacred text. So *Pippin* would be a real breakaway: stupid hippies singing secular text. With a book by Roger O. Hirson and Schwartz's score, *Pippin* might easily come forth as the second *Godspell*, in which case it would have closed on the first night.

Bob Fosse saved *Pippin*, and he had to bar Schwartz from rehearsals to do it. What Fosse saw in the material was very much like yet different from Schwartz's paradigm. Not a bunch of clowns but a bunch of really sharp theatre pros. Clowns belong in a circus, not in the Imperial Theatre.

Theatre pros can double and triple as courtiers, soldiers, merrymakers, and so on. They make the so very touching little show fade away like a one-reel silent from 1908. The Fosse cut and strut takes over, tart and hustler faces alight with smiles that aren't really smiles, dance with a hard-on. Ann Reinking, one of the *Pippin* ensemble and later a Fosse stylist, describes the Fosse look as "one part's very extended and one part's broken." But that's only what the dancer feels. What the audience feels is confidence in a master of the art who will furnish surprise and delight.

The opening always got applause: after no overture, the action began with hands and smoke, as if Fosse were a sorcerer conjuring up his people out of parts and effects. Sure enough, the number was "Magic To Do," ushering in Schwartz's very contemporary sound, solid theatre music

---

* "Godspel" is old English for "good tidings," meaning the Gospel, whose good news of Christian Redemption forms the basis of the show's reenactment of certain parables in Matthew.

leaning more toward rock than toward Sondheim, and toward the piano guys like Elton John rather than the guitar guys like Bob Dylan.

So "Corner of the Sky," the Hero's Wanting Song, is rock sung over a keyboard toccata, as if Bach were accompanying Paul Simon. "Magic To Do" starts on a bluesy piano vamp over an A bass, a paw-the-ground come-hither as the Leading Player (Ben Vereen) insinuates himself into view. There's a lot of that in Fosse's *Pippin*; it's a slinky show.

The Leading Player serves as emcee in the tale of Pippin, heir to the empire of father Charlemagne (Eric Berry) and, more generally, a wastrel in search of a quest. He outwits hostile forces at court, takes seize-the-day advice from his grandmother, moves in with a widow (Jill Clayburgh) with a little boy (Shane Nickerson), and ultimately decides that there is no quest. There's merely life. *Pippin* begins with Fosse at his most; it ends with Fosse shrugging. If that's all he wants, Fosse says, let him have it. So the stage empties of the ensemble, now bored with *Pippin*. They leave him with his little family, who kind of gesture or something and the lights go out the end.

With its pleasing ensemble cast, appealing score, and Fosse's endless inventiveness, *Pippin* was a novelty; for the lack of plot actually helped specialize it, distinguish it. It was trendy, too, now delving into anti-war irony, now sexually experimental. It was so wholesome that Granny's number, "No Time At All," was turned into an audience sing-along, with the lyrics presented on an illuminated manuscript dropped from the flies; and it was so earthy that Bob Fosse directed it. In the innocent 1950s, the essential Fosse number was the trio "Steam Heat," from *The Pajama Game*. In the 1970s, the essential Fosse number was what came to be known as The Manson Trio, a bit of guignol soft shoe for the Leading Player and two Fosse Chicks. Placed during *Pippin*'s war sequence, the spot was a grinning victory dance over the slain. Taped and televised without commentary, it was the first successful commercial for a Broadway show, and one reason why *Pippin* was such a big hit.

Another is the relatively small capitalization cost, about $500,000. The producer, Stuart Ostrow, couldn't raise the full budget, so Fosse's set designer, Tony Walton, had to compromise with bits and pieces on a bare stage. These combined well with Patricia Zipprodt's thrift-shop medieval costumes and of course the devious Fosse groupings, now so traditional (as in a minstrel-show lineup for "War Is a Science") and then all over the map (in the restless erotomania of "Simple Joys"). What Fosse did best in *Pippin* was to get so much content out of his staging of the numbers that they seemed to draw the action forward when in fact there was no action. The action was Fosse.

But can a director-choreographer *author* a musical? One person can write a musical—George M. Cohan, Noël Coward, Ida Hoyt Chamberlain, Sandy Wilson, Meredith Willson, Lionel Bart, John Jennings, Bob Merrill, Rupert Holmes. And one person can *stage* a musical, can't he?

Of course, too many persons shouldn't stage a musical, especially when they are all Michael Bennett, grabbing and shouting and making and firing. *Pippin* had a cast of eighteen. *Seesaw*, written by Michael Stewart with a score by Cy Coleman and Dorothy Fields, sprawled to almost fifty roles. What was this show based on, *War and Peace*?

By an irony almost too fine to be believed, *Seesaw* was based on a play with only two characters. William Gibson's *Two For the Seesaw* (1958) examined the temporary romance between Jerry and Gittel: an older man and a young woman; or a bourgeois and a bohemian; or the midwest and New York, depending on how one views it. Gibson viewed it from every possible angle in a skillful character study, often funny and heartrending at once. Even so, the play might have fallen through the cracks of a busy season, ending up as an arcane entry in an old *Theatre World* with a single photo of, say, Karl Malden and Ina Balin. Casting saved the show: Henry Fonda, on one of his occasional Broadway visits, and Anne Bancroft in her Broadway debut. He was tense and she had crazy charm; both were brilliant. Low running costs allowed the piece to play twenty-one months, and it successfully went Hollywood (with Robert Mitchum and Shirley MacLaine) in 1962. Now, about a decade later, was a right time to open it up for music.

Except. Gibson didn't conceive of a big story and then delete all but two of its people. He conceived the two people in a way that made the rest of the world extraneous. A bit of it is mentioned—the wife that he is divorcing and her overbearing father, the guy who gave the party at which Jerry and Gittel met, her friend Sophie. There is one unifying element, in their constant use of the telephone. But the play really is about these two only, as they bridge the cultural gap:

JERRY: I'm not a legal resident of this state.
GITTEL: Oh. So what state are you from, legally?

JERRY: Nebraska.

GITTEL: Nebraska. That's somewhere way out in California, isn't it?

then grow terribly close and eventually crash apart when he cruelly disengages to return to Omaha. He leaves her in utter despair:

GITTEL: *I love you, Jerry!*
   (Jerry is rigid; it takes her a moment to go on.)
   Long as you *live* I want you to remember the last thing you heard out of me was I love you!

Both of these snatches of Gibson are retained in *Seesaw*, suggesting how closely book writer Michael Stewart hewed to text. That is, when he wasn't Opening Up with those fifty small speaking parts. Director Edwin Sherin wanted to retain the flavor of the original play, so *Seesaw* was a sizable yet not opulent show. The costumes were New York casual and Jerry's lawyer suits, and choreographer Grover Dale was at pains to try to spark this plain piece with the magic fun that one expects of a musical.

The Detroit tryout was not going well, and that's when Michael Bennett took over. While *Seesaw* played through its tryout unchanged, Bennett and his Gang of Four—Bob Avian, Baayork Lee, Thommie Walsh, and Tommy Tune—rehearsed a new *Seesaw* for Broadway. This show drove hard and looked wild and fancy, albeit with a gritty realism stressing race and crime, the New York not of musicals but of life.

Sherin departed and Dale was shunted to the side while many in the cast were fired or demoted. Only one of the leads remained, Ken Howard as Jerry. In what was to have been virtually the star part of Gittel, Lainie Kazan had been perfect casting. But Bennett wanted to trade in Gibson's badly downtrodden waif for a confident musical-comedy leading lady. That would be Michele Lee.

Michael Stewart was furious, and Stephen Schwartz knows the feeling; he didn't like Fosse's *Pippin* any more than Stewart liked Bennett's *Seesaw*. Stewart took his name off the credits while the usual suspects tinkered with the dialogue and most of Gibson's Gittel disappeared into Bennett's determination to turn the show around. As songs were taken from this character in this scene and given to that character in that scene, new cue-in dialogue had to be devised. By whom?

How right were Schwartz and Stewart to resent this remaking of their concept by the director? Conversely, how right was Hal Prince to tell George Furth that some portion of his eleven playlets should be alchemically combined with a Sondheim score into *Company*, or to tell Sondheim and James Goldman that *The Girls Upstairs* had better be *Follies*, a completely different work? Maybe one person *can't* write a musical.

As Bennett continued to reinvent *Seesaw* in his favorite directorial attitude—ruthless—the show began to look potential. The Detroit rehearsals were pointing up something that had apparently eluded everyone before, the zany miscellany that gives background to any New York romance. The classic New York musical, *On the Town*, is loaded with it, made of it.

Of course, Bennett's everything included a lot of what football referees call "unnecessary roughness." For one thing, right after the opening number, Jerry gets mugged. It's supposed to be a comic scene, but it was a reminder of how dangerous New York was under the destructive mayoralty of John Lindsay, when hard-core leftists relished black-on-white crime as "enlightening." Missing the irony entirely, Lindsay himself performed a cameo early in *Seesaw*'s run, showing up in look-alike Ken Howard's part and giving *Seesaw* a boost not unlike that given to *Pippin* by its television spots.

The show needed boosting, for the reviews were very various, and the promotional infrastructure of airwave play was gone, leaving possible hit tunes unplugged. Gittel's "Poor Everybody Else" and "He's Good For Me" might have made it, along with Tommy Tune's specialty, "It's Not Where You Start (it's where you finish)," a gala piece staged with the dancers wearing black tights and colored balloons. The cast was in white suits for the opening, as the title tune quietly waltzed in on solo piano, the orchestra entering as Robin Wagner's screens slid down from the flies as if the scenery wanted to dance, too.

No question, Bennett had saved *Seesaw* from not working. But was it good? With all the Gibson material to work with, and with such added gimmick numbers as "Spanglish" for the barrio, the rocking "Ride Out the Storm" for blacks in sci-fi afros, and the down-and-dirty "My City" for the appearance of six prostitutes when Jerry is trying to use a pay phone, *Seesaw* was too much and not enough—not enough of what drove Gibson to get an entire script out of how these two very different personalities respond to each other, and too much of the ugly New York of the 1970s. It is worth remarking that a revival of *Two For the Seesaw*—if extremely well cast and superbly directed—might easily succeed today. But *Seesaw* could never be done again. And if one has not eradicated one's source material with the excitement of one's music, one has truly failed.

Bob Fosse would probably say, All musicals are originals, anyway. Once they are put into production, they become their own source material and can be taken in any direction. In other words: Bob Fosse's *Pippin*. Well, it worked, didn't it? Michael Bennett's *Seesaw* didn't work because one person cannot rewrite a musical, not from toe to top during a few weeks in Detroit. No one to this day can say who wrote *Seesaw*, though Bennett signed it: "Written, Directed, and Choreographed by Michael Bennett."

Did anything like *Pippin* occur in the more secure times of the Golden Age, when a showman altered a musical from its authors' vision to his own? No. Did anything like *Seesaw* occur, when a showman tore a work apart and put it together again? Yes, but it usually bombed, anyway.

Are we losing an essential clause in the contract between the writers and the stagers? Did Jerome Kern and Cole Porter work this way? Doesn't the eleventh-hour infusion of important new talent drive a show's capitalization sky-high, with all the extra percentages and per diems for the occupying crew? What if producer Florenz Ziegfeld had called in Michael Bennett and his team on the *Show Boat* tryout in 1927—would that have made history, or was it as well that *Show Boat* made its history by being written and then staged (by its librettist, by the way)? Was Michael Bennett the evil genius of the 1970s? Did *Seesaw* last out 296 performances partly because John Gavin replaced Ken Howard and gay theatregoers made multiple visits to celebrate Gavin's shirtless scene?

Did Lainie Kazan ever forgive Michael Bennett for firing her out of her only chance at a star role in a musical? And did Michael Bennett need to think of Tommy Tune as some gypsy graduated into a feature part in *Seesaw* only to see Tune advance to director-choreographer, in which role he could "steal" the 1982 Best Musical Tony from Bennett when *Nine* and *Dreamgirls* were up together, leading Bennett to try to take over Tune's star show *My One and Only* in order to destroy it?

Yes.

7

IT'S A BORE

THE DREARY MUSICAL

This is a seventies invention: a show without delight. Usually, its subject is gruesome, or its score is dead, or it is attempting to reuse used-up material. Not all dreary shows have nothing. The titles to be investigated herein include one with a score by *My Fair Lady*'s authors, another with a number that, given exposure, was certain to become an all-time standard, and another that won the Best Musical Tony. They're still dreary, because some vitiating quality overtook all compensating factors.

Were there no dreary musicals earlier? Every decade has a few—*Barefoot Boy With Cheek* in the 1940s, say; or *How Now, Dow Jones* in the 1960s. But these are accidents. They weren't trying to be dreary. In the 1970s, dreary is a genre. It is not that these shows hope not to please, of course. But some of them go to places in which it is all but impossible to give pleasure.

For instance, *Lovely Ladies, Kind Gentlemen* (1970) didn't just happen to close after two weeks at the Majestic, a very exposed place in which to bomb. This show was *destined* to do two weeks: because it was another of those adaptations of an old play that is no adaptation. It cut down the original script and inserted songs. Terrible ones.

The source work, at least, is sound entertainment: John Patrick's comedy *The Teahouse of the August Moon*, drawn from Vern J. Sneider's novel about the postwar American occupation of Okinawa. The fun lies in the way the locals manipulate their bosses, embodied in the wily but ultimately well-intentioned interpreter, Sakini. A personal triumph for David Wayne in the 1953 play and Marlon Brando in the 1956 film, the musical's Sakini went to Kenneth Nelson, the original Matt in

The Fantasticks and Michael in *The Boys in the Band*. The rest of the cast was comparably capable and not especially well known: Ron Husmann as the captain hero, Bernie West as his pompously clueless colonel, Remak Ramsay as another captain, and Eleanor Calbes as an innocently troublesome geisha. Add to this a book by Patrick himself, a score by Stan Freeman and Franklin Underwood, choreography by Marc Breaux, and direction by Lawrence Kasha, and one has a particularly vulnerable project, devoid of box-office pull. West was replaced by Broadway's choice lovable curmudgeon, David Burns; but still.

Even more vulnerable was the old hat treatment of the play, which was relatively familiar. Remember, one reason for the success of *Oklahoma!*, *Fanny*, and *Chicago* (to name three faithful adaptations from older work) is that the originals had vacated the scene. The musicals were thus fresh storytelling.

Lovely Ladies featured a lively opening, "With a Snap of My Finger," in which Sakini and the ensemble sang the exposition. However, after that it was a revival with songs. Sakini's character number, "Right Hand Man." The Captain's character number, "This Time." The *geisha's* character number, sung in Luchuan dialect. Or a party number for Sakini and the two captains in the new teahouse, "Call Me Back," one of those supposedly riotous events interrupted by old jokes:

HUSMANN: Did you hear about the pirate who had a wooden leg named Smith?
RAMSAY: Oh, really? What was the name of the other leg?

There was one interesting touch, when Burns suddenly barged in, breaking up the music. But surely one had learned by 1970 that an old story must be *reinspired*, not simply ensonged.

Even more dreary than the feckless adaptations were the shows that were simply terrible in every respect, lacking even a lively opening and David Burns. *Tricks* (1973) was the decade's worst musical after *Dude*. This, too, was an adaptation, of Molière's *Les Fourberies de Scapin*, and it wore its lineage heavily, with commedia dell'arte costumes and a black backup quartet called The Commedia and more zany posing than in the entire seventeenth century. The staging was very physical, with the cast popping out from behind screens, running offstage into the auditorium (and unfortunately running right back on again), grabbing straw hats and canes for one number, and making a big deal out of a character's fatuously antique wheelchair. At one point, an actor flew across the stage on a rope painted like a peppermint stick, landed on a slide, slid, and jumped to his feet to snap out a single line.

René Auberjonois and Christopher Murney played Scapin and his stooge, apparently dazzling audiences in Louisville and at Washington's Arena Stage. Somewhere along the way, Herman Levin saw it and thought it had a place on Broadway. Perhaps the rock score made him sense that he had the next *Hair* in tow; producers sometimes think like that. Levin also produced *Lovely Ladies, Kind Gentlemen*. But Levin also produced *My Fair Lady*. Doesn't he know what good music is supposed to sound like?

One might call *Tricks* one of the "why?" musicals: why do something so unnecessary? *The Selling of the President* (1972) was a "don't" musical: don't put on a show in which Karen Morrow doesn't sing. This prize belter, Babylove in *The Grass Harp* the year before, played a PR expert masterminding the television campaign of presidential candidate Pat Hingle. The folksily boring Hingle suffers from lack of "image." It's Morrow's job to give him one and, if possible, do a little for his scatterbrained wife (Barbara Barrie).

The idea for the show came from Joe McGinniss' bestseller of the same title, on the 1968 presidential campaign. But the musical wasn't "based on" the book. It simply bought the title and the notion of a candidate sold like product. There were no character or atmosphere numbers; the entire score, by Bob James and Jack O'Brien (the latter of whom also wrote the book and, without billing, directed), was the commercials. They were supposed to be spoofs, but in this genre it's hard to be sure. Then it turned out that one of the numbers, "Terminix," was a *real* commercial for a *real* product whose manufacturers were among the show's investors. A scandal broke out, but the true scandal was the mounting of a show that couldn't possibly have been any good because the idea was so stupid. A score made of commercials? As Karen Morrow bustled up the aisle of the Shubert Theatre, clipboard in hand, leading Hingle and Barrie on another marketing spree, did she look back on her Broadway début, in the bomb *I Had a Ball*, as a kind of *Wonderful Town* compared with this?

Dreary was a genre: because whole cycles of repulsive work appeared, united around a style of unsuitable music; or an extraneous adaptation; or some new economy in production costs. There was, for example, the miniaturization of what in more solvent times would have been full-sized shows, playing smaller houses like the Playhouse, the Ritz, and the Bijou, compromising especially on scenery and trying to double the speaking roles as chorus when needed. *Dear Oscar* (1972), on the latter part of the life of Oscar Wilde, tripled speaking roles among its cast of twenty-two, filling the stage with the great and near great of Wilde's life. Wilde's wife, Constance, his beloved Bosie and Bosie's hideous father, friends Frank Harris, Robert Ross, and Sir Edward Carson, and enemy Charles Hawtrey were all on hand; and Richard Kneeland bore a notable resemblance to Wilde himself. Caryl Gabrielle Young's book and lyrics were surprisingly forthright about the case but not interesting, and Addy O. Fieger's music added nothing. Some of the numbers seemed oddly askew, as in Mrs. Wilde's "Swan and Edgar's," about her response to the innuendo swirling about her husband's sex life: she goes shopping.

Soon (1971) was the "rock opera" version of this little-show movement, with Barry Bostwick, Richard Gere, and Peter Allen as band members on the rise in the big city. This show's level of intelligence can be read in its credits: "based on an original story by Joseph Martinez Kookoolis and Scott Fagan," this "adapted by Martin Duberman," with "music by Joseph Martinez Kookoolis and Scott Fagan" and "lyrics by Scott Fagan."

Did we really need all that for a show that didn't even last a week? We have to hear the songwriters' names over again even as they credit Duberman with (apparently) having doctored their unplayable script? One is irresistibly reminded of George Abbott's comment on the director-choreographer's expansive credit, popularized in the 1950s, as "Entire production directed by." Because the director already *is* the director of the entire production, Abbott likened this to "Entire role of the Mother played by Lizzy Flop."

Different Times (1972) was the Americana epic show, the kind that follows several generations of a family while tumultuous historical changes provide background. It is the last thing one would expect to see trying to get by with a pathetic three-level set of steps for scenery, though the costumes looked legit. And the doubling-up was extremely intense, as the narrative jumped at intervals from 1905 to 1970: women's suffrage, World War I, Prohibition, a dance marathon, and so on. Mary Jo Catlett played six small roles.

Here is another author writing an entire show himself, Michael Brown. He staged it, too, but that wasn't the problem. Some who caught *Different Times* during its three-week run at the ANTA kind of liked it. It was, at least, trying something out, though critics were bemused that David V. Robison's play *Promenade, All!*, which had opened at the Alvin but two weeks before, covered almost the same time period, with Hume Cronyn, Anne Jackson, Eli Wallach, and Richard Backus playing multiple roles as four generations of a family.

Different Times is the one with the song that should have been a hit, "I'm Not Through." Sung by Joe Masiell in the defiant hysteria of which he was unfortunately the unquestioned master, the number ends in deflation in the show's dramatic context. As a 45 single, however, it would have had an upbeat finish and thus could challenge "I Gotta Be Me" in the genre of food-aggressive first-person male vocalist solo.

The rest of *Different Times'* score is variable, with numbers spoofing old forms and some just spoofing in some enigmatic way. Mary Jo Catlett had an amusing bit as a Texas Guinan sort singing "I Feel Grand" through a tremendous hangover as her dancing Hazelnuts tap her crazy. "*Stop that!*" she tells her floor show.

Even so, the air of hungry underproduction dogged one's enjoyment. There was too little Mary Jo Catlett and too much panorama. At least Brown did not make Alan Jay Lerner's mistake, in *Love Life*, of thinking that the premise of an Americana epic is enough and that one can run out of story early in Act Two. *Different Times* burst with narrative right to the end. On the other hand, Lerner had Kurt Weill writing the music.

Worse than the reduced shows were the shows actually conceived to be small, trying to define virtue in a lack of scope. So *Park* (1970) had only four players in its one set of, yes, a park, with a six-man band playing in band costumes in a gazebo upstage. (The sound was largely Now, with an electric keyboard, guitar, bass, and drums; but also a flute and a French horn.) Young Joan Hackett and Don Scardino and the more senior Julie Wilson and David Brooks met as strangers, then turned out to be a family. Though it's always a pleasure to remake acquaintance with the delightful Wilson, the entertainment was modest, a loaded word that simply describes the piece's limited dimension but also its limited potential. Four people is not a Broadway musical—and the modest score by Lance Mulcahy and Paul Cherry was no help. It is worth noting that *Park*, like

Tricks, had originated regionally (at Baltimore's Center Stage), then was picked up for The Street. It marked a new development in Broadway history: producers were not necessarily commissioning and cultivating new projects but adopting someone else's issue as their own. It was cheaper.

Sextet (1974) could never have been mistaken for an import from the regions; this was strictly Manhattan in style. But modest. Two gay boy friends (Robert Spencer, Harvey Evans) host a dinner for two couples, Spencer's old college roommate (Jerry Lanning) and his wife (Dixie Carter), and Spencer's mother (Mary Small) and her new companion (John Newton). Oddly, *Sextet* was somewhat under the influence of that least modest of spectacles, *Follies*, for characters occasionally blurted out what they were thinking but surely couldn't be saying, and stage action took in flashbacks as alternate realities.

Thus, as Lanning was about to enter, Spencer recalled making sexual overtures to him in college, and Lanning walked into the party throwing a punch at Spencer in slow motion—obviously a memory "staged" for us in the theatre of Spencer's autobiography.

Director Jered Barclay kept *Sextet* brisk and busy, best of all when Carter overheard husband Lanning setting up an extramarital date, put down the phone, and immediately launched into "(He'll have) Visiting Rights" as she coldly planned the divorce. Still, a problem with little shows is that they're little. There isn't a lot for them to work with. Exhausting every situational possibility in "Nervous," "What the Hell Am I Doing Here?," "Women and Men," and so on, the Lawrence Hurwit–Lee Goldsmith score finally let Mary Small sing the nostalgic and utterly irrelevant "Roseland" in a spotlight. Modest. Professional. Drab.

If anything influenced *Rainbow Jones* (1974), it was *Carnival!* (1961), for here, too, the friendless heroine is adopted by four imaginary friends. In *Carnival!*, they're puppets. In *Rainbow Jones*, they're real animals, played by actors: a dog, a cat, a fox, and a lion. The set was platforms and pipes with another of those little bands right on stage, and whimsy lay heavy on the evening. Jill Williams wrote the entire show, whose reputation was compromised when critics noted that the director and the leading actress were married *and* the show's producers. None of these little shows ran, but *Rainbow Jones* had the distinction of opening with the closing notice already posted, in correct anticipation of unusually blistering reviews. "An idiocy," said Douglas Watt.

The Dreary Musical didn't come only in small packages or in sheerly mistaken notions such as *Lovely Ladies, Kind Gentlemen*. Star vehicles—Big Broadway at its Biggest—could also prove leaden, tired, or inept. Shirley Booth had captivated the public with her bawdy proletarian cutup in *A Tree Grows in Brooklyn* (1951), *By the Beautiful Sea* (1954), and, in the artistic version *d'après* Sean O'Casey, *Juno* (1959). Why did she make her long-awaited return to the musical as a nun? Not even an impish "How do you solve a problem like Maria?" nun, but the Mother Superior of a German order in New Mexico that needs a chapel. Sidney Poitier builds it for them—in the *movie*, *Lilies of the Field*. Booth's was the musical version, *Look To the Lilies* (1970), a lifeless blunder badly in need of Sidney Poitier and the score to *A Tree Grows in Brooklyn*.

Poitier's successor, Al Freeman Jr., seemed uninterested in the proceedings, and *Lilies*' music, by Jule Styne, was one of his most feeble efforts (though by no means the worst). Meanwhile, director Joshua Logan was then in the middle of the period in which he couldn't get anything to work. The show woke up now and then, when Patti Karr, Carmen Alvarez, and Titos Vandis came on as bordello workers and their boss. But this was one of the sleepiest shows ever made by major talents.

If Shirley Booth as a nun is a "don't" musical, perhaps Melina Mercouri in the title role of Aristophanes' *Lysistrata* (1972) is at least suitable. But this was Michael Cacoyannis' *Lysistrata*, for as adapter, lyricist, and director he emphasized the original's anti-war message with raucous updating that dwarfed even earthy goddess Mercouri. "Effete snobs" was heard, someone spoke of "the un-Hellenic Activities Committee," and there was even a "Fuck!" Cacoyannis had staged *The Trojan Women* very successfully at Circle in the Square in 1963, and he not only directed but wrote the movie *Zorba the Greek*. Yet his work here was vulgar and stupefying. The by now all but inevitable tacky unit set, with a ramp that wound up around the edge of the balcony, seemed like a spoof of itself.

Was this a musical? Composer Peter Link was hot; he had prepared the incidental score for the New York Shakespeare Festival's buoyant *Much Ado About Nothing* in Central Park the previous summer. But the Link-Cacoyannis songs suffered puerile lyrics, and were almost entirely for the star or the chorus, making this something like Melina Mercouri's nightclub act as written by Aristophanes, with bathroom jokes by Michael Cacoyannis.

THE DECADE IN PICTURES:
THE WORLD ACCORDING TO SWOPE

Boys and girls, I am so excited! The preeminent photographer of the age, Martha Swope, has accepted our invitation to guide us through an exhibit of a few of the greatest shows of the 1970s. To start: *A Chorus Line*'s song and dance, "The Music and the Mirror," as Donna McKechnie launches an informal tour of seventies divas. Will anyone ever dare try to restage the superb geometry of Michael Bennett's choreography? "And spoil that line?" Joan Crawford demands, in *Torch Song*.

All photos in this section © Martha Swope.

It's time for the Sondheim-Prince concept show, as in *Follies*, which was conceived and first written (as *The Girls Upstairs*) before the others. Above, the despair of *Follies*: Yvonne De Carlo comforts John McMartin. Above right, the intensity of *Follies*: McMartin sings "Too Many Mornings" to the girl he gave away (Dorothy Collins) and the girl he can't forget (Marti Rolph). But they're the same girl. Below right, I'll bet you've never seen *this* shot of "Who's That Woman?" before. It's the jazz of *Follies*, it's own music and mirror, with Mary McCarty at center, backed by Alexis Smith, Dorothy Collins, Ethel Barrymore Colt (hidden behind Collins), Helon Blount and Yvonne De Carlo. McCarty's ghost is barefoot. Is this the sly genius of Hal Prince, undressing the gaudy bauble of show biz? Or is she just barefoot? One of the many *Follies* riddles.

Company's spatting spouses Barbara Barrie and Charles Kimbrough crowd Dean Jones: lots of, or too much, *Company*? Right, visual splendor is a feature of Sondheim-Prince. At top, diva No. 2, Glynis Johns, recalls Florence Klotz's costumes for *A Little Night Music*. Below, the finale, after Hermione Gingold (far right) has died. Laurence Guittard and Patricia Elliott waltz upstage as Johns and Len Cariou contemplate a more nuanced happy ending. Note, at left, a few of the Liebeslieder singers and, right, George Lee Andrews bravely going on after they cut his only song, "Silly People." Martha will make it up to George Lee with major exposure a few pages hence.

Chicago brings us helpings of Forbidden Broadway, in sequences killed before the premiere. Above, agent David Rounds sings "Ten Percent" just before his entire role was dropped. Below, diva No. 3, Gwen Verdon, leads the Eddie Cantor Number, "Me and My Baby," cut to a single vocal chorus for the tiring star.

Two summits of musical comedy. Above, the sentimental form: *Annie*, with James Hosbein, Steven Boockvor, Bob Freschi, Donald Craig, Andrea McArdle, Reid Shelton, Sandy Faison, Mari McMinn. Below, the zany form: as George Lee Andrews rejoins us to dance with diva No. 4, Madeline Kahn in *On the Twentieth Century*.

Diva No. 5 is our own Martha Swope, giving us a thrilling shot of the last second of *Twentieth Century*'s first act. John Cullum, Imogene Coca, George Coe, and Dean Dittman look forward to her bankrolling of their epic drama about Mary Magdalene, so Cullum must find a way to separate Kahn (seated right) from boyfriend Kevin Kline (with Kahn) and her movie career. Silly people.

All right, then: Christopher Plummer as Cyrano de Bergerac. This is top-okay casting! And even if Plummer is no singer, he can Rex Harrison his way through the numbers on sheer magnetism while all the firecracker vitality of Edmond Rostand's poetic comedy spins about him. A *Cyrano* musical is irresistible, it seems. Victor Herbert got to it way back in the First Era, Mr. J. J. Shubert twice tried (and failed) to bring in his production during the 1930s, and, more recently, there were versions by Robert Wright and George Forrest, Ad and Koen van Dijk, and David Shire and Richard Maltby.

Plummer's *Cyrano* (1973) falls into this chapter because the score, by Michael J. Lewis and Anthony Burgess (who had adapted Rostand for a straight Plummer *Cyrano* in Minneapolis two years earlier), is so poor. True, "Bergerac," a duet for Cyrano and Roxane on their childhood together, rippled with doting joy. Later, Roxane's "You Have Made Me Love" was eloquent, especially in Leigh Beery's ecstatic rendering.

But Walter Kerr noted how musical the play is *without* music: "arias without end, mocking duets, passages of whispered counterpoint, the long lingering coda beneath fluttering fall leaves in a convent garden." To add music to *Cyrano*, one must discover in Rostand something amplifiable, something that Rostand himself missed. But he didn't. His play is filled to the brim with the lyrical, the flavorful, the splendid, everything raised to the utmost.

Christopher Plummer flopping in *Cyrano*? What next? How about Yul Brynner as Odysseus, in yet another attempt by composer Mitch Leigh, director Albert Marre, and co-star Joan Diener to reestablish the eminence that they knew in *Man of La Mancha*? The Homer adaptation opened in Washington, D.C. as *Odyssey*, and it made one, spending fifty-three weeks on the road before hitting Broadway as *Home Sweet Homer* (1976). The academic classicist and author of the novel *Love Story*, Erich Segal, wrote the libretto, but by the time the show played its opening-closing Sunday matinee both book and lyrics were credited to others.

This is never a good sign, though Brynner was as enjoyable as ever and some of the music has appeal. Diener's "The Rose," accompanied mostly on harp, is very beautiful indeed, and Brynner was given an interesting duet with his son, Telemachus (Russ Thacker), on the courtship of women. Called "How Could I Dare To Dream?," it was especially touching because Telemachus at that moment has no idea that the old man is his father.

However, unbelievably tiresome dialogue and an anything-for-a-laugh panic in Marre's direction at once befogged and overheated the piece. Brynner did some shtick in imitation of the slow-mo bumbler created by Tim Conway on television's *Carol Burnett Show* that stood out as a vulgar anachronism in a show that otherwise was more or less honoring its time scheme.

To sap the energy of both Homer and Brynner at once is something that one has to *try* to do, and that more than anything else makes the Dreary Musical. The combined runs of *Look To the Lilies*, *Lysistrata*, *Cyrano*, and *Home Sweet Homer* total 83 performances—something that cannot be said of the work of Jule Styne, Melina Mercouri, and Mitch Leigh in the 1960s. Something is going wrong in the 1970s: something more than economics. The chemistry of collaboration is souring more frequently than it used to. The prosperity of new work from old sources is going bankrupt in spasms of shockingly poor judgment. And now they're inventing new forms of the "don't" musical, such as musical adaptations of movies that already *were* musical adaptations. They're actually trying to stage films!

Such as *Gigi*, whose theatrical transformation launched a cycle that is yet under way as we speak. This is one of the worst signs of atrophy in the Golden Age, a virtual admission that Broadway is running out of ideas and is creating pastiche art. And isn't *Gigi* of all films untouchable because of its lavish décor, thrilling location work, and unmatchable cast?

Edwin Lester didn't think so. He had long wanted to produce *Gigi* for his Civic Light Opera in California. But Lerner and Loewe had broken up their partnership after *Camelot*, and the 1958 movie doesn't have enough songs for a stage show. Then Lerner coaxed Loewe into doing the film *The Little Prince* in 1971, and they had such a merry time that Lester finally caught them on a yes. Ironically, with a largely new script and a great deal of new music and lyrics, the stage *Gigi* was in the theatre by 1973, while *The Little Prince* didn't appear till 1974.

Anyway, now the trouble begins. Who is to play the Maurice Chevalier role? *Alfred Drake?* Is Lester resetting *Gigi* in Baghdad? Maybe Rodgers and Hammerstein should have thought of Chevalier for Curly when they filmed *Oklahoma!*. And what of the role of Mamita, so delicately played by Hermione Gingold—normally one of the broadest of comics—that she scarcely gets a laugh in the entire film? You want Maria

Karnilova? Tell Lerner and Loewe not to write any new songs; Karnilova will sing "You Gotta Have a Gimmick," "The Kangaroo," and "No Boom Boom."

Given the cut-rate France in the casting, Daniel Massey is at least suavely European in Louis Jourdan's role; better, while not a singer, Massey can field a high G for the climax of "She Is Not Thinking of Me."

But who is to be the next Leslie Caron? The charm, the youth, the voice? True, Leslie's singing was dubbed (by Betty Wand). They do that in Hollywood. They can't do it on Broadway—they shouldn't, at any rate. But the odd thing is that really good ingenues are very hard to come by, especially the kind that play a girl being groomed to be a courtesan against her will. One needs more than charm. You would think that Ethel Merman is hard to come by, or Alfred Drake, for that matter. Ironically, there were, even at this late date, more headliners than there were Extremely Effective Ingenues, and *Gigi* is impossible without one. Karin Wolfe, the final choice, was likable and musical, but less than Absolute Gigi.

So it's already not good. Lerner and Loewe are giving us more Lerner and Loewe, however, and that is worth celebrating. Isn't this team as good as any other in the Golden Age, even if they are never mentioned on those shortlists with Rodgers and Hart or the Gershwins? The stage *Gigi* dropped two of the heroine's numbers from the film, adding three excellent new ones. "The Earth and Other Minor Things" is her establishing song. "I Never Want To Go Home Again" brings down the second-act curtain, a joyous kick-up-heels-on-the-beach number that grows pensively cool as the older principals, gazing at *Gigi*, suddenly realize that she is a young woman and potential romance material. "In This Wide, Wide World" is a novelty, a Telephone Number of the sort much favored during the Second Age and after (as in "Hello, Frisco, Hello" and "All Alone"), in which Gigi Gets Boy.

There were some new lyrics for old music; and Drake, too, got a new number, another of Lerner's sarcasms on the erotic life, "Paris Is Paris Again." It offers some of the most forced rhymes in Lerner's career, as with "Gallicly" and "phallicly." The "Gossip" number from the film was expanded into "Da Da Da Da," as if this wild Offenbachian cancan cannot bear lyrics and must settle for nonsense syllables. (The vocal lines were cut before the New York premiere and the music used only for dancing.)

The number that got the most attention was "The Contract," nine minutes of haggling among *Gigi*'s rapacious aunt (Agnes Moorehead), Mamita, and two attorneys. Its centerpiece is a waltz refrain beginning "Seven Rooms." This had been written for the film as "A Toujours," a haunting farewell number. To represent it as a section of a business scene misguises its purpose—wastes it, in effect.

So, for all the new Lerner and Loewe, we also get a lot of bungling. As if aware of its twice-told nature, the overture tasted of the new songs only, though the curtain rose during it for vignettes of the *belle époque*. Then came the entrance of that *maître de la vie parisienne*, Alfred Drake:

DRAKE: (to the audience) Good evening...Bon voyage...Happy birthday.

Good evening "because it is." Bon voyage to his current ex-lover. And happy birthday "because it's hers": and Gigi came running in to blow out the cake candles to three chords on the celesta, harp, and glockenspiel. Those three chords were as continental as the show ever got. If the first few minutes were fresh—though traditional in feeling—it was not because of *Gigi* but because of some sharp teamwork between choreographer Onna White and dance arranger Trude Rittmann. Because as soon as Drake started in on "Thank Heaven For Little Girls," one could not avoid the realization that one had, after all, seen this show before.

Drake was at his best, pointing up the words, elaborating with his portamento, and crisping out the replies for "It's a Bore." He was game because he was so glad to be working again. Some shows have flop sweat; this show had flop confidence. After all, *Gigi* had been one of the biggest movies of all time. The stage version, however, was one of the least successful movies of all time, with a solid pre-Broadway tour but a ho-hum reception in New York and three months of only polite applause. From an international MGM triumph it had become the kind of thing that Renata Adler thinks of when she hears the word "musical."

And that's dreary. *Raisin* (1973) is dreary even with the Tony. Not that it's badly written—no less an authority than Richard Rodgers singled it out when asked what younger writers he admired. They were Judd Woldin and Robert Brittan, adapting Lorraine Hansberry's *A Raisin in the Sun*. Very faithfully, too. Very *very* faithfully. The play, about a black urban family contemplating a move to the suburbs, is serious and the musical is serious. But most serious plays, fitted up for music, become uplifted, spiritually lightened, like *Carousel*. *Raisin* isn't lightened. It's heavied.

Raisin's book, by Hansberry's widower, Robert Nemiroff, and Charlotte Zaltzberg, seems determined to retain every possible word of the original, though the songs keep gobbling up text, a genuine achievement. So a tiny breakfast spat in the play turns into "Man Song": the male wants to dare, to bust out; the female wants security. A new boy friend immersed in African culture presents a young woman with a Nigerian robe, and Woldin and Brittan find in this a wild waltz dream of major seventh and $^9_7{}_4$ chords, a chase over the veld.

It's still dreary. It's another revival with songs, this time of a play too powerful to sing. Woldin and Brittan did their work well, yet the dialogue overwhelms them. The characters resist them—pious, rock-solid Mama (Virginia Capers); her almost neurotically ambitious son, Walter Lee (Joe Morton); her daughter, Beneatha (Deborah Allen); Walter Lee's wife, Ruth (Ernestine Jackson); and their little boy, Travis (Ralph Carter, who, we recall, survived both *Dude* and *Via Galactica*). None of these has been perverted from his role in the play. Mama has two solos, one (about a flower) hopeful, "A Whole Lotta Sunlight," and one (about, well, life) titanic, "Measure the Valleys." The songs are finely judged. But they add nothing to what Hansberry wrote. They *are* what Hansberry wrote; that's the trouble.

Walter Lee is expanded somewhat; he has the bulk of the score. And little Ralph Carter enjoyed a delightful solo "shout" in the second-act opening, a church number called "He Came Down This Morning." (For a rare touch of show-biz smarts in this gloomy work, Mama sternly motioned him to his seat just before his solo ended and, as he sat, slyly finished it off for him.)

Still, *A Raisin in the Sun* is one of those pushed-to-the-limit pieces that cannot be intensified or redeemed. It's already *there*. Yes, *Raisin*'s chorus could give us a taste of the Chicago ghetto in an opening ballet of local characters; the play cannot do that. And the breathless "Runnin' To Meet the Man" frames the treadmill worklife that Walter Lee hopes to get off of. It firms his motivation. Yes. Yes. And the musical can end Act One with Walter Lee's bitterly ironic "You Done Right," ending on a chord that is virtually an act of violence, e+?, as the curtain comes down. The musical can even revive a comic character whose scene was dropped from the original *Raisin in the Sun* in 1959, the nosy Mrs. Johnson (Helen Martin, recently of *Purlie*).* Yes, the musical can cut from the entrance of the nervous white man representing the town whereto the family will move—we know what *he* wants—to Travis' wistful solo, "Sidewalk Tree." It's *still* dreary. It's even a "why?" musical: why try to improve on Hansberry? And that dumb title! This "raisin in the sun" refers to a line from Langston Hughes' poem "Montage of a Dream Deferred," that dream (in relation to Hansberry) being both the suburban house and black liberation, for the play is very political, among many other things. To reduce the line to one word that no longer bears any meaning suggests a risible attempt to emulate *Mame*, *Purlie*, and other one-word war cries.

Raisin's cast was at least up to the challenge of replacing the play's Claudia McNeil, Sidney Poitier, Ruby Dee, and Diana Sands. Unlike *Gigi*'s ghosts and placeholders, *Raisin*'s people formed in effect a superb ensemble for *A Raisin in the Sun*. One thing may be said at last: unlike *Green Grow the Lilacs* and *I Am a Camera*, *A Raisin in the Sun* has not been superseded by its musical. And that is what "dreary" means.

---

* The musical thus restored Hansberry's one joke, after Mrs. Johnson leaves:

> RUTH: If ignorance was gold...
> MAMA: Shush. Don't talk about folks behind their backs.
> RUTH: *You* do.
> MAMA: I'm old and corrupted.

Of course, Mama isn't joking. As in a Sheldon Harnick lyric, it's funny because *she* thinks it's reasonable.

8

KEEP IT HOT

THE CONCEPT MUSICAL

Within one twelve-month period, from mid-1975 to mid-1976, three shows greatly developed the most misunderstood form in the musical's history. What *is* a concept show? It is a presentational rather than strictly narrative work that employs out-of-story elements to comment upon and at times take part in the action, utilizing avant-garde techniques to defy unities of place, time, and action. To put it another way: *Love Life* gives *Allegro* a blowjob.

Chicago (1975), billed as a "musical vaudeville," is a book show with a score compiling old show-biz tropes—an Eddie Cantor number, a Helen Morgan number, a Bert Williams number. Because *Chicago* sees show biz as an overriding power in American culture—turning a murder trial, for example, into a circus—the out-of-story "presentations" of the numbers create an Alienation Effect at once Brechtian and Ziegfeldian. It's a peep-show *Follies*.

Pacific Overtures (1976) is completely different in every respect, though it also employs out-of-story devices—a narrator, for example. It, too, is presentational, combining elements of American and Japanese theatre that make it, like *Chicago*, more an intellectual than romantic experience. (For instance, all major roles are played by men, even the female roles.) But *Chicago*, above all, tells of one person in a brief period of her life. *Pacific Overtures* has no protagonist; its subject is history.

1600 Pennsylvania Avenue (1976) offers a cast in modern dress on a bare stage putting on a show. Thus a play inside a play, it covers the first century of life in the White House, this being a metaphor for American life. One couple portray the various presidents and first ladies; another couple play their black servants. Most of the numbers are sung by characters as part of the narrative, but these performers keep recurring in different eras, making a fantasy of the flow of historical time.

The three shows have little in common. All boasted scores by major writers, but *Chicago* is a musical comedy and the other two are musical plays. *Chicago* is drawn from a satiric piece of the 1920s, the other two from chronicle. *Chicago* was staged by a top director-choreographer, *Pacific Overtures* by a top director who is not a choreographer; and *1600* had staging problems. *Chicago* was built around two great divas, while *Pacific Overtures*' players were unknown and *1600*'s uncelebrated. *Chicago* performed in a unit set that actually looked like something, with the orchestra overhead on a giant drum. *Pacific Overtures* was a Boris Aronson spectacle. *1600* lacked visuals, though there were period costumes. And *Chicago*, underrated in its day, was nevertheless a hit. *Pacific Overtures* was a succès d'estime. And *1600* was a bomb.

But all three are concept shows that expanded the definition of the genre, as each concept musical tends to. No two are alike, because they favor such complex interaction between naturalism and stylization, between the integration of arts and the separation of arts.

Chicago is the simplest of the three in its "idea." The source, Maurine Watkins' 1926 play of the same title, has a large cast and climaxes with the heroine's murder trial on a crowded stage. Yet it tells a tidy little tale about Roxie's crime in a place that thrives on sensation and has no morals. Roxie's husband, Amos; Roxie's lawyer, Billy Flynn; Roxie's fellow murderess Velma Kelly; the matron of the prison; a sob-sister columnist, Mary Sunshine; and Roxie's confidant, a cynical reporter named Jake (played originally by the young Charles Bickford), are all the speaking parts of any size. When Bob Fosse began planning the scenario of the musical *Chicago*, he did nothing more to the dramatis personae than turn the cynical reporter into a cynical agent. This stresses the show's view that in America all types of fame are equal and all the famous are "stars" in show biz, whether they are performers or criminals. Maurine Watkins' heroine even mentions that she is headed for vaudeville, but it's just a line in passing. Fosse built it into his grand finale.

The project had been conceived as a vehicle for Fosse's wife and star, Gwen Verdon, in the early 1960s. Watkins was shy (though she did at least arrange for Verdon to get first refusal after Watkins' death). But by then Verdon did not want to carry a show alone. So the role of Velma Kelly was built up for Chita Rivera, inspiring an amusing line from Verdon as Rivera makes an exit: "She sure don't look like a Kelly to me." Adding Jerry Orbach as the lawyer, Barney Martin as the husband, and Mary McCarty as the matron, Fosse turned one trick in hiring a male (billed as M. O'Haughey) to play Mary Sunshine in drag, his falsetto suggesting the dippy high of the professional bleeding heart. David Rounds played the agent, acting also as the show's emcee. But tryouts led Fosse to drop Rounds, give his important lines to the matron, and let others in the cast play emcee at different times.

I say "Fosse" because *Chicago* was truly his work, though lyricist Fred Ebb wrote out the book material (much of it directly from Watkins) and though, of course, the Kander and Ebb score is not just one of the great ones but the center of what Fosse wanted to do with the format of the show. His "musical vaudeville" isn't dog or magic acts, but rather the songs that, together, summon up like those in *Follies* the American showbiz past. In these songs lie the ideas, the performers, the styles—the art that communicated certain notions that more or less everyone in the country agreed on as received truth.

So Verdon is on a piano for "Funny Honey," the Helen Morgan number about the undeserving guy who nevertheless holds her in thrall. The matron, in full nightclub kit, gets the Sophie Tucker number, "When You're Good To Mama." The venal lawyer enters with the Ted Lewis number, "All I Care About (is love)," and the drag-queen columnist takes the Marilyn Miller number, "A Little Bit of Good." (It even uses the vamp to "Look For the Silver Lining," from Miller's Ziegfeld vehicle *Sally*.) Marilyn Miller, the nation's heroine, as a drag queen! Fosse, you rogue. Other allusions take in Rudy Vallee megaphones, Bing Crosby boo-boo-boo, Texas Guinan, Eddie Cantor, and Zez Confrey piano novelties.

Not every number executes such precise archaeology. But the format clearly wants to unmask hypocrisy in American culture by unmasking the poses struck by "I love him so" numbers, "What's money?" numbers, "We're all God's creatures" numbers. Still, more important than Fosse's theme is Fosse's organization. This is a *very* integrated show, in the way that spoken dialogue interrupts and then alters or develops a song, and in the way that the music keeps coming in sequences. Every now and then there is a sizable book scene. But generally, *Chicago* is a *musical* vaudeville, racing through plot points to get to the next number.

At times, the songs travel in convoys. Near the end of Act One, the lawyer and Roxie give a press conference in which she plays dummy on his knee and he works her like a ventriloquist. This is "We Both Reached For the Gun," which climaxes when he holds a high note while "drinking" a glass of milk. As the song ends, several reporters phone headlines in, and the next number has already begun, "Roxie." It's a unique piece: first, Roxie's long speech in which she gloats over her notoriety. There's a lot of autobiography in it, as Roxie snaps her fingers and dances around in those Fosse life-is-nothing-the-moment-is-everything circles:

> ROXIE: I started foolin' around. Then I started screwin' around, which is foolin' around without dinner.

Already, she sees this spot as the basis of her vaudeville act. Six chorus boys have entered in Support, and the song has begun. Roxie even tenders an explanation for America's love affair with fame:

> ROXIE: That's because none of us got enough love in our childhood.

As the number concludes and the chorus men dance off to Roxie's "Those are my boys," more headlines are called out to us. Then a two-minute scene between Velma and the matron leads directly to Chita Rivera's tour de force, "I Can't Do It Alone."

This is a musical pile-on worthy of an operetta. *Chicago*, however, is the ultimate musical comedy, bawdy and satiric. This may have led some to underrate *Chicago*'s book and thus the show as a whole when it was new. Walter Kerr said, "The storyline with its built-in satire has really been lost altogether, sacrificed to stunts and soft-shoe." On the contrary, the story line had been jumped up by being carried by the score—in an oblique way. Because so much of the pop music that *Chicago* re-creates was specialty numbers, Kerr must have mistaken the purpose of *Chicago*'s songs. When Sophie Tucker puts over "You've Got To See Mama Every Night," the number has no purpose other than to please. Sophie is not Mama; Sophie is kidding. But *Chicago*'s matron singing "When You're

Good To Mama" is an explanation of the corruption on which The System works. This is *Chicago*'s story.

At that, the book is all the more remarkable for the way it complements the score. Because everything in *Chicago* that can possibly be turned into music has been so turned, the book consists mostly of deal-making and jokes:

> JUNE: (one of the murderesses) Mrs. Morton, if my husband, Wilbur, comes here to visit me, you tell him I do not want to see him.
> MATRON: June, your husband is dead, you killed him.
> JUNE: Oh well, forget it then.

There is one flaw: the trial. It did get a lively staging, with one player constantly changing his look to impersonate all twelve members of the jury. Still, it goes on forever while covering events that we already know of in ways that we can predict. Indeed, the sequence doesn't come alive till the scene changes to the prison, where Velma and the matron are following the trial on the radio. Velma fulminates at Roxie's use of Velma's tricks much in the way that a comedian treats a colleague stealing his jokes:

> MARY SUNSHINE: (on radio) Mrs. Hart . . . looks simply radiant in her . . . elegant silver shoes.
> VELMA: (suspiciously) With rhinestone buckles?
> MARY SUNSHINE: With rhinestone buckles.

It is worth noting that while the concept musical came into being in the late 1940s, it could not flourish until the 1960s, when staging policy had acculturated non-realistic design. Concept shows don't look like *Oklahoma!* or *The Music Man*. *Chicago* didn't really look like anything— yet the costuming was realistic, as if Jerome Kern had planned the clothes while Erwin Piscator had built the set.

Boris Aronson built *Pacific Overtures*, fourth in the seventies quintet of Sondheim-Prince collaborations. We knew that the sets would essentialize the work, as with *Company*'s glass-and-chrome apartment boxes and *Follies*' blasted temple of delight. With the *hanamichi* (the runway for entrances and exits through the house) and the elongated rectangular staging area, Aronson presented something like a Kabuki theatre, and his art had the look of Japanese woodcuts. Florence Klotz's costumes stood boldly against the backdrops, especially as the players were so made up that their faces disappeared as if behind masks.

They were figures in a play: exactly the point. John Weidman's book, about the forced opening of Japan by the West in the mid-nineteenth century, sees all people as Tolstoyan puppets of history. In Tolstoy's view, no one man can make history, and not even an entire people can stop it. History is going to happen. So, in another of those insanely brilliant opening numbers, "The Advantages of Floating in the Middle of the Sea," Sondheim presents the social condition of Japan, blithely secure in its lack of contact with the outside world. To the characteristic Sondheim repeated chord (e_2^5, so unexploited that Sondheim has virtually invented it), we are treated to the three elements of perfect civil order, "arrangements" of the screens, the rice, the bows: art, economy, and social degree. Even this soon, the Reciter (Mako) functions as interested party as well as Brechtian narrator. This is Epic Theatre, complete with Alienation Effect, political footnotes, and character development set against historical panorama. But Mako has joined us from a season or two among Americans, and he has some of our style in him. He makes jokes. He takes sides.

So *Pacific Overtures* is Kabuki and Epic Theatre *but*. It makes its own rules, adapting those of the other two genres to suit. Nothing in it typifies the Broadway musical, but it borrows here and there from forms that Jerry Herman would recognize. Again: *but*. What could be more revolutionary than a sort of Heroine's Wanting Song delivered by two Observers kneeling at sides of the stage while the heroine (Soon-Teck Oh, in one of four important roles) dances, not least because the heroine will commit suicide before her husband sees her again?

The song's lyrics are revolutionary, too, broken into the tiny declarations and wishes that, in typical Japanese style, combine into a truth. "There Is No Other Way" is spare and carefully expressed, with its recorder over hand drum. Then harp, then strings. It builds till, at an elegiacal expansion on the line "The bird flies," it seemed the most beautiful music yet heard on Broadway.

I remember thinking at the time that few will get this work. Simply the device of disintegrating this moment into its constituents would bewilder the slow. Any other musical, even another bold one, would have stated this scene in a duet for the wife and her husband, Kayama (Isao Sato). But only the two Observers sing, one about what is happening and the other "speaking" for the wife. Note that even Jonathan Tunick's orchestration is segmented; the entire show is. *Pacific Overtures* breaks this vast account down into the loosest and tightest of book musicals. Loose because it allows room for so much; tight because it never relaxes its grip on how the history is happening.

Some characters are introduced only to vanish. Others recur, such as the government councillor Abe Masahiro (Yuki Shimoda). Similarly, the score introduces many figures we never see again, such as a madam of geisha girls or three British sailors. Yet it never ceases to consider the turning of history's wheel—the madam's and sailors' songs treat the social dislocation caused by the Westerners' arrival.

Conversely, the obviously eventful day on which Japan signed its first treaty with America falls into the score in an offbeat way. "Someone in a Tree" is a beguiling discussion by characters who didn't understand what was happening—exactly what history is while it's in the present tense. The trade negotiations between Japan and its visitors are conducted in "Please Hello," a burlesque. Costumed as if for the senior-class operetta in a Japanese high school, the various Western admirals sing in pastiche. The American gets John Philip Sousa, the Brit sings Gilbert and Sullivan patter, the Frenchman a cancan; and the number climaxes with an evocation of a word that was very much in use at that stage of the Cold War, "détente."

Such an intricate pageant could not properly bear a protagonist. However, two figures do form a central story line in this *opera senza amore*, Kayama and his friend Manjiro (Sab Shimono, the original Ito in *Mame*). They humanize for us the growing crisis in Japan, between Westernizers and the reactionary élite. Ironically, the minor samurai Kayama goes Western, while Manjiro, at first a commoner who likes America, grows into a xenophobe devotee of aristocratic tradition.

These two also have a number that draws from the annals to develop character. Sondheim himself likes to cite "Someone in a Tree" because it centers the show's view of history. But "A Bowler Hat" is perhaps the outstanding number, in a coup de théâtre deftly blended of song, speech, mime, and the use of props. We listen to Kayama as he becomes ever more fluent in Western ways; we watch the silent Manjiro losing himself in the rhapsodic tranquillity of the tea ceremony.

It was a stunning experience in saying much with the most limited means, another aspect of Japanese art. Alien, exotic, and complex, *Pacific Overtures* represents more of the great disconnect between the musical and its public. Back when Ethel Merman and Cole Porter ran things, the notion of an intellectually challenging musical was unthinkable. Even the spoken theatre seldom truly challenged its public, except perhaps to persevere through the longer O'Neill works. *Pacific Overtures* encountered such a buyers' resistance during its Boston tryout that producer Prince had to spend his own money to bring the show to New York. There it got the most mixed notices in theatre history. One television idiot described the music as "atonal," and one of the supplementary papers actually called the show "loathsome" and "disgusting."

I think *Women's Wear Daily*'s Howard Kissel, of those who liked the piece, best appreciated what an Age of Sondheim meant to the enlightened theatregoer. "The most original, the most profound, the most theatrically ambitious of the Prince-Sondheim collaborations," Kissel wrote, because the best theatre is adventurous, not *Contact* or *Mamma Mia!*. "It is also," he continued, "the production in which the team that sets Broadway's highest standards most fully meets the astonishing objectives they set themselves."

One could not say as much of Leonard Bernstein and Alan Jay Lerner's *1600 Pennsylvania Avenue* (1976), one of the most self-evident of the Bad Idea musicals. That idea was to reduce all of American history to an *Upstairs, Downstairs* on race relations. Ken Howard and Patricia Routledge played various presidents and their wives; Gilbert Price and Emily Yancy played the ageless retainers Lud and Seena. There was to be none of *Chicago*'s plot motion, none of *Pacific Overtures*' unity of action; rather, *1600* was a revue with a throughline, embodied in the opening and closing number, "Rehearse!": democracy is ever in a state of rehearsal, ever refining and developing its liberal urge.

Unfortunately, Bernstein and Lerner were suffering from the sixties American version of the Disease of the West, whose symptomatic behavior obeys the rule, Democracies cannot be criticized enough and leftist fascisms cannot be criticized at all. The lack of patriotism in a Bicentennial musical is simply silly; the self-hatred is contemptible.

Worse, the show was bad entertainment, based as it was on little more than the usual white liberal obsession with black civil rights. The contents included the founding of Washington, D.C.; Thomas Jefferson's introduction of waffles and spaghetti into American cuisine; the War of 1812; the national crisis that led to the Civil War; the implication that James Buchanan was gay; and the age of the robber barons. This was presented as a minstrel show, just as in another musical with no plot, Lerner's *Love Life*. There was nothing of the opening of the west (with the genocidal elimination of the Indian, not a major leftist concern in the 1970s); the industrialization of the north; the expansion of the continent through the railroads; or the arts world's halfhearted attempts to identify an American style in music, painting, and theatre in the late 1800s.

The show's humiliating Philadelphia premiere found staff departing in exasperation that the material—or the authors—proved so intransigent. Director Frank Corsaro and choreographer Donald McKayle were replaced by Gilbert Moses and George Faison. Set and costume designer Tony Walton also left, taking his name off the posters. But his show curtain, a blueprint of the White House, was retained even so, complete with Walton's initials, unmistakable in the lower right-hand corner.

With some flops, one regrets the wasted time—in this case, four years of planning and writing. The Coca-Cola Company, *1600*'s sole backer at well over a million dollars, regretted the bad choice of PR and disavowed the production.

But *1600*'s participants must have regretted the loss of the music in the feast-or-famine system operating at this time. For Bernstein and Lerner created an astonishingly good score, even a synoptic all-American one, with fanfare, march, waltz, blues. It's Bernstein's most classical work for Broadway—more so than even *Candide*—with the expertise of the genius musician. Perhaps Bernstein wanted to make his own mark in the Age of (his onetime protégé) Sondheim, as in a number called "Sonatina": British Army aristos disdainfully pantywaisting around in the White House dining room. Bernstein laid it out in the orthodox three movements of sonata-allegro, minuet (on an English theme appropriated for "The Star Spangled Banner"), and rondo finale. Bernstein also revived a favorite trick, building much of the score on variations of an ur-theme. The melody is used most purely as the first lines of the show's anthem, "Take Care of This House." But it is heard throughout the evening, for instance tootling blithely in the woodwinds as punctuation during a scene between Washington and congressional delegates over where to locate the new capital, "On Ten Square Miles of the Potomac River."

Of our three concept shows, *1600* exploited the form least fully. *Chicago*'s vaudeville was "disguised" as character and plot numbers, a genuine innovation, and *Pacific Overtures*' Kabuki history was replete with curiosities. But *1600*'s concept eventually ran out of interest, especially because the two black leads and their servants chorus had little to do beyond reflecting the changes in racial integration and celebrating Lud and Seena's wedding in the irresistible "I Love My Wife," set to a Caribbean beat.

Still, every concept show does amend the catalogue of practices. There was one arresting touch in "The Little White Lie," when James and Eliza Monroe, sleepless in bed, bicker over the slavery issue. Accusing Monroe of accommodating racism, Eliza sings, "You knew it when you were Adams"—and Jefferson, and Madison. This is something new, a character's expressing knowledge of the show's non-realistic concept *while remaining realistically in character*. Another touch brightened the very end of the evening: as all but the two leads filled the stage for the closing reprise of "Rehearse!," the president and first lady entered upstage right, perfect replicas of Theodore and Edith Roosevelt. A sight gag: and the curtain fell.

The most lasting memory of *1600*'s *trompe l'oeil* impersonations fastens on "Duet For One," possibly the only genuine showstopper to appear in a show that ran but a single week. Ken Howard may have lacked the magnetism to play, among others, George Washington, John Adams, and Thomas Jefferson; but Patricia Routledge was a singer and comic of dazzling gifts. "Duet For One" offered the presidential inauguration of 1877. To bits of Rutherford B. Hayes' spoken oath of office, the incoming Lucy Hayes and the outgoing Julia (Mrs. Ulysses S.) Grant comment on the controversial election of 1876.* Routledge played both women, jumping

---

* Democrat Samuel J. Tilden won the popular vote, but the Republicans contested results in four states, stopping Tilden one vote short of victory in the Electoral College. Irregularities in the final results for the four states could not be settled by application of constitutional law, which was ambiguous on the matter. Ultimately, a compromise was reached: the Democratic South was liberated of Northern occupying forces and got other concessions; and the Republican presidential candidate, Hayes, was certified as the winner. Note an arresting coincidence in that Bernstein and Lerner could not possibly have guessed that their show would contain episodes relating to singular events of the millennium: the impeachment of a president (Andrew Johnson; Bill Clinton) and a disputed election (1876; 2000).

back and forth by flipping a movable part of her headgear. Routledge didn't merely change "hats": she completely changed in look and sound, from Julia's catty mezzo to Lucy's cooing soprano. The nine-minute number builds so extravagantly that the last big statement of the waltz refrain, "The First Lady of the Land," thrilled the opening-night audience into an ovation *during* the music.

The later history of our three shows is various. *Chicago*'s run was threatened early on by what seemed to be the entire world's refusal to give any more praise to Bob Fosse after he won a Tony, an Oscar, and an Emmy in the same year. Also, *Chicago* and *A Chorus Line* showed up almost simultaneously, and the usual revolutionists trumpeted preemptive hallelujahs for the latter show, not realizing that it is not revolutionary and that Michael Bennett was the latest in a line that Bob Fosse had helped to found.

Chicago got eleven Tony nominations (including Best Actress for both Verdon and Rivera) but lost them all, mainly to *A Chorus Line*. However, when Verdon suffered a throat ailment requiring an operation, Kander and Ebb favorite Liza Minnelli stepped in as Roxie. Minnelli was at the height of her powers and fame, and her nine-week stint put *Chicago* into sellout, with the usual spillover, after Verdon returned, from those who make a point of attending anything that sells out.

So *Chicago* eventually lasted 898 performances, though it never got its due till Encores! tried it in 1996. Concept shows generally do well in concert, because they seldom take place in specific locations and thus need no scenery. William Ivey Long dressed everyone in variations on hot black formal circuswear, Walter Bobbie and Ann Reinking staged the show in Fosse style; and Reinking, Bebe Neuwirth, James Naughton, and Joel Grey were excellent. Also, the cuts in the libretto were judicious rather than, as sometimes at Encores!, disfiguring. With Fosse no longer among us and sorely missed, *Chicago* was suddenly everyone's favorite show. Moved to Broadway, this concert staging became by far the most successful revival in Broadway history, going on to international popularity and a phenomenally successful film version.

Pacific Overtures, too, is better appreciated today. A relatively lavish Off-Broadway revival in 1984 got much better reviews than the original. (Those who couldn't grasp it the first time adopted the alibi that the original had been overproduced.) There was very little revision, mainly the dropping of two scenes, one in which the United States and Japan trade gifts (ours are a ton of cultural keepsakes, from Audubon's *Birds of America* to a locomotive; theirs are tiny treasures fastidiously wrapped), and one on the introduction of the rickshaw. The deletions help center the work. But it isn't written to be centered. It's history's "scrapbook," as Sondheim once put it.

This new staging, by Fran Soeder, strongly resembled the old one; is there but one way to perform this show correctly? The Prince-Aronson vision is virtually written into the text, and a 1987 production by the English National Opera, pinchpenny spare, recalled the original even so—though it was, surprisingly for an opera company, not at all as well sung.

Then, in 2000, and on tour in New York in 2002, a Japanese group mounted the show in somewhat different style. Director Amon Miyamoto sought to segregate the American input from the Japanese input in the composition by using the *hanamichi* not simply for entrances and exits but as a stage for the Western characters. Thus, the invasion of Japan is physicalized: the strangers come aggressively out of the audience toward the Japanese in the central playing area while a vast American flag unfurls overhead. Further, the Reciter (Takeharu Kunimoto) was an outright comic figure, lacking Mako's advocating intensity.

The production was comic in general, even gimmicked. Many of the original's most picturesque moments—Mako's grand-manner keening when Kayama discovered his wife's corpse, or the deadly quiet of Manjiro's tea ceremony while Kayama ebulliently flies on history's wings in "A Bowler Hat"—were gone. Apparently, the new cheap Broadway obtains in Japan as well, for the original orchestration for twenty-two players (not counting the stage band) was reduced to seven. They sounded terrible, and "There Is No Other Way" in particular was ruined. Nor, finally, was it useful to introduce World War II into the action* with a simulation of the destruction of Hiroshima and Nagasaki during "Next." We didn't start that war. Japan did.

---

* In 1976, given an already crowded evening, John Weidman (who was assisted on the book by Hugh Wheeler) wisely dealt with this matter obliquely, in lines spoken by Lord Abe: "We must appease the Westerners until we have learned the secrets of their power and success. Then, when we have become their equals. Then, perhaps. Then, if we are sure the time is right . . ." The belligerent threat is unmistakable, though of course the usual idiots missed it.

Alone of concept musicals, *1600 Pennsylvania Avenue* lives on devoid of its concept. As *A White House Cantata*, it is now less even than a concert staging: a concert. The "Rehearse!" frame is gone, along with a pair of numbers for the black singers. But virtually all the rest of the score is retained, even "The Red White and Blues," staged on Broadway as a striptease for the chorus men in the try-anything panic before opening night. An important duet for Lud and Seena, "This Time," a casualty of the tryout, has been restored, and the original scoring, by Sid Ramin, Hershy Kay, and Bernstein, has been improved to keep a full-sized orchestra busy. The work has even been recorded, with some cuts to hold it to a single disc, so at least the best of this Bicentennial monster is preserved.

And that is all one asks of this project, after all. The novel format that proved so intractable reminds us why so many producers fear novelty: it can go so awry. They want a sure thing. Not a good idea. A used one.

9

I Could Be at Home with My Seven Maids

THE REVIVAL

There is no surer evidence that an art is ailing than when it takes out a mortgage on its past to pay for its future. A Golden Age is spendthrift, greedy for new talent. Typically, when the Third Age began, there were virtually no revivals. The exceptions are outstanding—the Shuberts' elaborate mounting of *Florodora* in 1920, for instance, simply because its celebrated Sextet was *still* so famous a generation later that everyone wanted a look at the rest of the show. Florenz Ziegfeld put the original *Show Boat* production back on stage three years after it had closed, simply because the score had become so beloved that folks wanted to hear it again.

It was only in the 1940s that revivals started turning up in any significant numbers. Not counting the usual Gilbert and Sullivan from various groups, the City Center's spring season of limited-run resuscitations, or the cheap tours of operettas given a first week on The Street so the provincial posters could claim "Direct from Broadway," the 1940s hosted about a dozen revivals. This takes in *Porgy and Bess, A Connecticut Yankee, Show Boat* yet again, *Sally*, major Victor Herbert and German titles, and even something from the First Age, Reginald De Koven's *Robin Hood* (1890). One can only speculate on the reason for this retrospective flurry, for fifties Broadway was largely denuded of old work. True, the City Center's season was expanded, and television was broadcasting classic titles from *Naughty Marietta* to *High Button Shoes*. But of brand-new old shows on Broadway, there was only a flop *Music in the Air*, a flop *Shuffle Along*, a flop *Of Thee I Sing*, and a hit *Pal Joey*, which inspired a flop *On Your Toes*. After that, reviving was left to off-Broadway.

However, every so often there comes a production whose flash success creates an imitative cycle. It is not necessarily the first or the best. It is the most prosperous; and its news travels. And that is the *No, No, Nanette* of 1971, conceived by Harry Rigby as virtually a raising of the dead. Bygone talent would head the cast and even stage it. Indeed, *No, No, Nanette* beat out *Gigi* in bringing the movie musical onto Broadway, for Rigby's notion was, roughly, a Warner Bros. *No, No, Nanette* of about 1935: starring Ruby Keeler and Patsy Kelly and directed by Busby Berkeley.

A great deal of saga informs this event, especially regarding the firings, the surprises (Berkeley turned out to be an alcoholic zombie; Burt Shevelove took over), and, after the triumphant premiere, the legal battle for ownership between Rigby and his co-producer, Cyma Rubin. At the time, it was the talk of the town, especially when Don Dunn's book on the backstage of it all was serialized in *New York* magazine.

What matters now is how cleverly three creative elements conjoined to make *No, No, Nanette* into a fresh antique. Crisply and lovingly modernized, it nevertheless made no attempt to be taken at the same value as the new shows of the time. It wanted to be seen at a remove, as something of the 1920s for the 1970s. Not as something of the 1970s.

For instance, the height of the bickering between Nanette (Susan Watson) and her Tom (Roger Rathburn) in dialogue during the title number found her calling him "a flat tire" to his exasperated "You can go fly a kite!" This was not camping, but rather a styling of the "innocence" of the twenties musical. Even the long outdated "finaletto"—the dialogue-and-reprises ensemble number with which twenties musicals capped an act—was retained. The idea was to revisit the show on its terms as much as possible, which is why the book was largely rewritten but the score not much tampered with. A few minor numbers were cut, and one addition, called "Always You" and establishing the oldest couple (Keeler, Jack Gilford), made it as far as the Boston tryout. Later in Boston, another new number, "Only a Moment Ago,"* replaced it. This, too, was cut, because

---

* Who wrote these interpolations? Don Dunn's book credits "Always You" to Charles Gaynor, and "Only a Moment Ago" to Burt Shevelove and *Nanette*'s musical director, Buster Davis. The latter title was recorded for the cast album and left off the LP release but included in the CD reissue, whose liner notes inconsistently assign two different identifications of it: one, as a leftover item by *Nanette*'s composer and co-lyricist, Vincent Youmans and Irving Caesar; and, two, as Shevelove's versifying of an unused Youmans melody.

a song doesn't properly establish the famously dancing Keeler. While Patsy Kelly opened the finished show in a goofy battle with a vacuum cleaner, Keeler tantalized with some unimportant dialogue till she reappeared in tap kit to tear the house apart with the chorus boys in "I Want To Be Happy."

The three creative elements that conceived and perfected the *Nanette* revival are Shevelove, his musical staff (Buster Davis, dance arranger Luther Henderson, and orchestrator Ralph Burns), and designer Raoul Pène du Bois. It was Shevelove who figured out how much of 1925 worked for 1971, where to cut and where to improve. This is important history, because many revivals rewrite generally. Shevelove rewrote only where he thought rewriting necessary. Otherwise, why are you rewriting?

The musical staff made the most of one of the twenties' most tuneful scores. "Happy" and "Tea for Two" stand among the enduring standards. But "Too Many Rings Around Rosie," "You Can Dance With Any Girl At All," and the torch number, "'Where Has My Hubby Gone?' Blues," were marvelous rediscoveries. They provided Helen Gallagher with the best opportunity of her career (her role, Lucille, is arguably the revival's woman lead) as she alternated flippant with concerned, all-knowing with utterly lost. "Rosie," the first vocal in Shevelove's revision, is ground-zero musical-comedy philosophy. "You Can Dance" gave Gallagher and Bobby Van their challenge dance in different styles from maxixe to two-step. The torcher, an eleven o'clocker with Gallagher in blue silk backed by the boys in tuxedos, was so stunning that the show never quite recovered. One always felt that it ended fifteen minutes before it ended.

Du Bois' sets and costumes also helped focus the public's understanding of what Shevelove was doing. The girls' pleated skirts, the boys' art-deco sweaters, the cloche hats and beribboned dresses and men's belted suits were not merely authentification of period but a repositioning of musical comedy as a carefree adventure in an age of dark shows, dreary shows, and concept shows. The ruthless pastels, the hypnotic stripes and spangles, the onslaught of ukeleles in the finale: happyland. In the middle of a theatrical season in which God drowned most of humanity and show biz itself cracked apart in despair, *No, No, Nanette* reinstituted the kind of musical one meant by the word "musical."

This revival's phenomenal success sent the work to many stages, always with professional resurrections—June Allyson and Dennis Day with Judy Canova as the maid on one tour, Evelyn Keyes and Don Ameche with Ruth Donnelly on another. Near the end of its two-year run, the New York *Nanette* welcomed Martha Raye back to Broadway as the maid. It was a bit of a comedown after her Dolly, perhaps, but it is necessary to the survival of Western Civilization that our great performers get their stage time.*

Producer Rigby had found a formula for success after a long career putting on failures: revive outdated shows with old movie stars. His next offering was Harry Tierney and Joseph McCarthy's *Irene* (1919), with Debbie Reynolds in her Broadway debut. (Ruby Keeler and Patsy Kelly had been Broadway veterans.) The director was John Gielgud, a very odd choice, and the problem, right from the start, is that no one had any intention of reviving *Irene*. The show really was *Debbie Reynolds Hits Broadway* (1973), and after a disastrous tryout in Toronto, Reynolds demanded that Gower Champion—her director for an *Annie Get Your Gun* in California—take over. Champion had less interest than anyone in what *Irene* had been or could be. Champion wanted a Big One, for *The Happy Time* (1968) had failed and *Sugar* only scraped by. So now the show really was *Gower Champion's Comeback* (1973). By this time, in a tunestack made mostly of other songs by not composer Tierney but lyricist McCarthy, along with new ones by various hands, and in a new book also by various hands, *Irene* itself had all but vanished.

The rewriting of old shows did not start with *No, No, Nanette*. Most of the forties revivals had been reordered in some way. *Porgy and Bess* was given in a cut-down version with the recits delivered as spoken dialogue. *A Connecticut Yankee* was updated, *The Red Mill* cleared of its Second Age puns and slapstick, and *Show Boat* reconfigured from a musical comedy with operetta love duets to a musical play.

---

* Another personal note: I went back to *Nanette* for Raye, and found that Joy Hodges was playing Keeler's role. A few people clapped for Hodges' entrance, though hers was one of the lesser careers, taking in leads in *I'd Rather Be Right* (1937), *Dream With Music* (1944), the hideous *Nellie Bly* (1946), and not much more. Still, she took the trouble to show up, so I clapped, too. Behind me, someone whispered to his partner, "Who's that?," and an enraged queen answered, with a contemptuous snarl, "Nobody!" Whereupon my best friend, Bob Trent, turned around, noticed the queen, and told him, "You have to be cute to be that snotty." The two of them left at the end of the first act.

In the 1950s, *Pal Joey* was reinstated with very few changes. But the aforementioned *Shuffle Along* revival in 1952 eviscerated the original with an entirely new plotline and an almost entirely new score! However, this low-rent production folded up within its first week and went unremarked.

So it is fair to say that the promiscuous adulteration of old titles out of a lack of sympathy for what they represent came with *Irene*. The original work had inspired a cycle of urban Cinderella shows, often with an Irish inflection, that dominated Broadway in the early 1920s. In a tightly integrated score for a soprano heroine and various show-biz cutups, *Irene* paired its title part of an upholsterer's assistant with a society scion while she and two neighborhood friends became models. Their boss was Madame Lucy, an effeminate male played for gay laughs. There is little plot—no second couple, for example—and not all that much score. "Alice Blue Gown" and the title song were the hits, along with "Castle of Dreams" (whose theme was taken from the middle section of Chopin's so-called "Minute Waltz") and the jaunty "We're Getting Away With It." It was an intimate show, in a house limited to five hundred seats, and it made a star of Edith Day, who then played it in London and became so celebrated that they made her Queen of Drury Lane in three Hammerstein roles in a row, in *Rose-Marie*, *The Desert Song*, and *Show Boat*.

So we have an Irish Cinderella star part, and that the new *Irene* retained. It also kept the society boy (Monte Markham), his snobby mother (Ruth Warrick), Irene's mother (Patsy Kelly), Madame Lucy (George S. Irving), and the two friends (Janie Sell, Carmen Alvarez). It sang five of the original numbers. The changes it made are not as plentiful as those in the 1940 RKO version with Anna Neagle. Yet absolutely nothing in the 1973 *Irene* suggested an intimate period piece with ethnicity politics satirizing society hypocrites.

Nothing in it suggested anything. The city proles did Irish jigs and the society types did "The Riviera Rage," but there was no feeling about which step of the social ladder we were on. Raoul Pène du Bois was back on hand, yet *Irene* didn't look like much. This is a loaded word, but what it was was *slick*. Slick is good in that everything works; slick is bad in that it's product rather than a labor of love. Expensive product at that: for while the production ran long enough for Reynolds to be replaced by another MGM star, Jane Powell, the backers were not repaid because of the heavy expense of tryout corrections. An $800,000 budget had swelled by almost as much again while Champion revised the revision.

In the end, two things about *Irene* stood out. One was an added number, Wally Harper and Jack Lloyd's version of the Heroine's Wanting Song, "The World Must Be Bigger Than an Avenue." It is one of the best of its kind—better, really, than any title in the original score. The other thing was one of the poster credits, "Debbie Reynolds's Hairstyles by Pinky Babajian." That's important to know.

The critics, at least, were questioning the integrity of these revivals because of the corrupt scores. In *The New Yorker*, Brendan Gill called Rigby's series "show-biz body snatching" when the next one, *Good News*, came along in 1974. Each offering, Gill wrote, was "merely a shell of the original—a sort of brightly painted mummy case in which bits and pieces of other once celebrated cadavers have been made to mingle with a portion of the authentic remains." Walter Kerr, who could place the sources of *Good News*' borrowings from others of its authors' scores, likened the practice to the creation of "a smorgasbord of period echoes without any specific identity of its own."

From Warners and MGM, Rigby moved to Twentieth Century–Fox for his *Good News* stars, Alice Faye and John Payne. The DeSylva, Brown, and Henderson college musical of 1927 claimed a still-popular score, and Hollywood's 1947 remake, with June Allyson and Peter Lawford, has many partisans. It, too, is corrupt; but it has a quality of its own, a presence. Whatever quality that Rigby's *Good News* had was lost on a yearlong tour, during which adapter and director Abe Burrows and choreographer Donald Saddler were replaced by adapter Garry Marshall and director-choreographer Michael Kidd. *The Wall Street Journal*'s Edwin Wilson thought Burrows' version warm and lovely and Kidd's just another fast-food chowder.

Because it closed so quickly in New York—after two weeks, with Gene Nelson taking over for Payne—people assume that *Good News* was a disaster. It was no worse than Rigby's *Irene*, in fact, and based on a much better show in the first place. Some of it really jived. Try this lead-in to the first duet of the comic couple (Wayne Bryan, Barbara Lail), a livelier version of a scene in the 1927 original:

BABE: You're Bobby Randall, aren't you?
BOBBY: Yeah.
BABE: I'm Babe O'Day. The whole campus knows that we're in love!
BOBBY: What do you want with me? I'm only a substitute on the football team. I'm not handsome. All I have is four dollars—and that's tied up in IOUs.
BABE: I don't want a rich man. I don't want a handsome man. I don't want a clever man.
BOBBY: You want me.
BABE: Right.

And she jumps into the verse, unfortunately to "Button Up Your Overcoat." It's a fine number; so were most of the six other songs in this *Good News* that were written for purposes irrelevant to *Good News*' plot action. But why did we not hear Babe's establishing number, "Flaming Youth," spun off a catchphrase of the 1920s and a nifty piece of caricature? Why omit the duets that the authors wrote for Bobby and Babe, "Baby! What?" and "In the Meantime"? The former is a real curiosity—he sings the first word, she sings the second, then the orchestra takes over before the melody can continue.

There were some good things in this *Good News*—a personable cast of students, superb vocal arrangements by Hugh Martin and Timothy Gray, and the return of Stubby Kaye, with the running gag of leading on different animal mascots (a llama, a goat, a skunk, and finally a dog that licked his face while he sang). The overture was hardly begun when the curtain rose on "The Football Drill," with the team in the red-and-gray uniforms of Tait College manfully dancing their way through calisthenics. Donald Oenslager's sets were dull (though he had done the scenery for the original 1927 show), but Donald Brooks' costumes were, like Du Bois' for *Nanette*, a hoot.

I think Alice Faye and Michael Kidd killed it. Ruby Keeler wasn't an important talent, but she had a unique no-frills-just-me charm and she really could dance. Debbie Reynolds stormed through *Irene* with missionary zeal. But Faye, so pleasing in her film musicals, came off here as an inept Novelty Star. And Kidd tried to force a twenties piece into *right here now* when its only reason for coming back is that it originally was someplace else.

Only Harry Rigby wanted to raid old catalogues; others revived shows that were still vivid memories. However, the pumping and primping continued. *A Funny Thing Happened on the Way To the Forum* (1962) returned in 1972 with Phil Silvers, the Pseudolus whom it was written for. Surely this show defies editing, except when the Pseudolus can't manage the deceptive rhythms in "Pretty Little Picture." That song—and "That'll Show Him"—vanished. But two long-lost *Forum* numbers returned, undeservingly, "Farewell" (for someone who keeps not leaving) and "Echo Song."

There was more Sondheim, though only lyrics, in the rewrite that director Hal Prince and book writer Hugh Wheeler gave to *Candide* (1956). Seen in Brooklyn's Chelsea Theater Center in 1973 and on Broadway a year later, this new *Candide* marked the work's first critical and popular success in the most radical yet of its many revisions.

Possibly to avoid the disquieting picture of mature actors cluelessly screwing up again and again in Voltaire's black farce, Prince cast kids—twenty-two in something like eighty roles. He had Wheeler not rewrite Lillian Hellman's original book but lay out a wholly new one. He moved songs around, reassigned them, restored them and dropped them. He used a narrator, a Voltaire-Pangloss, and he turned the "comic operetta" of 1956 into a stupid musical comedy staged environmentally. The "stage" was fragmented, and the audience was so close to its bits and pieces that many photographs of the production include the public. Members were occasionally asked to hold an actor's coat while he fenced for his life, or whatever. It was *Candide* for children. It was *Candide* with children. The Pangloss, Lewis Stadlen, and the Old Lady, June Gable, gave the performance class and smarts. The rest of it was not well sung and even a bit coarse and bratty.

What do we do to *The Pajama Game* (1954) after that? This one got off lightly, in 1973. There was one added song and less dancing. The production, directed like the original by George Abbott, was cheap. For a novelty, co-producer (and co-author) Richard Adler presented a racially mixed cast, so white Hal Linden played opposite black Barbara McNair. Thus, instead of being simply antagonists in a management–labor dispute, they were now genetically ill-starred as well. It's dramatically valid. But after Linden challenged McNair on the matter early in Act One, the show never referred to the race thing again. The problem had evaporated along with George Abbott's attention span. Cab Calloway; his busy standby, Tiger Haynes; Mary Jo Catlett; and Sharron Miller graced this revival. But it was underproduced and deserved its short run.

Some revivals tried to pretend that they were new work. *Gentlemen Prefer Blondes* (1949) was now *Lorelei* (1974). *Kismet* (1953) went black as *Timbuktu!* (1978). What rinky-dink things they were, despite Carol Channing in the one and the glorious score of the other. They weren't as bargain-basement as *The Pajama Game*, true. But *Lorelei*'s supporting cast was not much above the understudy level, and *Timbuktu!* lacked the voice for one of Broadway's biggest scores.

Perhaps the silliest thing about *Lorelei* was the way it reapportioned the *Blondes* songs to different characters or even just different spots in the story, as if that in itself affirmed the renovation. This version of *Blondes* also gave a bigger role to Lorelei's "daddy" (Peter Palmer, the original Li'l Abner) and added a few uninteresting new songs by *Blondes*' composer, Jule Styne, now working with Betty Comden and Adolph Green.

Timbuktu! had a look. As director, choreographer, and costume designer, Geoffrey Holder made the show veritable eye-rape—stilt walkers, parasols, masks, feathers, amulets, streamers, bodice bangles, firefly wands, peekaboo mesh . . . really, everything but hairstyles by Pinky Babajian. The sets, planned by Tony Straiges, were simple, the better to set off the fashion show; and the setting was moved from ancient Baghdad to fourteenth-century Mali. No doubt they were dressing better in the new place.

As always, songs went missing while new ones appeared, though these at least were the work of *Kismet*'s original authors, Wright, Forrest, and Borodin. "Golden Land, Golden Life," drawn from the tenor's second-act aria in *Prince Igor*, has an authentic *Kismet* flavor, and might serve the show well in any future airing. On the other hand, the vocally demanding "Not Since Nineveh" had to be dropped, replaced by a dashing feminist rant, "In the Beginning, Woman."

This change was made for Eartha Kitt, definitely one of *Timbuktu!*'s assets. Try her entrance, amid a swarm of oiled bodybuilders who lowered her to the floor so that she could very slowly pick her way around them, prowl catlike to the true star's stage center, insolently cruise the house, and then add infinitely to the show's running time as she gargles out two sentences:

EARTHA: I'm...
        [...]
EARTHA: ...here....
        [...]
EARTHA: Anything new in...
        [...]
EARTHA: ...town?

Some revivals actually wanted to bring back an old show rather than some new piece under an old show's name. The first revival of the decade, *The Boy Friend*, in 1970, was simply *The Boy Friend*, with the unexpected embarrassment that critics preferred the unknown soubrette, Sandy Duncan, to the lead, television star Judy Carne. Meanwhile, in 1973, Lehman Engel supervised restagings of two twenties operettas by Sigmund Romberg without revision. *The Desert Song* featured David Cryer and Chris Callan, and *The Student Prince* had Harry Danner and Bonnie Hamilton. Both went out on tour and *The Desert Song* tried Broadway, to no avail. The *Post*'s Richard Watts Jr. had actually covered the first *Desert Song*, in 1926, and he found this production so faithful that he declared himself "tempted to reprint my original notice."

Most arresting was the reception accorded *On the Town* on its first return to Broadway, in 1971. The on-and-off Ron Field was a full-fledged smash-hit director-choreographer after *Applause*, so he dared take on the challenge of trying to erase Jerome Robbins. It was in fact the passage of time that had erased Robbins' original staging: no one living, including Robbins, could recall it. Nevertheless, Field's perceived hubris doomed the show, which was quite well produced.

Resisting the temptation to do Something Different and thus claim the work as his own, Field retained all the *On the Town* eccentricities: gabby Flossie and her friend, the blithely dippy announcer in the "Miss Turnstiles" ballet, the lobster-box chase scenes. Field also collected a capable cast (after some out-of-town firings). Ron Husmann, Remak Ramsay, and Jess Richards were the sailors, respectively opposite Donna

McKechnie, Phyllis Newman, and Bernadette Peters, who scored the first big win of her so far short but busy career. Driving a tiny, campy taxicab around the stage in her launching scene and taking over the place for a major "I Can Cook, Too," Peters caught the essence of *On the Town*'s New York. It is the crazy excitement of living in a place of adventure. This is why the three sailors are so stoked when they break into the opening scene: as if they knew that they were lucking into one of the great musical comedies.

The critics soured it up. They carped about Field's choreography, the casting, the attitude. Even authors Bernstein, Comden, and Green—now official darlings of the theatre community—were not given their due. No, it was another newly directed Robbins show, *Gypsy*, that got raves on *its* revival, in 1974. But *Gypsy* is much easier to do than *On the Town*; all you need is Angela Lansbury.

Gypsy, too, was revived without revision. How does one revise *Gypsy*, a perfect show? Besides, the author of the book, Arthur Laurents, was directing.

One thing was very different from the original. Ethel Merman's Rose was famously her first acting job—but except for "Rose's Turn," the songs did not bring out anything but the typical Merman bugle call. When Merman learned singing, one didn't act songs. One sang them. Lansbury acts them—in, for example, the catalogue of "stones" in "Mr. Goldstone, I Love You," where Lansbury is thinking them up, pouncing on each inspiration. Merman simply sang the list without inflection, because in Merman's theatre, characters don't think up anything. That's the lyricist's job.

Few stars of revivals have been as Compared as Lansbury was. Phil Silvers' Pseudolus was considered, to an extent, as Zero Mostel's successor, true. But there was not a lot of discussion about how *Timbuktu!*'s Ira Hawkins related to Alfred Drake as Hajj, or even whether the *Candide* kids improved upon their seniors of 1956.

However, Rose* is the musical's Norma, Manon, Marschallin. One must compare, because each great assumption expands our understanding. Many commented on the eerie ending of Lansbury's "Rose's Turn," when

---

* Will everyone please stop calling *Gypsy*'s protagonist "Momma Rose"? Her daughters call her "Momma" and Herbie and her father call her "Rose." Nobody calls her "Momma Rose" *and I'm not going to tell you again.*

she seemed to step out of character to bow to the applause. Except she kept on bowing even as the applause faded, even after it ended. At last we got it—this wasn't Lansbury acknowledging *our* applause in the Winter Garden, but Rose dementedly hearing the cheers that she had never got in life.

Rex Robbins sang a bit more than did the original Herbie, Jack Klugman, and Zan Charisse played Louise; but there really isn't much more to say about a *Gypsy* after assessing the Rose. One can't even critique the dancing, as in a *Pajama Game* or *Lorelei*, for the *Gypsy* choreography (Robbins' original was reproduced at this time) is functional rather than presentational. *Gypsy* dances only when characters are meant to be dancing in real life, in rehearsal or performance. Not till someone flips *Gypsy* the way Nicholas Hytner flipped *Carousel* for England's National Theatre and at Lincoln Center in the 1990s are we ever to reconsider *Gypsy* as a whole.

Even more faithful than *On the Town* and *Gypsy* was a twentieth-anniversary *My Fair Lady*, in 1976. The original producer, Herman Levin, decided to revive not just the show but the production: Oliver Smith's 1956 sets and Cecil Beaton's 1956 costumes, with reproductions of Moss Hart's 1956 direction and Hanya Holm's 1956 choreography.

This cannot be done successfully. The original director can, it is true, restage on his original plan *if he is there* to adjust it to suit the new participants. Moss Hart was dead, and his successor, Jerry Adler, lacked the authority to reimpose the direction. He had to copy it, which creates a pastiche performance, lifelessly imitative. The crowd scenes especially suffered. The opening action, outside Covent Garden, once so elegant and crisp, so clearly demarcated between the bourgeois and the proles, now came off as caricature: as people walking funny or making odd faces. That is not how *My Fair Lady* began in 1956.

What protected this revival was a mostly good cast. The Pickering, Robert Coote, was held over from the original; and what can one say of this portrayal but that one never knew whether Robert Coote was playing Pickering or Pickering was playing Robert Coote? George Rose was the Doolittle. Some thought Rose perfectly acceptable in everything he did, while others found him relentlessly flavorless, especially in a role this tasty. As Freddy, Jerry Lanning was miscast. The first grown-up Patrick in *Mame*, Lanning is captain of the football team; Freddy should be British, doltish, and silly.

The two leads were unquestionably well chosen. It is impossible to follow Rex Harrison and Julie Andrews, not least in a memorial production designed to provoke nostalgia. Andrews in particular is irreplaceable, because she gets so much out of doing so little. The other major twentieth-century show-biz stars really *worked* at it—Al Jolson, Sophie Tucker, Bert Lahr, Judy Garland, Milton Berle, Gene Kelly, Carol Burnett. Andrews need only show up to be marvelous. Christine Andreas sang a ravishing Eliza and hit all the right points dramatically, but it was Ian Richardson's tremendous Higgins that gave the show its class. An actor rather than a singer, Richardson nevertheless sang more of Higgins than Harrison even tried to, and he found many nuances in a character that Shaw may have written to be monochromatic. One might say that Harrison played Higgins with the experience of a veteran of boulevard comedy while Richardson played with the relish of a veteran of Shakespeare. Walter Kerr was so impressed that he devoted most of his review to Richardson, writing in such sated excitement that it nearly approached the homoerotic.

The most faithful revival was in fact more faithful than the original had been. This was the *Porgy and Bess* put on in 1976 by the Houston Grand Opera, which opened cuts made in the début in 1935. These were unavoidable. The Theatre Guild could not have afforded the overtime costs of an uncut *Porgy*, for the piece is a long one. So is the role of Porgy, and as there was no custom of alternate casting back then, Todd Duncan would have exhausted himself singing eight Porgys a week—without microphones, remember—unless the role was trimmed.

That's all there was to it: matters of economy and energy. There was no wish to dilute the vision of George Gershwin. Yet the hype surrounding the 1976 *Porgy and Bess* suggested that not till then was the work to be seen as Gershwin had intended. Perhaps prompted by incorrect press releases, writers stated that earlier productions were routinely denuded of important music and that the recits had been given as spoken dialogue. The implication was that *Porgy and Bess* had been subjected to cultural sabotage because of its black subject matter.

This is simply untrue. Only in the aforementioned 1942 revival were the recits spoken. *Porgy* has been an opera from the start. It had the honor to be one of the very few American operas to get recorded when it was new, by Lawrence Tibbett and Helen Jepson of the Metropolitan Opera backed by the original chorus and orchestra, with Gershwin supervising and even reinstating one of the cut numbers, "The Buzzard Song." Todd Duncan and his Bess, Anne Brown, made *two* albums a bit later. Columbia Records gave it a splendid full-length reading in 1951 using the prominent black opera singers of the time, albeit with substantial internal cuts. A four-year international tour (with, at first, Leontyne Price's Bess) took the piece to Russia. Samuel Goldwyn filmed it in 1959, an opera. The City Opera gave it during its spring seasons in 1961 and 1964. The only cultural sabotage in *Porgy*'s history was committed by the American music establishment, which tried to close *Porgy and Bess* down because a Jewish composer had produced the first really good American opera after generations of failure by the WASPs who ran Music in those days.

After all that, it's a relief to be able to say that Houston's was a superb realization in every way. Almost all the cuts were opened under John DeMain's very dramatic conducting. Director Jack O'Brien kept a big show very readable, with Clamma Dale's spectacular Bess, Donnie Ray Albert's gently powerful Porgy, and Larry Marshall's louche Sportin' Life. Spurred, no doubt, by Houston, the Met put on *its* uncut *Porgy* in 1985. An *opera*.

In truth, the seventies revival scene was less a question of how faithful to be and more a matter of sheer numbers, as old titles kept turning up. Tours would drop in with original cast members: *Man of La Mancha*, *Fiddler on the Roof*, *The King and I*, *Hello, Dolly!*. Black casts would take over, as with *Timbuktu!*: *Guys and Dolls* and *Stop the World—I Want To Get Off* in a Las Vegas version starring Sammy Davis Jr. Some of Goodspeed Opera House's adulterations would visit The Street: *Very Good Eddie*, *Going Up*, *Whoopee!*. How many different Jerome Kern shows provided the interpolations into this *Very Good Eddie*? Eight thousand? Circle in the Square got into the revival business with a *Where's Charley?* starring, for some reason, Raul Julia. Circle's *Pal Joey* was even more questionable. Ballerino Edward Villella was to make his musical-comedy debut, with coaching from both George Balanchine and Jerome Robbins, his choreographers at the New York City Ballet. It still wasn't working, so Villella walked. His co-star, Eleanor Parker, walked, too. The understudies played the run. Critics praised Joan Copeland and doubted Christopher Chadman. But Douglas Watt liked his "ratty charm," and *Variety*'s Hobe pointed out that Chadman was, after all, "a last-minute draftee for a tough assignment."

The revival king of the 1970s was Kurt Weill. Four of his German works and two American shows were mounted for open or limited runs on and off Broadway and in New York's major opera houses. Some of these zipped out of view in fast motion. A *Johnny Johnson* (1936) directed by José Quintero closed on opening night in 1971. Numbers dropped from the original were reinstated, but there was to be no altering of the script, for its author, Paul Green, was alive and touchy. A *Lost in the Stars* (1949) led by Brock Peters ran 39 performances a year later. The *Johnny Johnson* had been basically underpowered, but *Lost in the Stars* was a debauch. Gene Frankel staged it on a tilted circle with a hole in the center, with primitive tribal dances to cover set changes. This is ten-second thinking. The blacks in *Lost in the Stars* do not belong to any tribe. They are village Christians or city-dwelling bourgeois or lowlives. They don't wear masks or perform piquant native ceremonies. Unlike *Johnny Johnson*, this *Lost in the Stars* did no restoring. On the contrary, it cut two numbers and gave the soprano's "Stay Well" to Gilbert Price in a role that was originally non-singing.

Then there was the zombie-prom *Threepenny Opera*, at the Vivian Beaumont in 1976. Here is more (conductor) Silverman and (director) Foreman, in a translation by Ralph Manheim and John Willett touted as more authentic than others. Raul Julia was again miscast, this time as Macheath. Ellen Greene played Jenny and Caroline Kava the heroine, Polly, with C. K. Alexander and Elizabeth Wilson as the senior Peachums.

Lotte Lenya hated it. Where was the bawdy merriment of the Berlin original in 1928, the deadpan exposé of the famous 1954 mounting at the Theatre de Lys? That revival brought back not only *Threepenny* but all of Kurt Weill. And here, thought Lenya, was this Lincoln Center *thing* with the cast acting like goons and going through Chinese-box Brechtian motions, such as everyone's waving his hands in the air and running upstage at the end of the first act. In 1928 and 1954, the public was led to infer that the players would be having sex with each other right after the curtain. This Lincoln Center gang would be haunting a house.

Others found it a valid *Threepenny* with many interesting perceptions, one of those productions that committed theatregoers want to collect even if they won't like it. This was not the case with *Happy End*, originally the follow-up to *Threepenny* in Berlin in 1929 but lamed with a book so terrible that no one would take credit for it. (The byline was assigned to the made-up Dorothy Lane.) All Berlin was still *Threepenny*-mad and eager to enjoy *Happy End*. But it suffered a scandal and closed after 3 performances.

Set in Brecht's favorite American city, Chicago, *Happy End* treats the romance of Salvation Army lieutenant Hallelujah Lil and Bill Cracker, the chief of a criminal gang. The piece is inevitably compared to the much later *Guys and Dolls*, and it curiously anticipates it with a light-hearted view of crime. It has its sinister touches, true, but what particularly helps it along is one of Weill's best German scores. "The Bilbao Song" and "Surabaya Johnny" are well known, but every number fills the ear. And note that the score behaves quite differently from that to *The Threepenny Opera*, with more of those party pieces that characters suddenly choose to sing because they feel like it. But then, unlike some composers, Weill never wrote the same score twice.

Clearly, this was a work that the public needed to sample. *The Threepenny Opera* takes care of itself because it's so popular. Less-well-known Weill needs curating. *Happy End*'s standard English translation, by Michael Feingold, ideally restores the original story line while inventing lively new dialogue. Yale Rep staged this version in 1972 and again in 1976. This production was taken up in 1977 by the Chelsea Theater Center in Brooklyn, unfortunately in a redaction contaminated by Chelsea's director, Robert Kalfin. It was nevertheless moved to Broadway for a nine-week run, though the backstage troubles were compounded by the last-minute substitution, in the two leads, of Meryl Streep for Shirley Knight and Bob Gunton for an injured Christopher Lloyd.

While Feingold was able to save *Happy End* without altering its integrity, the City Opera's *Silverlake* in 1980 completely rewrote *Der Silbersee*. An opera company would have to, for Georg Kaiser's play of 1933 was just that: a play. Kaiser did not permit Weill to absorb his dialogue in music. Weill's score must be incidental, never to disturb Kaiser's fatuous symbolism and endless dialectical fiddlesticks. Clearly, such a work could not be revived in its original form. Kaiser is another of the many transitional figures in theatre history that had to exist in their day but needn't exist anymore.

It is Weill's music only that sponsors a *Silverlake* revival. In 1971, Josef Heinzelmann arranged a concert staging for the Holland Festival, cutting Kaiser down to little more than a narrator, Lotte Lenya. She also played the villainess of the piece, in one of her last appearances onstage in the theatre of Kurt Weill.

The City Opera could not concert its way through *Silverlake*. With a new script by Hugh Wheeler and English lyrics by longtime Weill associate Lys Simonette under the direction of Hal Prince, *Silverlake* was vastly overhauled. Other Weill music was filtered in for underscoring and for one new vocal number, and an arresting character was invented, a brutal dancing mime portraying the figure of Hunger. Joel Grey took the lead role, a policeman who wounds a felon (William Neill) and then virtually adopts him, and the original foggy, symbolic ending was clarified. It was bad Kaiser, good theatre, and, with Elizabeth Hynes, Elaine Bonazzi, and Jack Harrold under conductor Julius Rudel, excellent Weill. If the worst thing about *Irene* was Harry Rigby, the worst thing about *Silverlake* was Georg Kaiser. The work had to be changed so that the music could be heard.

The summit of the Weill Revival was the reclamation of *Mahagonny*, or, more properly, *Aufstieg und Fall der Stadt Mahagonny* (Rise and Fall of Mahagonny City), the opera of 1930 that Weill wrote with Brecht. This work frames our decade, at first in 1970 in that big old barn on lower Second Avenue where *Grease* and *Smith* played and then in 1979 at the Metropolitan Opera. Neither staging brought the work to public favor, but it remains the "biggest" of Weill's German stage works, with a tremendous reputation among musicians. For decades, all that survived of the opera were two 78 sides by Lotte Lenya and a little-known jazz-band medley. Even when Columbia Records took down a complete *Mahagonny* for release in 1958, one hungered to see this bizarre fable in which the Marxist Brecht deconstructs capitalism in a kind of end-of-the-world amusement park in which the only criminal is the man without money.

For years, the co-producer and director of the epochal de Lys *Threepenny*, Carmen Capalbo, had hoped to present *Mahagonny*. A man obsessed, he pursued his dream despite terrific setbacks, such as the death of the first translator and having to deal with Brecht's son. Capalbo finally got his show on, and the well-attended previews proved how much interest there was in the piece.

However, these previews went on for two months while Capalbo struggled with the classic revival question: how much of the work's intrinsic style can be respected when theatre styles are constantly evolving? Does one *Irene* it, *Candide* it? Reproduce it like *My Fair Lady*? Or give it a faithful resuscitation, a *Porgy and Bess*?

Alas, Capalbo decided to rock it. Wouldn't the rebellious Weill and Brecht, so avant-garde in the 1920s, have wanted a "now" *Mahagonny*? The brothel scene could defy the cautions with a porn clip. Larry Rivers can prepare color projections to work against Robin Wagner's set, a pile of twenty-four bordello rooms that, at one point, all flashed into view simultaneously, filled with working girls and their clients. It got a hand on opening night—and Barbara Harris, Estelle Parsons, and Frank Porretta were the leads, an impressive lineup for what was technically off-Broadway.

But Capalbo should not have tried to rock *Mahagonny*. Somewhere along the way the rock players were deemphasized and the orchestra brought more into line with what Weill had written. The various rockers in the cast—folkie and Bob Dylan cohort Dave Van Ronk was in it the night I saw it—had all vanished by opening night. Still, Capalbo had failed to trust the work. Maybe twenties musicals need some firming up if they are to play to a public instructed by Rodgers and Hammerstein. But operas live by other rules.

The Met's *Mahagonny* was authentic. Unfortunately, while Capalbo had the wrong staging but the right audience, the Met had the wrong audience. Metgoers don't like operas they haven't heard of. They like *Aida*. Director John Dexter could not live up to the ruthless abstractions of Brechtian gestural theatre, and so allowed his Jenny, Teresa Stratas, to emote with extreme prejudice when the penniless hero is condemned to death. Lotte Lenya, the first Berlin Jenny after the Leipzig premiere, wouldn't have emoted. One stands motionless, looking sly and Brechtian.

Still, one thing the Met does is spend the money, and it put on a big show with a few niceties, such as a la-di-da parasol for the ghastly hag that runs the place, sung by Astrid Varnay. The finale was as gigantic as the authors could have wanted, with hordes of supers carrying the picket-line signs right into the auditorium and up the aisles, a notable breach of Met decorum.

The downtown *Mahagonny* lasted only 8 performances once it finally opened; the Met version played in three seasons to very poor houses.

But this is a difficult work for most people, with its savage indictment of democracy by Brecht, a man who stooged for Soviet Communism, the most murderous slave empire the world has known. Weill lavished his best work on this libretto; why did he want to? Wasn't there someone in Germany with an Adele Astaire stolen-jewels plot for him to set?

Mahagonny has yet to make a place for itself in America. But another work brought back in this decade had a happier time after a tragic conception. In fact, this work was revived sixty-four years after its only performance during the composer's lifetime. A handful of invited guests saw no more than a reading of it, no one would produce it, and Scott Joplin died in despair. The problem with *Treemonisha* was: how does one present to the world a new kind of American opera when there are no American operas of any kind, much less one on a black subject?

At the time of *Treemonisha*'s one performance, in 1911, Americans were writing operas, but in a derivatively European manner no matter what the subjects. Even the great Victor Herbert couldn't crack the problem with his two operas. At least the first, *Natoma* (1911), did mark an attempt to fashion a native style. But—like Leonard Bernstein later on—Herbert was less interesting in the opera house than he was on Broadway. *Natoma,* with its Spanish California setting, American Indian heroine, and tenor naval lieutenant straight out of *Madame Butterfly,* sounded like a European's idea of American music. And the vainglorious libretto and war-paint dances were no help.

Joplin filled *his* opera with strophic ballads, chorales, and dances, the popular music of the day. Because the composer is famous for the ragtimes that came back into currency in the 1970s, *Treemonisha* is often called "the ragtime opera." In fact, though it contains ragtime, it is what Joplin called it on the title page of the published score: "opera." Joplin wrote his own libretto, in three short acts that follow the morning, afternoon, and evening of a single day in Arkansas in 1884, when the titular heroine is eighteen.

Strong women are not rare in opera, but this woman is a leader of her people. She spurs the action by defying the "conjurors" who take advantage of folks by peddling "bags o' luck." The conjuror chief, Zodzetrick, has Treemonisha kidnapped in Act One, to be thrown into a hornets' nest. In Act Two, she is rescued by her boy friend, Remus. In Act Three, Treemonisha inspires everyone to throw off superstition and forgive the wicked conjurors, whereupon the entire company closes the show with a big dance and vocal in grand style, "A Real Slow Drag":

Marching onward, marching onward,
Marching to that lovely tune.

It's a wonderful score, with many a treat tossed in, as when Zodzetrick gloatingly (and risibly) tells his followers that their power resides in the words "Hee hoo"; or when Joplin directs the chorus to sing downward glissandos, a captivating effect; or even in the score's one Leitmotiv, a chirping ragtime bit that, says Joplin, "represents the happiness of the people when they feel free from the conjurors and their spells of superstition."

There are flaws. The big story ballad, "The Sacred Tree," is laid out in seven long verses, too much for a static solo. Joplin uses fake rhymes and incorrect accents. Some of the libretto sounds naïve today, as when Treemonisha's mother considers buying a bag o' luck:

MONISHA: Will it drive away de blues?
An' stop Ned from drinkin' booze?

All the same, *Treemonisha* is another of those concoctions unique to American culture, the work that invents its own form. With nothing to draw on but his vision—without predecessors or models—Scott Joplin *created* American opera.

The ragtime revival gave *Treemonisha* its chance. As with *Porgy and Bess*, it was the Houston Grand Opera that brought the piece to Broadway, in 1975, in Gunther Schuller's orchestration. (Joplin's was lost.) Frank Corsaro and choreographer Louis Johnson staged the work with a single intermission (between Acts Two and Three) in a rendering at once *faux* innocent and African tribal: the bad guys wore intricately detailed masks, but one number was given over to dancers in childlike bear and alligator costumes. Carmen Balthrop (with Kathleen Battle as her alternate), Betty Allen, Curtis Rayam, Willard White, and Ben Harney led the cast, and except for the usual killjoys and a condescending Walter Kerr, the press was appreciative. But no more than that.

They liked it, yes. Still, very, very few people have the knowledge to see *Treemonisha* in historical context—to comprehend how comprehensively inventive the piece is when set next to such coeval "American" operas as *Mona* (1912) or *Shanewis* (1918). Druids, Indians, nonsense. Perhaps it will take some time before recordplay popularizes the music and inspires a revival; perhaps opinion-makers will be in a more grateful mood. After all the black junk that they rubber-stamped earlier in the decade for political reasons, it astonishes that they refused to give Joplin credit for his courage and self-belief. It's all but impossible—isn't it?—to be the first person to do something.

10

WERE YOU SAYING SOMETHING?

OFF-BROADWAY

The off-Broadway musical is a historical item that was barely developed in the 1950s, flowered in the 1960s, and was all but gone by the 1970s. There was still an off-Broadway and it still put on musicals. But the forms that off-Broadway created and by which it made its witness were missing: the sweethearted little show, the adaptation of an antique play, the burlesque, the modest revival, the eccentricity. Respectively: *The Fantasticks, Ernest in Love, Little Mary Sunshine, The Threepenny Opera, Promenade*.

By the 1970s, the off-Broadway musical was anything—anything not playing uptown at the moment. Off-Broadway shows would move to Broadway as if on a dare: as if there *was* no difference between the two places. Big shows like *The Best Little Whorehouse in Texas* (1978) were "off-Broadway." Authors graduated from off-Broadway to the David Merrick big time, such as Harvey Schmidt and Tom Jones, would return to off-Broadway, in their case with the early-Christian fable *Philemon* (1975), as if finding a more imposing artistic cachet in the small-time. Experimental shows like *The Me Nobody Knows* (1970) could leave the downtown Orpheum for the Helen Hayes, as if this collection of real-life inner-city kids' writing was not a bold idea.

Ghetto schoolteacher Stephen M. Joseph anthologized kids' poetry and prose; Herb Schapiro saw it as a musical. With a score by Gary William Friedman and Will Holt and direction by Robert H. Livingston, *The Me Nobody Knows* became a freak hit with its cast aged from seven to eighteen singing about race, drugs, violence, and their private longings for a lovelier life.

This is Broadway? Or how about *Blood Red Roses* (1970), Michael Valenti and John Lewin's epic-theatre look at the Crimean War? *Newsday*'s George Oppenheimer likened it to "a British Christmas pantomime written by Bertolt Brecht." In its antagonistic tone, it recalled the bourgeois-baiting credo of off-Broadway's radical element, its Living Theatre and Jean Genet. One song was entitled "How Fucked Up Things Are," though it wasn't listed as such in the program.

Ironically, at the last minute the piece was expensively recapitalized for a booking on Broadway (at the John Golden), where only blacks have baiting rights. Critics praised Ed Wittstein's pop-up toy-theatre sets; and actors Jess Richards and Philip Bruns as two soldiers, one young and the other doing Cockney music-hall jokes; and Jeanie Carson playing four roles, including Queen Victoria and Florence Nightingale. The ultra-contemporary language, however, offended the period nature of the piece, and Lewin was so eager to take on the Vietnam War that he cheated on his research. At one point, Big Ben was mentioned, although the Crimean War ended in 1856 and the giant bell was not cast till 1858. (Clive Barnes, alone of the critics, caught the error.) *Blood Red Roses* closed on opening night.

Well, why *not* take off-Broadway shows to The Street, when the off-Broadway of such dainty forget-me-nots as *Riverwind* and *Man With a Load of Mischief* was by now a threatened species? There were, at least, a few adaptations of old plays. Royall Tyler's *The Contrast* (1787) and Anna Cora Mowatt's *Fashion* (1845), classic American comedies satirizing the snobbery of parvenus, were made musical under their own titles by book writer and director Anthony Stimac and songwriters Donald Pippin and Steve Brown in, respectively, 1972 and 1974.

Ty McConnell played a lead in both, but in *Fashion* he was the only male among nine women. It was Stimac's joke that a women's theatrical sodality is putting on the show, coached by their director, McConnell. *Fashion* ran longer than *The Contrast*, perhaps because of a particularly tuneful score that serves as plot and character numbers while spoofing the forms themselves. Aficionados and the laity alike can enjoy it; but each group in effect attends a different show. Mary Jo Catlett delighted as the socially ambitious Mrs. Tiffany, leading the opening "Rococo Rag," anticipating prominence in "My Daughter the Countess," and tricking the big number of the Merrick-Champion genre with "My Title Song." The trick is that the word "fashion" never quite gets uttered.

Something closer to modern-day theatre turned up—twice—in versions of John Millington Synge's *The Playboy of the Western World* (1907), on how Irish villagers thrill to the exploits of a rebellious young patricide, only to turn on him when his father shows up alive. *Christy* (1975), named after the playboy himself, lasted 40 performances at the Bert Wheeler Theatre with a non-union cast that most critics found too cute and perky. Lawrence J. Blank's music and Bernie Spiro's libretto faced the same problem that bedeviled *Cyrano*'s authors: with all that tantalizing Irish poetry, the play is already a musical. The other adaptation, Stanley Walden and Jacques Levy's *Back Country* (1975), lost the Irish poetry for a new setting in late-nineteenth-century Kansas. This one never even came in.

Carson McCullers' *The Member of the Wedding* might make a sweet musical, with all its emotional content. Or is it completed as is? Perhaps G Wood's *F. Jasmine Addams* (1971) could have been thought of as a revival of McCullers' play with songs. The first musical ever mounted by Circle in the Square, *F. Jasmine Addams* offered Neva Small and Theresa Merritt in roles created by Julie Harris and Ethel Waters, and Luther Henderson favored G Wood with his usual superb arrangements of the music. One likes the credits, but the show gave up after a week without a public.

Off-Broadway could at any rate host work of special-interest groups. As black drama had flourished in the 1960s, the 1970s welcomed gays. Revues could cover many aspects of gay life—cruising, dating, breaking up, and the more profound themes, such as The Right Haircut For You. Al Carmines' *The Faggot* (1973), in the Reverend Carmines' Judson Memorial Church, featured a scene in a bar in which the rejected suitors of a smug cutie physically assaulted him in comic revenge. *Lovers* (1975), by Steve Sterner and Peter del Valle, touched on some unusual issues, such as the untimely death of a lover. (It was unusual then, of course. AIDS was unknown.) *Lovers* had numbers such as "Role-Playing," "The Trucks" (a no-no cruising place), and "Belt and Leather," the last sung by two clones, each waiting for the other to make the first move. Unfortunately, *Lovers* made the typical mistake of trying to get an anthem out of politics, not unlike trying to discern a melody in Marc Blitzstein's *The Cradle Will Rock*. "Somehow I'm Taller" even included the preposterous cry "The sky's the limit!" Ladies, it doesn't make you taller.

There were no political agendas in Bill Solly and Donald Ward's *Boy Meets Boy* (1975), one of the last of off-Broadway's pastiche burlesques. In its gladsome lack of reason and Solly's rudimentary songs, *Boy Meets Boy* is something like twenties Broadway with a gay sensibility written in sixties off-Broadway style. True, *Little Mary Sunshine* already did that, in a vastly superior way. But *Little Mary* is a parody of old genres, while *Boy Meets Boy* sillies about in no particular direction.

It's a Cinderella tale, set in London and Paris in the 1930s. The prince is Casey O'Brien (Joe Barrett), an American journalist. Cinderella is Guy Rose (David Gallegly) and the stepsisters are merged in Clarence Cutler (Raymond Wood), Guy's jilted fiancé. The score dimly recalls thirties styles, more so in the Cole Porteresque "Let's!" and less so in "(Tell me, please) Does Anybody Love You?" Guy's ode to the sleeping Casey, it sounds a bit like something that Walter Willison might have refused to sing in *Two By Two*. More telling was the lifeless moan of the synthesizer in the tiny orchestra, a sign of the techno encroachments of the electronic era. The *No, No, Nanette* revival had been celebrated for not using any plug-in "sweetening," and *Timbuktu!* was castigated for the hum and screechback that haunted its sound system.

The Last Sweet Days of Isaac (1970) actually reveled in its bulky handheld mikes, stainless-steel boxes, and televisionland attitude. But this was a satire on modern technolife and another side of off-Broadway: the experimental. "A 1970 musical" was the billing, and the show seemed as much to love as to giggle at the trendy idiocies of the day. With music by Nancy Ford and book and lyrics by Gretchen Cryer, *Isaac* offered Austin Pendleton, Fredricka Weber, and a band called The Zeitgeist in two one-acts. First play: trapped in an elevator. Second play: two leftist protesters in jail watching television reportage of *his* death.

It's existential. But, again, in a satirical way. Sample line: "Who are you anyway? In the ultimate sense, I mean." Some loved it, because it was a painless way to experience...well, The Zeitgeist. Others thought it claptrap and wondered if it might be true that women can't compose music any more than women can have hard-ons. Otherwise, why are there so very few women composers? In any case, there has seldom been so loaded a program description as *Isaac*'s "Time: the present."

All this leaves us with an off-Broadway despoiled of its artistic entitlements. We don't want works too dizzy for The Street. We want works too special for The Street, the kind that defy rules, work well small, and have "unusual" music. I know: another staging of a movie musical. But this one will play in English for the first time, in a unique recreation by Andrei Serban that turns cinema into theatre. *Gigi* didn't even try to, which is why it is a Dreary Musical. *This* show reinvents its film in avant-garde creativity that makes it a Very Interesting Off-Broadway Musical:

The Umbrellas of Cherbourg (1979). The 1964 film, an opera, tells how Geneviève loves Guy, how she becomes pregnant while Guy is off doing his military service, and how her mother arranges for Geneviève to marry a wealthy older man. The entire script, by the film's director, Jacques Demy, is sung, to Michel Legrand's music. The score, though, is made not of numbers but of sung conversations. These very occasionally coalesce into what could be called a song, as in the older man's marriage proposal (recorded by Tony Bennett as "Watch What Happens") or the very famous lovers' duet, "I Will Wait For You," which recurs many, many times. Norman Gimbel's English lyric for the number, used in pop singles in the mid-1960s, was retained for the stage version; the rest of the score was translated by Sheldon Harnick and Charles Burr.

Serban's approach backed a bare stage with the skyline of rainy Cherbourg and, using a few pieces to establish locale (a garage, the mother's umbrella boutique), built the entire production out of twelve Plexiglas panels mounted on casters. Constantly moved about in evocative patterns, the panels became a visual equivalent of the ever-flowing music, played by a band of eleven and sung by a cast of fifteen.

Dean Pitchford and Stefanianne Christopherson were the young lovers, Judith Roberts and Laurence Guittard the mother and older suitor. But the evening's stars were Serban and his set designer, Michael Yeargan. Together, they devised stage pictures that might have been planned by Marcel Marceau in conference with Federico Fellini. So, for once, a musical film was not stifled on stage but enchanted. Its limited run of one month saw many a show-biz potentate paying his respects at the Public Theater, reminding some of the days when *A Chorus Line* had just started performing there and limousines lined the block. It was heavily rumored that Mike Nichols was going to bring *The Umbrellas of Cherbourg* to Broadway.

That never happened. Was the project too special for the Broadway audience? Was it too sad? For Demy and Legrand close their story in great sorrow. Four years after her marriage, Geneviève stops her car for gas—but the station belongs to Guy, now married himself. Worse, his child, named Françoise, is in the car with Geneviève. "I Will Wait For You" wells up in the orchestra as the lovers part for the last time, and there the curtain sadly falls.

If nothing else, *The Umbrellas of Cherbourg* proved that there were still kinds of musicals that were feared not to prosper in the big houses, and that off-Broadway was still the place where they lived. The identifying features of the "off-Broadway musical"—the dippy ditties, the high-school gym décor, the wannabe-pro cast members—are gone. What remains is the venturing idealism that put on the Theatre de Lys *Threepenny Opera*, which founded the off-Broadway musical. This idealism knows that the survival-of-the-fittest economy of Broadway was useful quite some time ago in killing off the junk. Today, it may be killing off the jewels.

11

HAVEN'T WE MET?

THE REVUE

Once one of the musical's most popular genres, the variety show collapsed in the 1950s. The revue was, simply, a musical without narrative: songs, dances, and sketches, with a special interest in satirizing the topics of the day. In fact, the first revues, made on the French model, were called "reviews," as retrospectives of the previous year's news, celebrities, and novelties.

In its heyday in the 1920s and 1930s, the revue was so popular that it attracted showmen eager to outdo one another in spectacle, and unique talents topped the bills. "Revue" was everywhere—radio was virtually made of it, movie palaces featured mini-revues between the feature and shorts, and when television came in, headliners' revues like Milton Berle's *Texaco Star Theater* dominated the ratings lists.

Alas, all these star-studded network revues sated the public's interest in variety. How could stage revues compete with Ed Sullivan or, later, Carol Burnett? This was a show-biz disaster, for variety had formed a money-and-talent infrastructure since the nineteenth century. As the theatre and concomitant venues such as vaudeville expanded, more opportunities were created that had to be filled—and if one is casting for talent, talent shows up.

To pick just one very famous instance, back in 1930 a producer putting together his latest musical heard of a sensational unknown singer performing between screenings onstage at the Brooklyn Paramount. The producer ran out there and, properly impressed, took the singer to audition for his composer. The singer was just a piece of talent trying to find a place in show biz; she earned her living as a stenographer. But there was so much employment available that she had no trouble getting the job that leads to The Job. The composer was George Gershwin, the producer was Vinton Freedley, and the stenographer was Ethel Merman, hired for *Girl Crazy*, her Broadway debut.

However, when show biz starts to contract, it loses its support system, and this in turn causes more contraction. With fewer opportunities for specialists in song, dance, and comedy, the working specialists retire without replacement. And the revue, dependent on specialists, becomes extinct.

There still were revues, but only as another example of an art cannibalizing its heritage to create "new" work: the songwriter anthology. *Berlin To Broadway With Kurt Weill* (1972) is not untypical: Jerry Lanning, Hal Watters, Margery Cohen, and Judy Lander sang the classics and some other Weill, and Ken Kercheval narrated. As the title suggests, the structure was chronological, with the obvious tutorial advantage.

The show played the de Lys, home of the historic *Threepenny*, and the cast changed attire and played with props to decorate each next sequence—suitcases for arrival in Mahagonny, circus trappings for *Lady in the Dark*. Most important, Newton Wayland's musical arrangements stretched his little band to respect Weill's originals (though an insufficient clarinet in the accordion, flute, and oboe line in "Train to Johannesburg" and some Las Vegas styling by the singers destroyed that number).

There's a problem in the singing overall. This cast of young Americans lacked the listening experience or the coaching to encompass the diverse modes that Weill's music adopted. He enjoys Weimar liberty and defiance, flees Nazi Germany, lands in America during the political 1930s, then reinstructs himself to make opera on Broadway with *his* version of opera, *his* Broadway. *Berlin To Broadway*'s four singers have talent, but their Kurt Weill suggests high-schoolers in Shakespeare. It's a good education for them. It's not good for us.

Oh Coward! (1972), on the contrary, was stylish with skinnier means, *very* off-Broadway. Three players in unchanged evening dress did Noël Coward in any old order, occasionally grouping a few songs by theme; and there was in general a very English feeling in the air.

That's good planning. Without that feeling, Coward would sound as wrong as Weill did at the de Lys. Roderick Cook, who put the revue together, *is* English. Jamie Ross, on hand for his sweet tones in ballad, is a Scot. Barbara Cason is from Memphis, Tennessee; but she, too, had the style down cold. The Master himself attended, with Marlene Dietrich, and announced that he was pleased.

Most authentic of all was *Words and Music* (1974), because this time the Master was right on stage, performing: lyricist Sammy Cahn. With self-effacing charm, a brace of backstage anecdotes, and just-barely voice and piano, Cahn wowed the public. Professional pianist Richard Leonard and singers Shirley Lemmon, Jon Peck, and Kelly Garrett (who went directly, and briefly, into the woman lead of *Mack & Mabel*) spelled Cahn. But what really entertained the public was the realization that so many song hits had been the work of a man whom, till now, no one had ever heard of. "Three Coins in the Fountain," "All the Way," "I Should Care," "Thoroughly Modern Millie," and "Papa, Won't You Dance With Me?" were among the titles summoned, and one great pleasure was that, unlike the Kurt Weill and Noël Coward standards, these songs hadn't been overperformed in recent years. "Bei Mir Bist Du Schoen" had turned up in the Andrews Sisters' encore finale to *Over Here!* earlier that year, and it still sounded fresh.

Rodgers & Hart (1975) was not authentic. The cast made a point of noting that every one of them had been born after Lorenz Hart had died. "When do the stars come out?" Alfred Drake growled to Russell Nype during intermission at one performance. This was Broadway, after all, not some gewgaw at the Theatre de Lys. Or was Drake—who had created roles in both Rodgers and Hart and Rodgers and Hammerstein—irritated at not having been invited to sing himself?

In fact, the twelve performers were all gifted; and Jimmy Brennan, Virginia Sandifur, Wayne Bryan, Tovah Feldshuh, David–James Carroll, Laurence Guittard, Stephen Lehew, Rebecca York, and Barbara Andres had all taken or would take leads on Broadway. Drake was correct in feeling that *Rodgers & Hart* didn't play well, but the performers were not the problem. The problem was the "concept by Richard Lewine and John Fearnley," because there was no concept. On a bare stage of steps and platforms, in sporty clothes in primary colors, the singers came out, started singing, and never stopped, hitting nearly one hundred titles by the trick of starting the next one three seconds into the current one. It would have been fascinating to hear such rarities as "A Lovely Day For a

Murder," "How Was I To Know?," and "The Gateway of the Temple of Minerva"; but we *didn't* hear them. Burt Shevelove and Donald Saddler staged the show to move and move and move, determined to comprehend the entirety of Rodgers and Hart but failing to *listen* to the songs. There were some quaint surprises, such as handing "Zip" to one of the boys, dressed in leather. Under his jacket, his T-shirt read "Mother." Ladies, it doesn't make you taller. The show was not bad, just unconceived—and it never recovered from the floppo opening of having the cast come out pair by pair with their arms spread out to sing the title of the show over and over, jumping a step in key with each repeat.

The greed for shows of this type led to one focusing not on writing talent but on a performer. Linda Hopkins opened Me and Bessie (1975) with some spoken lines beginning, "I ain't Bessie. But there's a whole lot of Bessie in me." There was. In fact, even given the odd rules for blues singing, in which the non-voices have all the advantage, the amplevoiced Hopkins presented the material far better than Bessie Smith ever did. Assisting were one male and one female dancer, to play small roles in the evening's more dramatic second half.

But doesn't a certain monotony creep in? One person singing song after song, especially so many rave-ups, as in Me and Bessie? Isn't this less theatre than a performance piece, even a club act? Me and Bessie played Los Angeles' Mark Taper Forum and then the Ambassador Theatre, true. Even so, one step beyond Linda Hopkins singing Bessie Smith is a performer not just reviving the work of a bygone entertainer but replicating the entertainer in look and sound. It's a party trick, like one of those evenings of, say, Ethel Merman put on by someone pretending to be Ethel Merman. Isn't this something to be left to your Aunt Agnes after one wine too many at the Thanksgiving party, at that for at most thirty seconds?

Arthur Schwartz and Howard Dietz got their turn in *That's Entertainment* (1972). As with *Rodgers & Hart*, there was a heavy tunestack and the chance to meet rare titles. Most interesting was director Paul Aaron and choreographer Larry Fuller's attempt to give this thin format some body by letting the nine performers carry on romances and breakups, using the song lyrics as text. *Rodgers & Hart* had staged some of the numbers, but abstractly or momentarily. *That's Entertainment* looked for continuity.

Even more substantial in this line was *Gershwin!: A Celebration* (1974), off the beaten track in the ground-floor cabaret room of the Manhattan Theatre Club's old building on East Seventy-fourth Street. To Steven Blier's dazzling piano, director Christopher Alden folded Gershwin into a scenario in which roué Ed Dixon gave pickup tips to juvenile Glen Mure while Martha Williford and Cayce Blanchard flirted with the boys. So "(You've got to treat them) High Hat" was Dixon's advice to Mure, "Drifting Along With the Tide" was Williford's establishing song, "Innocent Ingenue Baby" was Dixon's attempt to pick up Blanchard, and "Nice Work If You Can Get It" was a duet for the girls in the powder room.

Ironically, though Broadway and off-Broadway teemed with these anthology shows in the 1970s, it was the English that brought the form to its summit, sometimes with American subjects, in a series mounted at the Mermaid Theatre. *Cowardy Custard* (1972) quite outdid *Oh Coward!* with a larger cast of mostly brilliant players including Patricia Routledge, who ran her usual gamut from A to Z. Not content with reviving the bizarrely twee "Spinning Song," she actually found a way to deliver "I Went To a Marvellous Party" as if one had never heard it before.

Like *Oh Coward!*, *Cowardy Custard* grouped some songs by theme—a "Travel Sequence," a "London Sequence"—and assigned bits of Coward's autobiographical writings to the performers. One even got excerpts from the plays. There was an orchestra, there was dancing, and there was, thoroughly, a sense that very smart people had given the concept some thought. (Gerald Frow, Alan Strachan, and director Wendy Toye were credited.) The medleys had logic—even musical logic, as when the very end of Una Stubbs' "Try To Learn To Love" was inundated by the $\frac{3}{4}$ of Jonathan Cecil's "Kiss Me," rushing in with the determination of $\frac{4}{4}$; or when the last two notes of Tudor Davies' "Go Slow, Johnny" seemed to be echoed simultaneously by the first notes of Peter Gale's "Tokay."

The Mermaid's *Cole* (1974) was comparable, with more of those Sequences. But at least none of the Mermaids fell into the trap of trying to stuff too many songs into the program. On the contrary, the aim was to set off the songs individually, utterly to complete their potential. Our own Kenneth Nelson sang the greatest "I Worship You" ever to be heard, right at the center of Porter's heathen hedonism. Debonair juvenile Peter Gale was back from *Cowardy Custard*; the brilliantly versatile

Julia McKenzie sang the title number from the one Porter show we never hear anything of, *See America First* (1916), and also the withering "Thank You So Much, Mrs. Lowsborough-Goodby." Nothing in this chapter so far compared to these Mermaid shows for sheer stylistic authority. And then came Sondheim!

So the Brits will preach to us on the text of *our* Master? For *Side By Side By Sondheim* (1976) of course moved to Broadway (as the previous pair did not), taking its original cast of Julia McKenzie, Millicent Martin, and David Kernan, with interlocutor Ned Sherrin. This was not a Mermaid project, though it played that house. It was Kernan's idea, for an intimate Sondheim sing, with a narrator but no trimming. There was none of *Cowardy Custard*'s or *Cole*'s costumes, orchestra, or *production*—and very little of the Sondheim archeology that in itself furnishes the material for shows and CDs today. It was a bit staid, though Kernan sang "Could I Leave You?" and joined the two women in "You Could Drive a Person Crazy."

Still, the show hit The Street in 1977, between *Pacific Overtures* and *Sweeney Todd*: just when the American theatregoer was beginning to absorb Sondheim's music. It was also his or her second exposure to most of these songs, and they were thus easier to take.

Meanwhile, the American wing of the songwriter anthology movement got its first hit, *Bubbling Brown Sugar* (1976), in which three old show-biz blacks (Josephine Premice, Avon Long, Joseph Attles) take a white couple (Barry Preston, Barbara Rubenstein) and a black couple (Chip Garnett, Ethel Beatty) on a tour of Harlem. What they get is a tour of black entertainment history, from Bert Williams to Duke Ellington. The staging had presence, even in the by now hopelessly typical unit set, an ugly one. Attles showed up in the biggest necktie ever fastened, and Premice wrestled her feather boa to death.

It was a silly evening rather than a pridefully historic one; and no one songwriting team was featured. So Vivian Reed could thrill in the ancient "Sweet Georgia Brown" and then move to a Billie Holiday number, "God Bless the Child." The songwriter was black music in general. "God Bless the Child" rather stood out, though, among all the period sass and swagger. Yes, it's jazz. But it's devotional, like something out of Vinnette Carroll's *Your Arms Too Short To Box With God* (1976), a black equivalent of *Godspell* with songs by Alex Bradford and interpolations by Micki

Grant. *Your Arms* was well liked, but *Bubbling Brown Sugar* was a two-year hit, begging Broadway for more black anthology revues with genuine Harlem snap.

So the key work was *Ain't Misbehavin'* (1978), another entry in the Manhattan Theatre Club's cabaret series. Moved to Broadway, this revival of songs composed or simply performed by Fats Waller gave fine opportunities to Nell Carter, Andre De Shields, Armelia McQueen, Ken Page, and Charlaine Woodard. Richard Maltby Jr. was the director, but Luther Henderson had the music control. Henderson was a curator of old musics; his arrangements and orchestrations made *Ain't Misbehavin'* absolutely faithful to its source and absolutely new-minted. Maltby claimed the by now inevitable "concept" credit, like George Abbott's Lizzy Flop expanding her program exposure. On the contrary, it was the lack of concept that empowered *Ain't Misbehavin'*. The set was nowhere special, the songs just came at one (in full, no bits and medleys), and the staging was enjoyable but devoid of secret quest. This was pure musical celebration. There were no explanations, no educating, no dialogue at all. The singers played with ad-libs—at one point, Nell Carter would point out a man in the front row and say, "I been out with him." But mainly, they were there to put over the songs of Fats Waller.

The black anthology revues continued with *Eubie!* (1978), the biggest production yet and made entirely of singing and dancing. Eubie Blake was the subject, the title being his sobriquet, from his middle name, Hubert. However, where *Bubbling Brown Sugar* had all of black show biz to draw on and *Ain't Misbehavin'* had Fats Waller's irresistible rhythm and comedy numbers, *Eubie!* was stuck with a song catalogue so antique that some of it was no longer in copyright. Blake was born in 1883, and his career really peaked with *Shuffle Along*, in 1921. Lyricists of the early 1920s, especially those that Blake worked with, were not as liberated as Waller's collaborators in the 1930s and 1940s. However vital the performers, these songs were staying up past their bedtime.

Like Sammy Cahn, Eubie himself showed up onstage, in his nineties and, endearingly, wearing a hat. Everyone clapped and thrilled. Still, this was one of the less interesting of the revues.

What about a revue comprised of choreography? Was Bob Fosse making war on writers in *Dancin'* (1978), when he created a show exclusively out of Bob Fosse? The score was a ragbag, from Dan Emmett, George M.

Cohan, and John Philip Sousa to Neil Diamond and Melissa Manchester; and three separate acts and many short bits made this a painless sit for those in search of short and painless. *Dancin'* was a smash, but it wasn't a musical. People have feelings in a musical; and they sing about how they feel.

So *Working* (1978) was a musical, a theme revue. The theme was your job—any job at all, whether firefighter or mill worker, advertising copy writer or paperboy. Stephen Schwartz devised the show, directing (with choreographer Onna White) and eliciting contributions from Craig Carnelia, Micki Grant, James Taylor, and Mary Rodgers and Susan Birkenhead. Some of the numbers failed to probe the subject: the conflict between how one's job defines one and how one defines oneself. But a few of the songs served as tiny one-act plays. "Nobody Tells Me How," Bobo Lewis' complaint about how schoolteaching has changed during her career, was really the life story of a compassionate conservative. Homemaker Susan Bigelow, in "Just a Housewife," found a trenchant irony in that "just." In Lenora Nemetz' spot, "It's an Art," a waitress draws a parallel between table-waiting and show biz.

The book material came from Studs Terkel's volume of oral history, also called *Working*. However, the score is what has made *Working* popular with amateur and regional companies after a mere three weeks in New York. The novelty of these songs is that, for all their craftsman's finesse, they speak to people who don't often find themselves addressed by musicals.

One revue there was that doubled as a book musical: *The Magic Show* (1974). Was it because its producers wanted to present magician Doug Henning but feared that an evening-length magic act wouldn't go? So they erected a story show around Henning that seemed to incorporate him while not really doing so? Such as that he never took part in the music? And because two of the three producers had also put on *Godspell*, they asked Stephen Schwartz for a score? And Bob Randall would write a book about a seedy nightclub in Passaic, New Jersey, where there is this alcoholic old magician and Doug would replace him but the old-timer would then try to sabotage Doug's act?

It may sound like the musical as gimcrack, but it ran for 1,920 performances. This was, first, because Henning really did have a wonderful act, and, second, because the frame was amusing enough. Director-choreographer

Grover Dale gave it atmosphere, David Ogden Stiers as the cast-off magician was a wily piece of camp, and Schwartz's score is capable and surprising. Cheryl Barnes and Annie McGreevey sang noisy Pointer Sisters numbers, Dale Soules dealt out the ballads, Anita Morris handled the "babe" number, "Charmin's Lament" (which rhymes "whisked off by a warlock" with "hear his bedroom door lock," a couplet of E. Y. Harburgian panache), and Stiers had the cleverest number, the explosively name-dropping "Style."

Stiers was using "Style" to try to crush Doug Henning for his lack of grandeur; but that was Henning's charm. The most ingenuous of magicians, a skinny, long-haired, mustachioed kid dressed all in white with red-and-white oxfords on his feet, Henning quite simply dazzled. And with the orchestra onstage, as so often now, perched on a catwalk along the back wall of the place, one could sit up close and still be mystified as Anita Morris was sawed in half and Dale Soules levitated.

The Magic Show stands as exceptional in the line of the seventies revue, for the form was so preponderantly a songwriter anthology that it was, in effect, nothing else. Such shows were easy to put together, never risking that curse of the story show: book problems. And audiences flocked: because revues are easy to see. One's mind can wander for whole swatches of running time and one hasn't missed anything.

To be fair, *The Magic Show* really wasn't a revue, for while the book-show part of it was going, it really was a book show. Still, there seemed to be a possibility here, a way to entertain an undiscerning public by tricking out a bookless theatre piece with just enough unity of action to make it appear to be a musical. So Robert Stigwood reassembled his *Jesus Christ Superstar* team of director Tom O'Horgan, designers Robin Wagner and Randy Barcelo, lighting man Jules Fisher, and even sound man Abe Jacob for a Beatles show.

Sgt. Pepper's Lonely Hearts Club Band on the Road (1974) gathered the twelve cuts from the *Sgt. Pepper* LP along with a goodly helping of other Beatles tunes. A very slight throughline followed the odyssey of Billy Shears (Ted Neeley) and his girl friend Strawberry Fields (Kay Cole) as they defy Maxwell's Silver Hammermen (Allan Nicholls, William Parry, B. G. Gibson) and encounter the Sun Queen, Lovely Rita, Polythene Pam, and, of course, Sgt. Pepper (all played by David Patrick Kelly; as the Sun Queen he's Marilyn Monroe as the Statue of Liberty).

The fifteen-piece band (onstage, naturally) was the real thing, fielding the usual axes but also mandolin, E flat cyclotron, soprano recorder, euphonium, and even Wagner tuba. But the big and busy staging was strangely unimaginative after *Superstar*. It was literal, which the *Sgt. Pepper* songs certainly are not themselves. The Hammermen appeared as, yes, hammers, and "Mean Mr. Mustard" brought out a big dancing mustard jar. Reviewing *Superstar* three years earlier, *Time*'s T. E. Kalem coined "O'Horganitis," defining it as "the metastasis of spectacle over substance" typified by "bloat, inanity, hallucination, sexual kinkiness, and contagious vulgarity."

Yet the O'Horgan era was over by 1974—and note that *Sgt. Pepper* couldn't get a Broadway booking and had to content itself uptown at the Beacon, a rock palace. Nor was it successful at 66 performances. It was indistinguishable from an arena show or a rock concert, but it was where the revue form had gone to die.

12

I Really Don't Want to Write a Musical About Some Man Who Is Running from the Nazis. I Want to Do Something with Showgirls

MUSICAL COMEDY II

One inescapable fact about late-seventies musicals: almost every one of them is a commercial failure. But wasn't it always true of musicals that most of them failed?

No.

During the Second Age, the nation counted so many theatres and theatregoers that a musical attracting little attention in such show-biz capitals as New York, Chicago, and Seattle could tour the hinterland and do quite well. "New York's just a stand," Minnie Maddern Fiske once said; and she was an outstanding actress of the day. Acting was touring.

During the Third Age, a well-attended production could pay off in months, even into the 1950s. By the 1960s, however, a show could run a year and not break even, though it might have earned back much of its investment and, in time, through concomitant income such as stock and amateur rights, might gratify its investors.

In the 1970s, more musicals fail, often losing their entire investment, which by then runs over a million dollars. There are a few smash hits, and some just hits. There are respectable failures. There are no-good failures. And there are crazy bombs.

There have always been crazy bombs. One songwriting team made a career out of them: Carlo and Sanders. The king and queen of the "don't" musical, Monte Carlo and Alma Sanders billed themselves by last name only; and they actually did have one hit, *Tangerine* (1921). However, its success was attributed to reasons other than their score, and thereafter

Carlo and Sanders knew mainly heartbreak. True, *The Chiffon Girl* (1924) lasted 103 performances in a good booking right on Forty-second Street. But *Bye, Bye, Barbara* (1924) collapsed in two weeks, *Princess April* (1924; their third show that year) managed only three weeks, and *Oh! Oh! Nurse* (1925) lasted four weeks at the Cosmopolitan on Columbus Circle, generally regarded as the worst house on Broadway.

It was not that Carlo and Sanders were trying out unusual themes or formats. On the contrary, they were slaves to genre—the Irish Cinderella tale in the 1920s, the burlesque-with-a-story-line farce in the 1940s. The "don't" in their work inhered in Carlo's radio-jingle tunes and Sanders' idiotic lyrics.

At least they did wait five prudent years before daring The Street again. But *Mystery Moon* (1930) may be the only musical to close on opening night before *Kelly*, thirty-five years later. Then, like Evita's corpse, Carlo and Sanders disappeared for seventeen years. Their comeback, *Louisiana Lady* (1947), ran 4 performances.

But such shows were exceptional—till the 1970s. Then the crazy bomb proliferates. There are the relentless attempts to Do the New Music, as in *Rockabye Hamlet* (1976), one of the few crazy bombs brought in with a major name on the poster, Gower Champion. (Yes, it's a rock *Hamlet*.) Or *Got Tu Go Disco* (1979). Or *Saravà* (1979).

Mitch Leigh is back. He is a sometimes excellent composer, and like most of his flops, *Saravà* has some good music. It has a good story premise, too. Didn't *Man of La Mancha*, *Cry For Us All*, and *Home Sweet Homer* all turn on interesting personality clashes? Cervantes versus the Inquisition. An unseen woman whose impending death controls a big-city mayoral election. A hero takes on the gods.

Based on the Brazilian novel and movie known up north as *Dona Flor and Her Two Husbands*, *Saravà* treated the romantic triangle, but with a twist. It's one woman and two men. One man is nice. One man is dead.

The dead guy (P. J. Benjamin) is Dona Flor's former husband. The nice guy (Michael Ingram) is her current husband. The problem is that not only does the first husband refuse to rest in peace but he's really hot, even as a ghost. How can nice rival hot, especially in Latin America?

Amid all this is Mitch Leigh's desire to reestablish himself with a genuine musical comedy: exotic fun stuff with a lot of Brazilian street parties. The tunestack includes "Makulele," "Viva a Vida," and "Muito Bom."

The character numbers are more traditional, and Leigh has even abandoned his characteristic construction in which the voice sings the melody while the orchestra plays a dizzy rhythmic accompaniment. Leigh was going for a popular hit, easy to enjoy, with N. Richard Nash's book and lyrics and a curiously unknown director-choreographer, Rick Atwell.

Indeed, the show amused some folks, not least because of a paradox: one rooted for the nice guy even though the hot guy clearly outclasses him as sheer pleasure. And the nice guy knew it:

TEO: Maybe I am not as romantic as your husband. And there he has the advantage over me. But I have one great advantage over him.
FLOR: What's that?
TEO: I'm alive.

There is this as well: Tovah Feldshuh gave a tremendous performance, albeit in a season that saw other Tony-nominated turns by *Platinum*'s Alexis Smith, *Ballroom*'s Dorothy Loudon, and *Sweeney Todd*'s Angela Lansbury, who won.

What makes *Saravà* a crazy bomb is less the show itself than its attempt to run without opening; and it nearly worked. A lively television commercial was drawing the public till the critics realized that *Saravà* might succeed entirely without their consideration. It's not nice to fool Mother Nature. The daily reviewers held a vote, with the *Times* and the *News* carrying the motion to rush in, buy tickets, and tell the tale. It was a slaughter—but the television spots did not falter and *Saravà* ultimately played 140 performances.

The Utter Glory of Morrissey Hall (1979) ran a single night, and this one was a crazy bomb because it was terrible. Sad to say, a good deal of effort was wasted on it, for this look at an English girls' school needs a big cast and keeps them all relentlessly in motion. Inspired perhaps by Ronald Searle's St. Trinian's cartoons and the films based on them, *Morrissey Hall* had a score by the author of *You're a Good Man, Charlie Brown*, Clark Gesner, and a book by Gesner and Nagle Jackson, who directed. A very few of the songs were almost tuneful and one or two jokes landed. Still, the cast, headed by Celeste Holm as the headmistress, had nothing to work with.

It must have been the idea itself that persuaded the producers to bring in yet another regional entry, this one from the Pacific Conservatory of the Performing Arts, because the idea suggests a funny family show. If the idea is sound, then the show must be, too? Gesner's girls are not the outright criminals of the St. Trinian's series. They are at worst disobedient and mischievous; as a recurring gag, arrows are constantly flying across the stage and just missing someone. The faculty have their personal problems to contribute to the action, and one of the girls has a boy friend who arrives inside a trunk. "The Letter" (from the boy friend) typifies the show's lack of judgment. The melody works well enough, and the moment is right for a number: the girl reads the boy's letter aloud while the boy materializes (on a wire, overhead) to sing some of the contents himself. Throughout, the other girls comment. It's ordinary stuff, but it *could* go over—that is, if the girls' comments weren't so stupid, if the lyrics weren't so feeble, and if the whole affair didn't take on such a contagiously floppo quality that the entire rest of the act suffers.

Not that *Morrissey Hall* was any good up to that point. Out of town, Celeste Holm's predecessor was Eileen Heckart, who was asked to leave and glad to go. If a show cannot use a sharp talent like Heckart's, something must be wrong with the show. We've seen plenty of failures cascading through the decade. Some were old-fashioned, like *Molly*. Some were wrongheaded, like *1600 Pennsylvania Avenue*. But few were as simply bad as this one. *Saravà* was better.

Next we come to the Dreary Musicals, not outstandingly poor but contaminated in some overwhelming way. *Something's Afoot* (1976) came to Broadway from San Francisco's American Conservatory Theatre and Goodspeed Opera House as a good idea—a takeoff on the Agatha Christie who'sdoingit, in which characters are murdered one by one in an isolated mansion. For novelty, it is the house itself that does the killing, booby-trapped to murder by exploding staircase, electrocuting light switch, and the like.

You already know the house party: the mannish woman detective, the roué, the old colonel, the two youngsters who bond romantically, the haughty lady, the saucy maid, and so on. At Goodspeed in 1973, Mary Jo Catlett played the detective; on Broadway, it was Tessie O'Shea, known especially for her rousing music-hall vocals in Noël Coward's *The Girl Who Came To Supper* (1963). O'Shea was the only name of note, though sweetheart Barbara Heuman had succeeded to the title role in the *No, No, Nanette* revival with great charm, saucy maid Neva Small will attract our notice presently, and roué Gary Beach would eventually luck into an important role in *The Producers*. (The other sweetheart, Willard Beckham, went on to a similar role in *The Utter Glory of Morrissey Hall* three years later.)

Of course, a small show like *Something's Afoot*, booked into the little Lyceum, cannot afford an all-star cast. Yet it must not play like summer stock, either, for its very structure calls for a series of characterological "turns." True, Agatha Christie's comparable title *The Mousetrap* has been running for whole generations in London with nobody in it. But musicals function more flamboyantly.

So maybe this show isn't such a good idea. For the A.C.T. and Goodspeed, fine. Broadway's public expects the best, and *Something's Afoot* was—here's that word again—*modest* in every way. One could try to praise it as "unpretentious," with its unit set and four-man orchestra: but is there supposed to be something pretentious about a big show that plays superbly?

Something's Afoot was another off-Broadway musical trying to get by on The Street. The performers weren't the problem (though Tessie O'Shea was miscast), and director-choreographer Tony Tanner made the most of what he was given. The problem is the authors—four of them, occasionally getting off a cute joke but mainly plodding; and the score is suffocated with imitation numbers. Of course, parody is the intention. But the sweethearts' "I Don't Know Why I Trust You" has the horrible tinkle of every forgotten bomb that played the Sheridan Square Playhouse; and "The Man With the Ginger Moustache" gets all its effect from the haughty lady's singing Helen Morgan torch. Writing these *Boy Friend* scores isn't as easy as it looks.

Sometimes Dreary is simply the same old *kind* of show without compensatory refreshment—rich atmosphere, exciting performances, wonderful music. *Angel* (1978) offered yet another adaptation of an unsuitably serious play with a book co-written by the playwright *and* yet another pop-theatre score by Gary Geld and Peter Udell *and* yet another risible reduction of the play's title—*Look Homeward, Angel*—to a single word. But "Angel," in this context, is meaningless.

Thomas Wolfe's novel *Look Homeward, Angel!* and the 1957 play drawn from it by Ketti Frings tell of a troubled southern family with an artistic, alcoholic father, a naggy mother, and an older brother who looks after the sensitive young protagonist but dies during the course of the story. There's no role in it for Adele Astaire, which means that the music had better be of the *A Time For Singing* or *Titanic* kind, a beautiful Big Sing.

Angel's isn't. Geld and Udell catch a rustic flavor, but with tired old ditties of no account; and their continued use of false rhymes has become extremely irritating. But then, parents Fred Gwynne and Frances Sternhagen were non-singers, and sons Joel Higgins and Don Scardino field only decent Broadway voices, not the gala instruments these dark shows need, if only to soothe the tragic heart of the piece. Many a flop has at least started invitingly. Even *The Utter Glory of Morrissey Hall*'s introductory "Promenade" has a lilt. But from the rise of *Angel*'s curtain, boardinghouse guests chirping through "All the Comforts of Home," this was a dismal show.

So was *The Act* (1977), even with Liza Minnelli, Gower Champion, and Kander and Ebb. Minnelli and Martin Scorsese must have had a wonderful time making the movie *New York, New York* the previous year, for she then drew him into her world of the theatre to direct *In Person*, a Las Vegas headline act deconstructed by the star's memories. Retitled *Shine It On* and then *The Act*, the show had to be the most exhausting star vehicle of all time. Minnelli had only one actor in support, Barry Nelson as her sometime husband; and of course Nelson doesn't sing. No one did, except Minnelli, occasionally aided by a six-person corps: twelve numbers, each a big one.

There was a Shaker Hymn Number, "Turning," performed twirling on poles in a red silk outfit that was about as far from the ascetic Shaker worldview as one can get. There was the indispensable Kander and Ebb Make It Here Number, "Bobo's," the Kander and Ebb Cakewalk Number, "City Lights," the Kander and Ebb White Gospel Rave-up, "Shine It On." One number had no genre, a piece about adultery called "Arthur in the Afternoon," originally written for and cut from *A Family Affair*, where the lover was not Arthur but, for Shelley Berman, Mamie. No wonder Minnelli had to resort to some lip-synching to tape, though she got blasted for it all the same.

Scorsese proved unable to pull a hit together and Champion replaced him, though he had only a few weeks in which to revise. Book writer George Furth blamed Scorsese for all the show's problems, but Scorsese's version had done terrific business on the prolonged tryout that became almost routine in this decade. Anyway, how is one to effect much revision in what is in effect a one-woman singing act with flashback book scenes? With its unit set and little corps, *The Act* would have made a bundle if it had been any good. It is not only Kander and Ebb's weakest score but their only poor one. The book material seems an excuse to turn a nightclub stand into theatre. Could it be that Minnelli wanted to return to Broadway but simply couldn't find a good story to play? Are we running out of stories—is that what all these revues and revivals tell us?

Credit *Platinum* (1978), then, with giving Alexis Smith a new book show. Playing old-time movie star Lila Halliday, Smith, too, had to make do with a unit set, though this one was David Hays' realization of a high-tech recording studio. It includes a movie screen, a Jacuzzi, and so many mikes that conversation effortlessly carries to a recording producer's invisible subordinates, and orders are instantly obeyed. So when Smith declines to record a disco version of her old hit tune, the producer can simply say, "Erase Miss Halliday." And Smith—with her bygone movie-star Hollywood and its Irving Berlin and Harry Warren and Frank Loesser—is erased.

There was potential here, in a confrontation of old show biz and the New Music. Its crass side was embodied in the record producer (a superb Stanley Kamel) and a snotty young singer (Lisa Mordente). Its dumb side was a trio of backup girls (Damita Jo Freeman, Robin Green, Avery Sommers), one of whom disarmingly calls the elegant Smith "Miss Lady." Its attractive side was a top rocker with hidden sensitivity (a very winning Richard Cox, who was to play the serial killer in the movie *Cruising* two years later). Smith teaches the backup girls the time step; they teach her the Attitudes of Rock. More important, Smith and Cox become an intimate team, at least for a while.

So *Platinum* is about how old and new can learn from each other. Fair enough; and it is true that, one year after *Platinum*, Ethel Merman released an A&M LP of disco readings of her old anthems. But too much of Gary William Friedman and Will Holt's score was ugly pop, and too much of the book, by Holt and Bruce Vilanch, was dull. Vilanch is one of the funniest men in America, but the jokes clunked:

> SMITH: (to herself) You can take a chance on making this record. Or continue to play Mame for the rest of your life (pause for mild audience laugh) in summer stock (pause for second mild laugh) in Columbus, Ohio! (Third mild laugh, mainly in loyal support of Smith)

or:

> YOUNG BACKUP CHICK: Oh, you've been on the road?
> SMITH: My dear . . . I *am* the road!

Cox, as one Dan Danger—"I am a heavy-metal crotch-pushing parody of myself!"—had some conflict to play, and he was game enough to provide some trendy nudity (backal only) in the Jacuzzi. But in all there was too little story and not enough fun, though Joe Layton was in charge. The piece needed a subplot, more something, stronger rock. It was better than dreary, perhaps, and not at all the horror that many supposed it to be. If nothing else, it was the only other chance to see Alexis Smith in a Broadway musical after her debut in *Follies*; and she did get a Tony nomination for her Lila Halliday. Cox was nominated, too.

I Remember Mama (1979) was supremely Dreary, if only because it had sounded like such a good idea: a Richard Rodgers show starring Liv Ullmann as the extraordinary Norwegian–American matriarch who had already provisioned commercial and artistic successes in fiction, theatre, film, and television. That *Working* number "Just a Housewife" comes to mind when considering this archetypal figure, so basic yet so resourceful. Thomas Meehan wrote the book and Martin Charnin collaborated with Rodgers and directed, till the Philadelphia tryout opened very glumly. The action lacked action, and the score was even more variable than that for *Rex*. Then, too, Ullmann had trouble with the songs and seemed somewhat less the actress than one knew her to be. She and Charnin did not get along; Cy Feuer stepped in as director.

Worse, the genial but unimportant Papa, little more than furniture in earlier incarnations, vexed the scenario. If he didn't sing, it would look odd; once he sang, in "You Could Not Please Me More," he became suddenly important—and the Papa, George Hearn, has too much presence to play furniture in any case. What to do with this intrusive nonentity of a character? Meehan's solution was to rid the show's middle third of Hearn on an implausible pretext, giving *Mama* the wrong story and too little of it.

Rodgers was nearly seventy-seven years old and not in good health. He still had his gift, in "Ev'ry Day (Comes Something Beautiful)"; in daughter Katrin's "A Writer Writes At Night," a wonderful new excuse for kids staying up late; and, working in Philadelphia with lyricist Raymond Jessel, "A Little Bit More." But the half of the score dealing with Mama's family was poor. These are flimsy characters, people beyond music.

What *I Remember Mama* lacked was Oscar Hammerstein. The work was not, speaking fairly, Rodgers and Hammerstein material, for—except in "The Hardangerfjord," a number for celebrating Norwegian neighbors—there is none of the folkish community background that typifies their shows. True, *Mama* is a bit reminiscent of *The Sound of Music* in its focus on one family group. Had Rodgers and Hammerstein written *I Remember Mama* in 1959, who knows what they might have done with it?

The 1979 *Mama* collapsed after exhausting the three months' advance sale, despite a relentless television campaign in which Ullmann crowed, "I am singing Richard Rodgers' music!" An exaggeration. *Mama* did tally up a better run than that of *Rex*, but one cursed by acrimonious comments from the participants and by Rodgers' death a few months after the show closed. The oddest note in all this is that, years later, when the score was recorded, our own (naturalized) Sally Ann Howes sang a perfectly judged Mama, accent and all.

Enough of the Dreary. Let us proceed to enjoyable flops, with the intriguing scores, the novel subject matter, the dazzling staging. These are aficionados' collectibles, such as *Music Is* (1976). Did we need yet a third adaptation of *Twelfth Night* after the two off-Broadway tries in the 1960s? And was 1976 too late for the typical humdrum George Abbott book that lacks drama and wit? His many book collaborations tended to protect him. A co-writer such as Betty Smith, Douglas Wallop, or Jerome Weidman could supply the content while Abbott shapes it through sound theatre practice. For all the writing that Abbott did—very often of smash hits, too—he was less a writer than an editor and manager. He was the guy in charge who knows how plays work.

Music Is enjoyed the typical Abbott casting of newcomers and not-thereyets. Catherine Cox and Joel Higgins were the siblings, David Holliday was Orsino, and Sherry Mathis was Olivia. All were fine, and Higgins made history by being the only actor ever to call Abbott by his first name instead of the worshipful "Mr. Abbott" required by unwritten thespian law. The choice portrayal, however, was the Malvolio of Christopher Hewett, at once the most Shakespearean of the players and a big silly camp. "I'll play the dandy!" he vowed in his rampageous solo, "I Am It," putting into a single line all the growly eros of the born lecher who has never loved till now.

In all, the Richard Adler–Will Holt score was, at its best, sound musical-comedy writing. George Abbott musicals don't usually feature bel canto the way, say, Rodgers and Hammerstein shows do. An Abbott vocalist is Nancy Walker or Harold Lang: very pleasing, but a good way short of *Carousel*. *Music Is*, however, took Abbott somewhat into grander reaches. Holliday, an almost opera-weight baritone, was given little to sing. But Mathis gave good tone, and Higgins had much more to work with here than in the paltry *Angel*. In particular, Cox gave an outstanding reading of the evening's best ballad, "Should I Speak Of Loving You"; it really was one of the most *musical* spots in the entire decade. At that, Hershy Kay's orchestrations were superb, and William Cox's dance arrangements dug into Adler's melodies with zest, putting them through every conceivable decoction, including one section for harpsichord and dizzy coloratura soprano.

The show was a music festival. Choreographer Patricia Birch fell in with the spirit by setting the set changes as dance crossovers and topping the show by having chorus boy Denny Shearer take off his baseball cap and plop it onto Catherine Cox's head just before the lights went out.

So everyone was in top form—except George Abbott. Like Richard Rodgers, he, too, was aging now, though he was in perfect health for a man who was days away from ninety. But then, Abbott shows know certain flaws, especially character inconsistencies and irrelevant or even incorrect song numbers. After landing on the beach after the shipwreck, Joel Higgins had a duet with a character of absolutely no importance in the plot, "Hate To Say Goodbye To You." Why would they hate to part when they hardly know each other? Because it was time for a barn-dance cheer-up number? Abbott should have cut it; and we can guess what

Hal Prince would have said had Adler and Holt sung it for him: "That'll do very nicely for a dinner theatre in Tucson. Or were you writing this show for Broadway?"

Audiences loved *Music Is*, which may be why Abbott did almost no work on it during the tryout. He did not even stick around after the Washington, D.C. opening. Then *Music Is* came in, to withering reviews. For the week that it ran, audiences—now informed about its quality—sat there stone-hearted, implacable.

So Long, 174th Street (1976), another fast failure, suggests a George Abbott show in its juvenile high spirits: a high-schooler who wants to become an actor against the wishes of his family fantasizes about fame, money, and sex. With sidekicks, girl friends, and thirties New York, it sounds like *On the Town* without the war. However, *On the Town* is one of the Third Age's classic titles because of the unassuming way in which it makes art out of pop. It wasn't supposed to be great: it was supposed to be a musical comedy.

So Long, 174th Street was also just supposed to be a musical comedy, and that is all it was. Stan Daniels wrote the score, for a book by Joseph Stein based on Stein's 1963 comedy *Enter Laughing*, from Carl Reiner's autobiographical novel. And it was not an Abbott show; Burt Shevelove directed.

It's a risqué piece, with rather a lot of time devoted to the hero's puerile erotic obsessions. There are *two* songs about them, "Undressing Girls With My Eyes" and "You Touched Her (breasts)." Yes, youth has to go through this phase; but the audience doesn't. Daniels' score was more appealing when stylizing the sensual, as in "Bolero on Rye," in which *faux* Ravel accompanies an imaginary lunch at a Jewish delicatessen. To the waiter's dully murmured repetitions, the hero and his date order the entire exotic menu. Finally, the waiter (Gene Varrone) reveals an expansive tenor with Pavarotti stunting, and the two young people get to the main course. "I'll have him," says the girl; and the hero responds, "I'll have her."

That was Robert Morse, too old by now in a part fit for a *jeune premier* just ready to break through to stardom. In other words: Morse as he was in the 1950s. George Abbott would have cast Morse's understudy, Jimmy Brennan, whose youth would have kept all the sex hunger innocent. The older Morse gave it too much texture. Imagining himself a movie star, Morse envisions his butler (George S. Irving) fielding a call from a love-smitten Greta Garbo. She's out of luck; Morse is booked up for months. "He's screwing Dolores del Rio" is the first line of "The Butler's Song," and shock brings out a laugh. However, with the naïve Brennan as wish-maker, it's a lark. With Morse, it's every man's cheap reality, and the fun squirms out of reach.

Much of the show was quite humorous even so, with a rare score that is made almost exclusively of comedy numbers. The opening, "David Kolowitz, the Actor," pictures the world at Morse's feet, including President and Eleanor Roosevelt, John Barrymore, and even the Pope. Later, when Morse visualizes his funeral in "Boy Oh Boy," his friend Marvin (Lawrence John Moss) greets the mourners:

> MARVIN: (To the Roosevelts) Right this way, Mr. President. (To the next arrival) Oh, Mr. Barrymore! (Turning to a newcomer) A yarmulke? (It's the Pope) Your Holiness! (Who of course is wearing a Vatican skullcap) Oh, you got one.

Part of the fun is that Morse was playing someone without a shred of talent, the kind that knocks over scenery. However, it isn't enjoyable to find him so dogged by a parental determination to run his life. For a novelty, Morse had not a Jewish mother but a Papa (Lee Goodman), using emotional blackmail to try to wrestle Morse into the pharmaceutical business. "My Son the Druggist" is actually rather amusing. But "If You Want To Break Your Father's Heart," sung during a fantasy trial scene, is outrageous. If Papa wants a druggist in the family, why doesn't he enroll in a pharmacology program?

Alan Jay Lerner and Burton Lane had a habit of teaming up but once a decade: first, the movie *Royal Wedding* (1951); on Broadway, *On a Clear Day You Can See Forever* (1965); in 1979, *Carmelina*. Georgia Brown played a single mother in an Italian village, and Cesare Siepi, as in *Bravo Giovanni* (1962), owned a tavern. Siepi loves Brown, but she is cool. Why? Lerner never figured that out, which is partly why this one, too, closed in two weeks. A *Mamma Mia!* subplot found three American ex-servicemen coming to visit Brown to meet her daughter, sired by one of them. This is also the theme of the 1968 film *Buona Sera, Mrs. Campbell*. The tale is a true one; apparently, the authors of three different works all read the same newspaper item.

Of course, any score by Lane and Lerner will be worth listening to. But neither was at his best here. Even with two fine singers like Brown and Siepi, there's nothing with the lyrical outpouring of *On a Clear Day*. The lack of substance in Lerner and Joseph Stein's book seems to have infected everything. Oliver Smith's scenery looked ordinary. Siepi and Brown paired badly. A merely capable number such as Brown's "Someone in April" stood out for its clever absorption of plot exposition in a character number; but it also stood out because nothing else did. The music simply wasn't on the level of Lane's *Finian's Rainbow*, the lyrics dinky after Lerner's *My Fair Lady*.

Was the whole decade to be a graveyard for craftsmen? And whose idea was it that José Ferrer could stage musicals? Was the decade running out of competent journeyman directors as well? It was Ferrer who enervated the dashing *Oh Captain!* (1958), who scraped all the charm out of the *State Fair* remake (1962), and who numbed *Carmelina*. If you want a flop director, invest in Ron Field. He sometimes had a hit, and he will give you a brilliant staging. So *King of Hearts* (1978) at least *looked* like the real thing. There was first of all Santo Loquasto's spectacular set, a collection of sticks and surfaces fitted together before the public's eyes to turn into a French village. This was mounted on a revolve to include the local insane asylum, cockeyed at impossible angles of view. The inmates were the dramatis personae, along with an American soldier who tries to get them to evacuate the village, mined to explode by the retreating Germans.

You may know the film, Philippe de Broca's 1966 World War I farce of the same title, with Alan Bates as the soldier. Another product of the Disease of the West, the movie fondles the notion that people in power are insane and incarcerated people are reasonable. Right. Winston Churchill and Franklin Roosevelt are insane. Charles Manson is reasonable.

King of Hearts is insane. Its aim was to cash in on the film's popularity. But the audience for sixties cult movies—even one with Bates' famous backal nude shot—isn't a Broadway-going audience. And had this public troubled to attend the show, it surely wouldn't have liked the score, traditional in sound. Peter Link's music has charm. But lyricist Jacob Brackman is deaf. He'll rhyme anything, including "scandalous" and "abandoned us."

Don Scardino, replacing Robby Benson (of the tryout) as the American, successfully held the show's center as the only sane character.

He naturally goes over to the other side—not to the Germans, but to the asylum inmates, in recognition of the true insanity, war. Actually, the true insanity lay in trying to stretch a slender plotline over the course of an evening.

I will say this again: in a musical, each number must accomplish something to the public's satisfaction or the structure collapses. Let's pause for a moment to consider a perfect score, that to *My Fair Lady*. It isn't just good music and clever lyrics. Every single number defines or develops major characters or advances plot or establishes the timeplace. Obviously, a high quality of invention is essential. But the score must above all function *correctly*.

King of Hearts' score did not function correctly. It lacked motion: so did the plot. This show was so imprecisely realized that it started out with a book by Steve Tesich, reached Broadway with a book by Joseph Stein, and is now available for performance with a book by Steve Tesich. Goodspeed Opera House presented Tesich's humorless version in 2002, giving one the opportunity to remember how irritating it is to watch actors playing nuts. Worse, one of them's a mime. It was thrilling to renew a spectator's relationship with *Georgy*'s Melissa Hart; but she deserves better than the role of the bordello madam. It's a stupid part, a flop part. *King of Hearts* has some good music, but it's a flop show in either version.

Michael Bennett had a flop, too, and his also was an eyeful. *Ballroom* (1978) was Bennett's first show after *A Chorus Line*, an impossible situation. Tharon Musser, the lighting designer for both titles, said, "No matter what we did . . . we would have had our throats cut." Bennett did try to avoid comparisons with *A Chorus Line* by choosing a vastly different project. *A Chorus Line* is a gritty piece about ambitious young people. *Ballroom* is gentle. It's about old people.

Or even: *A Chorus Line* is extremely integrated, with dialogue and song so intertwined that there is no division between the book and the score. *Ballroom* is broken up into book scenes and songs; some of the songs are performance pieces, not integrated at all. *Ballroom* has no underscored dialogue; *A Chorus Line* is loaded with it. *Ballroom* also has none of *A Chorus Line*'s up-and-down dramatic rhythm, being built of one arching rise. And note that *Ballroom* has a love plot that ends sort of happily. *A Chorus Line* ends with people being accepted or rejected for work.

Of course, *A Chorus Line* tells us that this work is love; but that's two chapters away. What matters is that Michael Bennett thought that

Ballroom was as far from *A Chorus Line* as one could go, whereas one can't in fact go *anywhere* from *A Chorus Line*. It's like *Show Boat* and *Oklahoma!*, right at the center of its culture, unique and expansive.

Ballroom was based on a teleplay by Jerome Kass, one of the few people that Bennett met on his brief post–*Chorus Line* Hollywood jaunt whom he liked. *Queen of the Stardust Ballroom* followed a new widow's reentry into life in a Bronx dance palace, where she meets a married man with whom she has an affair. Coincidentally, the art came from life, just as *A Chorus Line* did, for this was the story of Kass' late mother.

Not coincidentally, *Ballroom* shared with *A Chorus Line* Bennett's preference for writers who were not Broadway honchos. Possibly because of the tremendous fight that he lost with Hal Prince during the Boston tryout of *Follies*, Bennett liked working with talents he could intimidate. Kass wrote *Ballroom*'s script, and Billy Goldenberg composed the music to the lyrics of Alan and Marilyn Bergman. Their best line, from "Dreams," is the theme of the show. "Trust your dreams," it urges. Trust them and nothing else: "for they know who you are."

Like half of *Ballroom*'s numbers, "Dreams" is sung by the Stardust's two bandstand vocalists. Concept commentary, perhaps? Not really. Their first spot, "A Song For Dancing," could be their credo, as a pleasantly undistinguished couple providing musical background to the show biz of old nobodies.

But then, in Michael Bennett's world, everyone has a right to a show biz of some kind. The healing quality of show-biz success is why the *Chorus Line* auditioners are so eager to work and why the Stardust regulars love to dance: it reimagines them. This must be why Bennett wanted very little plot or character music for this show. There is no music in one's drab life: it's all in the ballroom.

So that's where Bea Asher (Dorothy Loudon) goes, prodded by a friend who says, "It took me six months after *my* husband died to realize that they only buried one of us." Bea meets Al Rossi (Vincent Gardenia), and it might as well be Cinderella and the Prince. Indeed, Bea's intolerant in-laws and children are kinds of stepmother and stepsisters. Not a one of them has a shred of sympathy for the enchanting new life that Bea has created for herself; they fancy her baby-sitting for them and being bored.

Interestingly, Bennett staged the back-and-forth between the real life of Bea's junk shop and living room and the show-biz dream of the ballroom without transitional punctuation. Under Tharon Musser's lighting specifications, Robin Wagner's set designs could turn on a dime. This allowed Bea to travel across town by simply turning upstage. Further, Bennett laid *Ballroom* out in a single act, like *A Chorus Line*. (And like *So Long, 174th Street*, for that matter; this was a decade increasingly devoted to one-act musicals.) The material was too thin for a full evening—or, one might say, too concentrated. One can plot its curve in a sentence: Bea hears of the dream, enters the dream, and finds love in the dream. For it knows who she is.

Ballroom is an extremely romantic show, clearly, even if it treats the old folks who seemed *so* old in *70, Girls, 70*. Remember "Do We?"? It turns out that they do. Dorothy Loudon, so often lumbered with unworthy parts, had not her biggest success but her finest role as Bea Asher. She must have loved playing it, for her chemistry with Vincent Gardenia, with the Stardust dancers, and even with her repulsive relatives ran at highest potency. Loudon had long been a wonderful singer and comic, but here she was a life force, someone who doesn't ask for a lot but is bound to have something. Her eleven o'clock song, "Fifty Percent" (that is, of the married Gardenia), dissolved movie-style into the ballroom in formal dress-up for the trying on of the slipper: Bea's coronation, with King Al, as Queen of the Stardust Ballroom.

Yet the show failed, like every show in this chapter so far. Strange to say, *Ballroom* was too daring. Bennett had juxtaposed two utterly separate worlds, one made mainly of dialogue and one made mainly of dance. The dialogue is your life. The dance is your dream. The show teaches us how to move into the dream, a basic lesson that the American musical has been teaching since Irving Berlin and Jerome Kern took control of pop music in 1915.

However, the public of the 1970s was not accustomed to entertainment so tightly self-defining. Where were all the plot twists, the kibitzers, the stuff? *Ballroom* today would be a sensation. They love dance pieces now. There was talk, too, that the Majestic Theatre box-office help was discouraging would-be ticket buyers with false tales of sellout, to hustle the crippled show out of the house and thus welcome in a possible hit. Certainly, the clueless reviews were no help. One wonders what would have happened if Bennett had followed up *A Chorus Line* with the irresistibly dazzling *Dreamgirls*.

Jerry Herman's *The Grand Tour* (1979) is, on the other hand, a conventional show, albeit with unconventional source material. Franz Werfel's *Jacobowsky and the Colonel*, produced here in 1944 by the Theatre Guild in S. N. Behrman's English adaptation, follows the partnership of an arrogant Polish army officer and an endearing Jewish survivor as they transport essential documents to England while the Nazis overrun France. A love triangle develops, because the colonel's French girl friend takes a shine to the unpretentious Jacobowsky.

There's a lot to work with here—three interesting characters, the suspenseful wartime dynamics with spies and passwords, even a train and a boat. *King of Hearts* was a visual feast on the other world war, but it sorely needed the textual weight that S. N. Behrman gave *The Grand Tour*'s book writers, Michael Stewart and Mark Bramble. Following the play's plotline and absorbing many of its scenes more or less verbatim, Stewart, Bramble, and Herman invented enough to beget something new, rather in the way that Rodgers and Hammerstein did in adapting used-up Theatre Guild plays into *Oklahoma!* and *Carousel*.

This was Joel Grey's third star vehicle at the Palace. He was not entirely right for the role of Cohan in *George M!* (1968), bringing too much energy to that lifelong underplayer; but the show was energetic generally. And the title role of *Goodtime Charley* was misconceived. But it is hard to imagine a song-and-dance man better suited to Jacobowsky than Grey. Here is a quiet and agreeable guy, one used to letting other people enjoy getting their way, and this is how Grey played him.

He would have made a flavorful counterpart to the Polish colonel had the authors not coarsened that figure into a comic stooge. For the Theatre Guild, Louis Calhern played Colonel Stjerbinsky as suave, chivalrous, and superior, an aristocrat who shows his contempt for the world by having better manners than everyone else in it. He even plays the violin, alerting his girl friend to his arrival with a serenade.

The musical's director, Gerald Freedman, had Colonel Ron Holgate posturing and growling yet always a figure of fun and anything but heroic. Werfel and Behrman were trying to observe how a combination of Stjerbinsky's power and Jacobowsky's intelligence equals one hero—that Nazi ruthlessness can be conquered only by a war of the heart and mind. This is what gave the play its charm in 1944, especially given that the pair have a couple of hair-raising near misses with the Nazis. The musical retains these, including one scene in which an S.S. officer (George Reinholt) goads Stjerbinksy when the colonel and Jacobowsky have him at gunpoint:

> S.S. CAPTAIN: I know you, Colonel. You are a survivor from a vanished past, and your code of honor as a soldier will not permit you to shoot an unarmed man.
> COLONEL: You Nazis do it.
> S.S. CAPTAIN: That is different. We are not distressed by codes.... Our soldiers are trained to kill without being troubled by senseless guilt.

Signaling to imaginary Nazis behind the colonel, the S.S. captain bolts, but Stjerbinksy shoots him after all, capping it with a line right out of Werfel-Behrman:

> COLONEL: I have broken my code ... and it feels wonderful!

What held *The Grand Tour* together was the music. (There was no *Mack & Mabel* mischief this year: Herman got a Tony nomination.) If Jerry Herman's best score is that to *Mame*, his greatest hit is *Hello, Dolly!* and the cult favorites are *Dear World* and *Mack & Mabel*. So *The Grand Tour* is his unappreciated title. It has one abiding flaw, a lack of European flavor. Herman's renovation of Louis Calhern's violin solo, "Marianne," is one of his most beguiling melodies, but it is too American in its evocation of such other names as "the Jennies" and "the Janets." In France? It does at least ennoble the accordion without which no Broadway musical set in France would be complete; and Marianne's own establishing song, "I Belong Here," was superbly sung by Florence Lacey. But the Jerry Herman $\frac{6}{8}$ cheer-up march, "For Poland," does not remotely suggest the thinking of Polish nationals or, indeed, anyone in Europe. Comparably, Cole Porter's *Can-Can* and Harold Rome's *Fanny* do not make this mistake.

Even so, on its own terms, the work collects situation and character songs that couldn't pass in any other piece. "Wedding Conversation" is the first of its kind, a comic duet for a man who thinks he's meeting with his espionage contact and a man who thinks *he's* meeting the rabbi who is to conduct a wedding. Best of all is the song that frames the evening,

"I'll Be Here Tomorrow." Once again, we see Herman's ability to work strictly within traditional forms while tilting them toward character, making them site-specific and universal at once. "I'll Be Here Tomorrow" belongs to a long line of hero-defies-the-world anthems. A fox-trot of mounting urgency, it turns Jacobowsky into music: gentle yet capable of great expansion. It's a survival song, obviously, heartening us at the very top of the show and then reassuring us at the end. It has to: because only the colonel and Marianne will cross the Channel to England and freedom. Jacobowsky must stay behind and continue to outwit the enemy just to stay alive. But he will—the music says so. As Grey hit the vocal's last three big high notes that sound like a long and happy life, the sun came up, Grey threw his arms out, and the show went into freeze-frame. And that's where the curtain fell.

Or, rather, that's where the last blackout came. By this time, shows that went out of town generally spared expenses by playing a single city and avoiding traveling costs. *The Grand Tour* previewed in San Francisco, where Tommy Tune was invited to aid director Freedman and choreographer Donald Saddler in perking up the piece. It may well have been Tune who substituted the cinematic "end-of-shot" lighting effect for the venerable falling of the curtain, because the blackout finale was relatively new at this time and favored by hotshots. It has the advantage of surprise, but it loses that five-second "departure" of a show that the curtain fall creates—that farewell kiss, so to say.

The Grand Tour ran only two months, most disappointing for a born audience show. One problem was two bad write-ups in the *Times*; another was the relatively late date for the recording and release of the cast album and, in any case, the lack of playing venues for it on the air. It's not a great score, but it gives pleasure, with all sorts of fizz—a train number, a circus number, a tango in which Marianne and the colonel simultaneously air their opposing reactions to Jacobowsky.

The best music of all this group is that of *The Robber Bridegroom*, Tennessee foolery with a country score. Alfred Uhry based his book on Eudora Welty's long short story of that title, and Robert Waldman composed the music to Uhry's lyrics. Briefly presented in workshop in 1974 in the Theatre at St. Clement's, *The Robber Bridegroom* went to the Harkness Theatre in 1975 with the Acting Company, in ambitious repertory with *The Three Sisters*, *The Time of Your Life*, and Marlowe's *Edward II*.

Kevin Kline played the robber and Patti LuPone, otherwise Irina, Kitty, and young Edward III in travesty, was the heroine Rosamund. Gerald Freedman had directed from the start, and Donald Saddler choreographed in 1975. In 1976, the two gave the show its first full-scale production, now on Broadway with a cast including some from St. Clement's and new ringers. Barry Bostwick had the best opportunity of his career as the debonair footpad Jamie Lockhart, exploiting the vocal riffs that country delights in, and Rhonda Coullet (heroine) and Barbara Lang (mean old thing) were the women leads in an enchantingly crazy romance.

Who made the rule that country scores written for Broadway bring out the best in their authors? Those unfamiliar with the sound assume it to be a monotonous jukebox of love laments and odes to rustic trivia. But *The Robber Bridegroom*'s opening is a concept-setter as adept as anything that Hal Prince ever okayed for production. "The Pricklepear Bloom" sets off Barbara Lang's villainess' spite in words, music, and even orchestration, as the fiddles hit one whining chord too many after each verse, too appalled to keep time. "Deeper in the Woods," a piece for true lovers (who speak) and chorus (who set the scene), sounds like a debauched Christmas carol.

It is as if the entire score has been skewed, not by the country style but by the authors' determination to set Welty's bizarre fable to music—really *set* it, not just lend it some of Broadway's venerable know-how. And yet nothing could put this show over, neither enthusiastic reviews nor a PR flurry when Bostwick fell during a rope trick in one of the last rehearsals and had to play the opening with his arm in a cast. *The Robber Bridegroom* lasted four months. Still, its unique savor will keep it from dating, and it may well please Broadway on a future visit.

At least we have exhausted the flops and reached the few hits. They are not an overwhelmingly impressive group. *I Love My Wife* (1977) is a beach-read musical, a time-passer. The subject was, as one song put it, "Love Revolution": swinging. As in the 1969 film *Bob & Carol & Ted & Alice*, two married couples who are longtime friends end up all in bed together. And do nothing.

The film was a little dangerous in its exploration of the love revolution's new etiquette, as when Natalie Wood excitedly introduced her husband, Robert Culp, to the man with whom she had just cheated on him. Michael Stewart's book for the musical never got near anything so risky, though it was based on a French play entitled *Viens Chez Moi, J'habite Chez une Copine*, which is, roughly, *Come Do a Threesome With Me and My Girl Friend*.

The musical was also almost off-Broadway in size, with a cast of eight but only four speaking roles in any true sense. (The other four were musicians and choristers.) James Naughton and Joanna Gleason were one couple and Lenny Baker and Ilene Graff the other, differentiated mainly in Naughton's alpha male and Baker's avid nerd. At the climax, as the two men were about to get into bed with the women for their love revolution, Baker made a play-within-a-play of undressing—fastidiously smoothing and folding, blowing into and then delicately rolling up his socks, de-pantsing as if skinning a peach. When it was Naughton's turn, he kicked off his shoes and instantly butterflied out of pants and shirt, the ever-ready man.

With so small a story and so tight a space to tell it in, the score, by Cy Coleman to Stewart's lyrics, invested heavily in incidental novelty. "A Mover's Life" was attached to the action only on the technicality that Baker played a mover. The second-act opening, "Hey There, Good Times," for the four extras, was excrescent. Even the one outstanding number, "Someone Wonderful I Missed," was presented outside the narrative, with one of the four extras pretending to be a Nashville radio announcer as Gleason and Graff took up the hand-helds with the trailing wires to sing a tuneful country spoof.

Gene Saks directed to make the most of the material, and some of the book was funny, as when Naughton, Graff, and Baker play the truth game:

NAUGHTON: Ask me anything. The more intimate, the better.
BAKER: Were you ever in the Boy Scouts?
NAUGHTON: That's not intimate.
BAKER: It depends on the scoutmaster.

Still, *I Love My Wife* won its two-year success because it uttered the S word without having any: as kids ring a doorbell and then run off giggling.

The Best Little Whorehouse in Texas (1978) tackled its sexual theme straight on, and in an odd form unlike the neatly packaged *I Love My Wife*. The latter show leaves ends dangling in its unintegrated numbers and stereotyped characters, but it's a tidy piece all the same. *Whorehouse* is messy, earthy, and individual. It's authentic, like it or not.

Four Texans made it: Carol Hall wrote the score and Larry L. King and Peter Masterson the book, from King's magazine piece about a bordello that flourished more or less openly. Masterson and Tommy Tune staged it in yet another drab unit set, though Tune found amusing things to do with it. From the first, there was debate among the communicants about whether or not to include "Whorehouse" in the show's title. Masterson figured that they might as well let the public know what the subject matter was right up front, if only to discourage professional innocents.

That typifies the work's honesty. There is no question that the four Texans gave Broadway a healthy dose of Lone Star lingo and attitudes; and the whorehouse was a whorehouse. But many of the things that one takes for granted in just about any musical were missing, because they didn't belong and also because the production team didn't include an old pro who knows the ropes and fears leaving them untied. So there was no love plot, for instance involving one of the house girls and a local boy. Even the two good-guy leads, the whorehouse madam (Carlin Glynn) and the sheriff (Henderson Forsythe), didn't make a love plot. There is strong sentiment between them from some time in the past, yes; but it's nothing formal. Of course, when Universal filmed the project in 1982, it made sure that Dolly Parton and Burt Reynolds were romantic intimates in present time: because it's the usual thing to do.

There is nothing usual about the stage *Whorehouse*. At times, its nonconformist approach creates a flaw, for example when waitress Doatsey Mae (Susan Mansur) sings an establishing piece in which she assures us that there's more to her than the Blue Plate Special. Mansur's easy belt soared into soprano range over a plaintive solo violin, a telling effect. So confidential and outgiving, "Doatsey Mae" really takes one's attention. But then this character vanishes from the narrative and reappears but once, in passing.

It's a rare error. Generally, *Whorehouse* makes good use of its odd construction, as in the downbeat ending, in which the corrupt governor (Jay Garner) and television snitch (Clint Allmon) mime Pecksniffian self-congratulation at having closed down the whorehouse. The onstage orchestra strikes up a reprise of the opening number, "Twenty Fans." It's lively music, but we feel amusingly unsatisfied: the bad guys won.

This was an amateurs' show, one might say; that's praise. Hall's previous musicals were unproduced, Masterson was ignorant of musicals, and King hated them. Only Tune was oriented, which explains why the writing of the show is strange but its staging very self-assured. *Whorehouse* ran 1,639 performances (including a return engagement after a two-month jaunt to Boston), playing to an audience of more than the usual confirmed local theatregoers. As with *Grease*, another show of rare flavor that started in the Eden Theatre and moved uptown, *Whorehouse* appealed to folks who, like Larry L. King, don't like the musicals that the rest of us do.

One reason why is the show's abundant atmosphere—the colorful idioms, the knee-jerk suspicion of anyone with habits different from one's own, the heavy overlay of religion. Consider this radio interview with a cheerleader during football halftime:

> SPORTSCASTER: I know that you girls have high ideals and look up to the people who embody the qualities you most admire. Could you tell us quickly your three all-time Great American Heroes?
> CHEERLEADER: (caught off-guard) Oh, Jesus!
> SPORTSCASTER: That's one, now name two more.

One expects a country score to match the country doings, though Hall's songs are too pointed to suit a country concert. Hearing the music to "The Sidestep," one might assume that it's a merry dance number; it is in fact a piece of political chicanery, as the governor fields the press' questions by not answering them. "Good Old Girl" is the sheriff's summation of his feelings for the madam—and this *could* stand country airplay without a word of contextual explanation. Yet the show turns it into a kind of plot number, once again defying the musical-comedy handbook by giving it to the men's chorus after the sheriff starts it. As they sweetly pour it out, the sheriff phones his good old girl to tell her that he has to close her down.

Any other show would present that scene in dialogue, so we can hear how it affects their relationship. But it is Hall's point that "Good Old Girl" tells us all we need to know. These are two unusually well-adjusted people who have the secret of high-quality survival: anything you can't conquer, you get over.

Larry L. King and Carol Hall spelled Henderson Forsythe and Susan Mansur on their vacations, and *I Love My Wife* found its replacements easily enough, bringing the Smothers Brothers back from the 1960s to play opposite Barbara Sharma and Janie Sell, then turning the show black. The next of our three hits was also easy to recast. It may well be one of the easiest hit musicals to put on in any case: only two characters, with a chorus of six and a simple set plan of projections and pieces. Yet this is a front-and-center show, not a *Park* or *Rainbow Jones*. How did David Merrick miss this one? You produce it on a *Waiting For Godot* budget and it yields *Hello, Dolly!* profits. It runs over two and a half years and is done all over the world and everyone loves it.

It's *They're Playing Our Song* (1979), with a Marvin Hamlisch–Carole Bayer Sager score and Neil Simon's book. Boy Meets Girl becomes Composer Meets Lyricist: and that's the whole show, because he loves and then gets her. Nothing else occurs, except Simon's most adept series of running gags, especially about her possessive ex–boy friend, Leon, and her crazy clothes, costume leftovers from various theatrical productions:

> SONIA: (referring to her dress) This is from *The Cherry Orchard*.
> VERNON: I don't know that store.
> SONIA: It's not a store. It's a play by Chekhov. My girl friend wore it . . . for thirty-eight performances and six previews.
> VERNON: You're lucky they didn't go out on tour.

So, later, when she arrives one day and twenty minutes late and rushes into his bathroom to vomit:

> VERNON: (into tape machine) She is wearing another one of those dresses that seem to cry out, "Enter Olga Petrovka from stage right."

And here's the twist:

> VERNON: Those look like normal clothes. Where'd you get normal clothes?
> SONIA: I have a friend who does Geritol commercials.

And here's the zinger:

> VERNON: (who has finally met Leon) He even remembered what you wore that first day he saw you running across the campus.
> SONIA: I can't remember. What was it?
> VERNON: A naval officer's uniform.
> SONIA: Of course. *Mister Roberts*. I was late for dress rehearsal.

The best running gag is that the two are supremely unsuited because Vernon (Robert Klein) is impatient with eccentricity, and Sonia (Lucie Arnaz) is eccentric. To be fair, she doesn't deserve the happy ending, because she cultivates exasperating phobias rather than trying to conquer them. It's that old case of what would be intolerable in life playing on stage as hysterically funny.

What greatly helps is the score, a highly enjoyable one. Sager's lyrics are almost terrible, filled with false rhymes and the cliché attitudes that cheap pop music run on. But Hamlisch's contribution to the nine numbers is good old-fashioned tunesmithing. None of the songs became a standard, because very little on Broadway can land on the national level anymore. But they have that reassuring "What show is that from?" friendliness. "Fallin'" is a touching ballad, "Workin' It Out" dancey pop, "If He Really Knew Me" is another touching ballad, and it continues so till one almost hopes for a dud just to break the pattern. Then Act Two starts, "When You're in My Arms" cuts into an irresistible Latin swing, and one wonders why there wasn't more of this in Hamlisch's edgy, jagged music to *A Chorus Line*. The score to *They're Playing Our Song* is a little like an evening full of "What I Did For Love."

Two characters handling an entire score might have led to irritation in the house. But someone among the authors, and director Robert Moore, and choreographer Patricia Birch thought up the "voices"—his three and her three, filling out the pair's psychology but also their vocal lines while lending a dancey variety to the stage pictures. When Vernon goes into the hospital with a broken leg, Sonia brings him a toy piano. "It's a Steinway grand," she explains. "Someone left it out in the rain." This leads to the last of the show's touching ballads, "Fill in the Words," in which the piano notes supply the line he can't utter. (Yet.) Amusingly, his three voices appear, all in hospital gowns like his, all playing toy pianos.

The best of this chapter's few hits was a financial failure. However, it ran over a year and felt like a hit, and it remains for many theatregoers one of the outstanding musical comedies of the decade, and even of all time. Unlike so many seventies shows that played as hapless miscellanies of unruly parts, *On the Twentieth Century* (1978) was a very stylish event. From Nicholas Gaetano's poster art in creamy pastels framed by skyscraper chrome, through the smoke that blew out of the locomotive show curtain during the train-trip overture, to the unseen movie-musical chorus that rained from heaven as the curtain fell, *On the Twentieth Century* was smart, dressy, and zany in every element, burlesque as Gesamtkunstwerk. Even the music was art deco.

Hal Prince directed, in an atypical foray out of the Higher Musical, but musical-comedy masters Betty Comden and Adolph Green wrote the book and lyrics, to Cy Coleman's music. The source material claims a peculiar history. Charles B. Milholland wrote a play called *The Napoleon of Broadway* about a flamboyant producer and his former protégée, now a movie star, taking the deluxe express from Chicago to New York. Milholland had worked as a press agent for producer Morris Gest, a Broadway Character whom everyone would detect in the producer character, Oscar Jaffee. A number of other producers, primarily David Belasco, had had tempestuous relationships with actresses they had discovered, presented, and acrimoniously parted from. This would add to the *à clef* fun.

Producer-director Jed Harris optioned the piece, contracting for a complete rewrite from Ben Hecht and Charles MacArthur, authors of Harris' hit *The Front Page*. Surely these pair added a touch of Harris into the character of Oscar Jaffee. For if Morris Gest was flamboyant, what to call the evil, scheming, exhibitionistic Harris, on whom Laurence Olivier modeled his Richard III? Hecht and MacArthur never finished their rewrite of Milholland, however, and now the option had passed to George Abbott and Philip Dunning, authors of another Jed Harris hit, *Broadway*. With two writers now producing *The Napoleon of Broadway*, the script was completed somehow or other, and the retitled *Twentieth Century* was a hit of the 1932–33 season. Hollywood filmed it in 1934 with John Barrymore and Carole Lombard, Barrymore pulling off one of his greatest hoaxes as, probably, a combination of every theatre psycho he had ever met; but now Oscar Jaffee was indelibly associated with Barrymore and *his* flamboyance.

So the musical darkened John Cullum's hair and gave him a mustache: Barrymore. Madeline Kahn was Lily Garland, his find, star, and love. The role of a religious fanatic, heretofore male, was refashioned for Imogene Coca. Kevin Kline played Kahn's brilliantined gigolo with a spoofy physicality, for example flying about their drawing room at the sight of Kahn in a negligee as if he were a leaf borne on winds of awe. George Lee Andrews played Max Jacobs, Jaffee's former office boy and now nemesis, a successful producer himself; and George Coe and Dean Dittman were

Jaffee's faithful retainers. Robin Wagner accepted the challenge of fitting a moving train into the St. James Theatre, Larry Fuller staged the musical numbers, and Hershy Kay, whose orchestrations have brightened many a so-so evening in these pages, filled out the roster.

Some shows fall because some of the team envisioned *this* show while others were working on *that* show. On this project, everyone was working on the same piece, a burlesque. It mocked show-biz pretension (Hollywood materialism but also thespian pomposity); it mocked fancy music and silly music; it mocked hypocrites and true believers; it mocked racial stereotypes, amateur writers, train trips, and every musical that ever lived.

It mocked with expertise. Yes, the overture simulated a train's start-up, acceleration, and voyage, entirely with themes from the score, for instance stoking up on a four-note cell drawn from "Together" and gathering speed by running themes from "I've Got It All" and the "Sign, Lily, Sign" Sextet concurrently. The score in general tended toward operetta, but parodistically. It wasn't your father's Sigmund Romberg: it was Cy Coleman's. It was even Robin Wagner's Romberg, when everyone in the show learned that Imogene Coca was an escaped asylum inmate and the stage was filled with a set designer's version of what Coleman's music was doing: funning up old show biz. As Coca ran through the train posting her "Repent for the time is at hand" stickers and everyone else ran after her, Cy Coleman and Robin Wagner got a duet out of silent-movie chase music and thisa-thata railroad visuals: two miniature trains passing each other; the great wheels of the engine plowing the iron road as Coca climbs down to slap another sticker on; and Coca spread-eagled on the locomotive's front, the whole thing in a "How do they *do* that?" defiance of the physical limitations of the stage.

There had to be pauses amid the craziness, so the public could relax and the action reprogram its energies. An obvious moment would be "Our Private World," in which Cullum and Kahn could admit their feelings for each other in intertwined soliloquies, each singing alone, inches apart in separate drawing rooms. With a Schubertian purity of melody, much of it built on the most basic harmony, the song is a kind of serious relief, the opposite of a clowns' scene in Shakespeare.

Similarly, Kahn had a solo in the middle of that comic Sextet in which Cullum and his team urge her to sign a contract to play the Magdalen in a religious pageant while Kline tries to stop her, going through a series of pratfalls and contortions as the others foil him. Again, the slapstick matches the drollery in the music.

But something more was needed at this point, to tell us exactly how Lily reacts to the contract—really, to Jaffee himself. Her solo, "Together," was given earlier in the show to Jaffee and, mainly, the chorus, as a goof on the American idolatry of celebrities. Now it is reclaimed as a worried love song, because, after all, she has *escaped* from the theatre, escaped from the manipulative Jaffee, who is Morris Gest, Richard III, and John Barrymore rolled into one. Ultimately, of course, the heroine can't get out of her romance any more than Don Murray could get out of *his* musical in *Smith*.

The bulk of this score is comic pastiche operetta, of course. The very absurdity of the tale, with the flop thespian railing at Hollywood fakery even as he conceives his own phony pageant and the fanatic slapping stickers of religious exhortation on everything, called for absurdity in the music. As always, Coleman legitimized parody as expression in its own right, utterly Jaffee-izing Cullum with a "hero defies the world" establishing song in "I Rise Again" and a hat-and-cane eleven o'clocker, "The Legacy." Kahn made her entrance in flashback, as a piano accompanist destroying an audition of "The Indian Maiden's Lament," one of those Gitche Gumee rhapsodies with the rolled chords and yodeling melismas, the bane of the amateur musicale during the Second Age. Then, under Cullum's prodding, Kahn let down her hair and tore off her geek outfit to stand revealed in French tricolor silk with sword and shield. Robin Wagner set her against a cardboard crowd in black and white and a vast silver Arc de Triomphe for "Veronique," which might be the best set of lyrics that Comden and Green ever wrote. Moreover, as the flashy characters need flashy music, that music needs flashy singing, and Kahn's role was studded with berserk high notes.

Perhaps the best of the spoofs was "Babette," in which Cullum's Christian epic vies for Kahn's attention with George Lee Andrews' latest option, a play by Somerset Maugham. Andrews pitches it to Kahn in lines whose avid inanity would occur only to Comden and Green:

MAX: Half-brittle, half-sardonic, half-tragic . . .
LILY: Yes, yes . . . three halves . . . bigger than life!

Script in hand, Kahn conjures up the Maugham play. It treats "the Mayfair set," for whom elegance is a mania and insincerity a drug. The stage crowds with society snakes, including Babette's husband, Rodney, and her lover, Nigel. A confrontational *scène à faire* appears imminent—but a spotlight enthralls Kahn as Hollywood Bible music peals out. Cullum's religious show and the Maugham play now do battle, while Coe, Dittman, and Coca wander through the Mayfair crowd in *Greatest Story Ever Told* getups, the daffiest touch of the evening. Even Cullum shows up thus, Kahn warding him off with the Maugham script as one raises the cross at a vampire.

Some thought of *On the Twentieth Century* as *Kiss Me, Kate* on a train. But the earlier show, despite its marvelous score, mixes a messy chowder of Shakespeare, operetta, and vaudeville, while the later show is above all consistent. John Cullum's entrance, for example, was a *train* entrance, a *comic* entrance: as Coe and Dittman reveal that he must have failed to make it on board, we see Cullum behind them, *outside*, climbing along the window line. He bangs on the car and, as they turn, his hat blows away in the wind.

In fact, Cullum played a tremendous Oscar Jaffee, revealing a satirist's slyness that none could have expected from *Shenandoah*'s Charlie Anderson. Cullum's "I close the iron door!" when (of course temporarily) renouncing impedient vassals, or even just his pronunciation of the word "dirrrrrected," made a tasty study in the higher theatrics.

For her part, Madeline Kahn found Lily an exhausting workout. She missed a number of performances, luckily with Judy Kaye as her understudy. But Prince—exasperated by a long battle with Kahn through rehearsals and previews—now insisted that she give place to the dazzling Kaye, who took over nine weeks after the opening. While both Cullum and Kahn were nominated for Tonys, only Cullum won, presumably because of Kahn's bad PR. *Twentieth*'s producers were so angry with her that when the song folio came out, its printing of the show's poster reflected the new billing, and the photos presented only Kaye, as if expunging Kahn from memory.

But all this tells us how good a Lily Kahn was. Prince exasperates easily, and he would not have waited all that time to replace Kahn if he had thought the show could do without her. In truth, Kaye sang the role better, with that free glory that she exults in on high, that "operetta is *yes*" sound in her voice. But Kahn was a uniquely enchanting imp.

The show went on to London in 1980, with two songs cut for tighter playing and Julia McKenzie not only reveling in but expanding Lily's supersonic vocal range. The show was not a hit there; but then, it was not a hit here, even at 453 performances. Nor has it attained classic status.

However: its adherents look upon it as typifying the intelligent fun that the musical now has lost. Writers used to be really smart, and their playing field was the land of joyful madness—again, Jacques Offenbach's *genre primitif et gai*. That combination of brilliance and glee makes *On the Twentieth Century* something like the last great musical comedy: one in which the authors, the stars, and the production team are working on the genius level. One doesn't have to be smart to write *The Full Monty* or *Mamma Mia!*.

13

Evolution Papa

THREE "DON'T" MUSICALS

Doctor Jazz (1975) didn't close out of town, but only because it didn't go out of town. Like so many seventies shows without advance-sale insurance, it tried out in New York. The marquee names were leads Bobby Van, Lola Falana, Lillian Hayman, and Peggy Pope, the more or less sole author, Buster Davis, and director-choreographer Donald McKayle, who was superseded before the opening by John Berry, billed as having "supervised." The action concerned the dissemination of black music in the early twentieth century, and the desperation among the members of the production team recalled many an out-of-town implosion of the past. Like *Mata Hari* and *Breakfast at Tiffany's*, *Dr. Jazz* was a big show with complicated problems that no one could solve.

Doctor Jazz folded in 5 performances, but it did have one really good thing in it, unfortunately not an element crucial for success. It offered spectacular dance and incidental arrangements (and orchestrations) by our unsung hero of the decade, Luther Henderson. Because so much of this backstager about the rise of jazz was made of showcase instrumentals and dance numbers, Henderson had the job of keeping all that ragtime, Dixieland, and blues authentic in ring but seventies in appeal. He brought it off so superbly that while *Doctor Jazz* always behaved like a bomb, it sounded like a smash hit.

Not that Davis' music and lyrics were all that good. They did at least jive in with the obscure old tunes with which he peppered his own work— a title song by King Oliver and Howard Melrose; "Cleopatra Had a Jazz Band," by J. L. Morgan and Jack Coogan; or even just "I Love It," by Harry Von Tilzer and E. Ray Goetz. Any theatregoer who failed to examine the program would have had no idea that the score was a mélange, though he would surely have noticed the lack of story and character numbers.

The real problem lay in the book, which like the score was written by Davis with (here uncredited) contributions from others. The score never accomplished anything, but it was an earful. The book simply never accomplished anything. Bobby Van played a trumpeter who is the gigolo of theatre manager Peggy Pope. Hayman keeps a brothel but has an innocent niece, Lola Falana. She can dance. Van wants to present her to the world—and somewhere in all the jazz playing and jazz dancing and even jazz brothelkeeping, and in the traveling from New Orleans through Chicago to New York, we are supposed to discover the elements of American Music.

In fact, all that *Doctor Jazz* gave us was clumsy indications, constant "onstage" numbers, and unmotivated decisions. The few character songs that did turn up struck generical poses that, in the chaos of the book, came off as non sequiturs. Van's "Anywhere the Wind Blows" is meant as the silhouette of the rootless hero. But Van wasn't rootless. He was scriptless.

Van himself was a problem. His approximation of the lovable rogue depended upon not characterization but on rapid delivery of lines so lightly learned that he kept stepping on the other actors' speeches or simply threw them off. This is the kind of performance appropriate for nightclub joshing, not for portrayal in a book musical.

Like much of the production team, Van had been involved in the *No, No, Nanette* revival, playing opposite Helen Gallagher. For some reason—I suspect Gallagher's intolerance of unprofessional behavior—Van wasn't as irritating on that outing. In *Doctor Jazz*, however, he had the charm of a snake-oil salesman. Nor could his part save him, obviously, for Davis never decided whether this white man was an enthusiast of black music or simply hot for Lola Falana's character, Edna Mae. Was the show metaphorical, or just another Boy Meets Girl? Even if Van wasn't meant to represent anything, who was he at all? Other characters called him "Dr. Jazz," yet he seldom took part in the music. Of course, he would be presented as irresistible to women. When he wants to become Falana's manager, Hayman vociferously resists:

VAN: You got it all wrong, it's not what you're thinking.
HAYMAN: It's not what I'm thinking that worries me. It's what *you're* thinking!

VAN: Come on, I'm not thinking nothing like that.

HAYMAN: Oh, let's see—you're not blind, you're not paralyzed, and you're not dead. *That's* what you're thinking!

VAN: You got a one-track mind.

HAYMAN: And you stay off that track!

Wasn't this cheesy stuff old in the 1940s? And do you see now why some of us find it bizarre that some critics weren't appreciating how far above this drivel stood the books of the Sondheim shows?

The irony of it is that *Doctor Jazz* was not a bad idea. An idea is not a book, of course, and there are usually more good ideas for shows than there are good writers of books. Joseph Stein is a good writer of books. With Will Glickman, he created a classic instance of the efficiently narrated, very funny show with a strong emotional foundation in an original work, *Plain and Fancy* (1955). On his own, in adaptation, Stein wrote one of the best of the more serious modern shows, albeit still very funny and with strong emotional content, *Fiddler on the Roof* (1964). Stein was the principal consultant in the attempt to turn *Doctor Jazz* around during its previews; surely he saw the lack of definition in the script. Van was not defined, his interest in Falana was not defined, and the work's attitude to the white management of black music was not defined. Why didn't Stein define them?

In fact, *Doctor Jazz* was so incoherent that it had no ending. At a certain point, Van was directed to shrug wryly, toss his trumpet in the air, and catch it. And there the curtain fell. "Nothing happened at the Winter Garden Theatre on Wednesday night," Clive Barnes wrote. "*Doctor Jazz* opened."

Stein wrote the book of our next show as well, this one adapted from a movie. *Beware movies!* Some pour themselves onto the stage, but others simply will not change form. Remember, a musical sets emphatic punctuation into the action at the end of each number. If the numbers don't further the action—or if they further it incorrectly, for example by calling attention to a character the audience doesn't care about—the work is crippled.

Making a musical of Marcel Pagnol's 1938 film *The Baker's Wife* was not a smart idea, because it has very little plot. The baker loses his wife to a cute young guy, the baker stops baking, and his hungry fellow villagers find the wife and bring her home. That would scarcely get Edna

St. Vincent Millay through a mannered one-acter, let alone provision a David Merrick musical with a score by Stephen Schwartz. However, the show that put Merrick onto the roster of Big Broadway Producers was *Fanny*, an adaptation of Marcel Pagnol cinema. There was logic in the choice, if only to David Merrick.

He was not the first to option the property, and other writers, too, had flirted with it over the years, for the movie is so full of picturesque detail that it doesn't *seem* plotless. Inspiring the great actor Raimu to give the baker a simplicity akin to holiness, and focusing on the marquis, the curé, and the schoolteacher as exponents of village attitudes, Pagnol created unique cinema. This is not easy when one is a thespian who regards movies as contemptible, as Pagnol was. He resolutely refused to adopt the grammar peculiar to film, the narrative intensity of editing, of the long shot and close-up. Pagnol wasn't making movies. He was filming plays. Even so, critic Richard Roud has called Pagnol "a precursor of neo-realism" because *The Baker's Wife* does anticipate filming in natural locations, emphasizing the social realities of ordinary folk, and even, where possible, casting non-actors to play themselves.

No wonder so many have sensed a latent musical in *La Femme du Boulanger*. So much of it is effervescent and life-affirming: isn't that what musical comedy is? Topol, the Israeli actor who led *Fiddler on the Roof* in London and on screen, was to play the baker, with Carole Demas as his wife and Kurt Peterson as the chauffeur she runs off with. (In the movie, he's a shepherd.) The three leading villagers were marquis Keene Curtis, curé David Rounds, and teacher Timothy Jerome. Joseph Hardy directed and Dan Siretta choreographed, and as six months of tryout (in 1976) unfolded, Merrick began The Firings. These were mainly of Topol and Demas, and Hardy and Siretta, replaced by Paul Sorvino and Patti LuPone, and John Berry and Robert Tucker. But eventually even orchestrator Thomas Pierson was replaced, by Don Walker. Yes, that must be why *The Baker's Wife* was failing: the orchestrations.

Failing it certainly was, and this one did close out of town, having played Los Angeles and San Francisco for the Civic Light Opera, then the St. Louis Muni, Boston, and Washington, D.C. Then Sorvino, LuPone, Peterson, and cast member Teri Ralston recorded the bulk of the score, and that recording is why *The Baker's Wife* is the only out-of-town disaster that keeps getting performed. Other titles that died in tryout have been recorded, of course, even staged here and there. But *The Baker's Wife* actually got a major West End mounting, in 1989, because director Trevor Nunn kept hearing songs from it in auditions, and the songs were unusually good.

So that is why *The Baker's Wife* lives on in a way that *Prettybelle* will not: as one of the decade's outstanding scores. The three leads' numbers in particular are wonderful character studies, but the sheer abundance of melody is what attracts the ear. Like Harold Rome in *Fanny*, Schwartz outdid his earlier work in composing Provence into his music. The framing philosophy-of-life number, Teri Ralston's "Chanson," is sung partly in French; and "Plain and Simple," the baker's recipe for bread, has the pipe-and-drum flavor of the Provençal *tambourin*.

Still, most of the score is pure Broadway, and very much more traditional in style than the whiz-kid sleight-of-hand spots that Schwartz filled for *The Magic Show*. Those numbers trick the rhythm and rock the beat. *The Baker's Wife* numbers are Golden Age, as if by a kid who grew up wanting to write shows that Rodgers and Hammerstein would recommend to their friends. The number that establishes the baker, "Merci, Madame," occurs just after he and his wife step into their new home. Note the cue lines:

THE BAKER: Do you really like it?
HIS WIFE: I really like it.
THE BAKER: (to their cat) Did you hear that? She likes it.

Rather ordinary conversation, isn't it?—except the melody begins on the third line, the song cutting into the dialogue because it's time. This practice has been in use for decades, but only the best writers know about it. Moreover, the melody itself is first-class, a sparkling polka with delightful lyrics that instantly give us the baker's character: charming, inventive, considerate. He'll hurt easily, however—and his bride is so unsuitably youthful that the villagers took her for his daughter. Her great number is "Meadowlark," which rivals *Lolita, My Love*'s "Sur les Quais" for the title of Best Song From An Out-Of-Town Closing. But her most telling number is a duet with the chauffeur, "Endless Delights," a self-replicating waltz that has the sound of guiltless marathon sex. They're young and beautiful, so they belong together and the music knows it.

So does the music of "Any Day Now Day," the baker's drunken insistence that his wife's return is imminent. The thought is fronted by yet another polka; but this one's a lie. The sad truth is that the baker cannot give his wife anything but his insufficient love, and the odd truth is that this proves sufficient after all. Tiring of her heartless sex, she returns; the baker storms a bit—a formality—and forgives. There is one last thing: together they will light the oven for the next day's baking, and as they start to, our *commère* Teri Ralston appears, to launch another airing of "Chanson." She knew it all along.

The villagers of course have their numbers. The movie dotes upon a dispute between the curé and the schoolteacher about whether or not Joan of Arc *thought* she heard or *actually* heard voices, and Schwartz adopted this for "If It Wasn't For You." We might also have expected the aroma of the baker's first working day to inspire a chorus of thanksgiving, "Bread." As the tunestack varies with each major staging, sometimes the villagers have more to do and sometimes less. The less the better, probably, because their music isn't on the high level of the leads' music; and of course a parade of numbers by people we tire of quickly only emphasizes their irrelevance.

On the other hand, doesn't the show need them to fill out the slim scenario? Trevor Nunn must have thought so, for the London production was overrun with villagers. Alun Armstrong, the ruthlessly child-abusing Yorkshire schoolmaster in the Royal Shakespeare Company's *Nicholas Nickleby* (which Nunn co-directed), rendered a heartbreaking baker. He was a genuine naïf, so bewildered by his wife's betrayal—and so drunk in "Any Day Now Day" that while staggering about the crowded tavern scene he went flying toward the orchestra pit, only to be pulled back at the last possible moment. Nunn's then wife, Sharon Lee Hill, was excellent as the errant Geneviève. In fact, the whole thing was excellent, and it closed quickly and suddenly.

It would appear that the lack of plot is going to haunt this score for all time. *Doctor Jazz* had a lack of plot, too; but *Doctor Jazz* was also utterly incoherent, a book musical without a book. *The Baker's Wife* has a book—by now, it has several—but little action. Worse, revivals seem reluctant to shave the wordy dialogue down. At Goodspeed's second stage in 2002, the work dragged and sagged even with "Plain and Simple" and "Endless Delights" cut. Lenny Wolpe, Christiane Noll, and Adam Monley headed a fine cast (with an especially attractive commère from Gay Marshall). But all that talking vitiates the singing.

Our third "don't" musical has less plot than the other two, being something like *The Baker's Wife* without the chauffeur. This one, too, closed out of town: *The Prince of Grand Street* (1978). Bob Merrill wrote all of it—book, music, and lyrics—to be a vehicle for Robert Preston as another of his lovable rogues. After Harold Hill, Preston's Pancho Villa, Ben Franklin, and Mack Sennett were all real-life figures. Yet even while changing his look for the swarthy Villa and the ancient Franklin, never did Preston alter his plastique or vocal delivery. *The Prince of Grand Street*, then, marked Preston's most bizarre defiance of verisimilitude. For while he returned to playing an invention, it was as one Nathan Rashumsky, a star actor of the Yiddish theatre of New York's Lower East Side in 1908.*

This is *Funny Girl* territory; Preston's Rashumsky was not unlike the Fanny Brice that Mary Martin would have played. Yes, they asked her first. Yet *The Prince of Grand Street* has more Jewish flavor than *Funny Girl*, more even than *Fiddler on the Roof*. The cultural background and the entire dramatis personae (except, in one scene, Mark Twain) were Jewish, whereas *Funny Girl* treated the very mixed world of American show biz and *Fiddler* included some of the shtetl's Russian Orthodox neighbors. Moreover, Merrill's music is ethnic in the extreme, digging deeply into cultural memory in plaintive minor keys.

Casting the rest of the show was tricky, for if everyone but Preston has a heavy accent, the show becomes preposterous. So some of the players had sort-of accents. Preston's romantic vis-à-vis, Neva Small (one of the youthful singing sensations of Merrill's *Henry, Sweet Henry*), employed a strangely intense delivery of the dialogue with no accent, Preston's severest critic (Werner Klemperer) had a slight German accent, and only Sam Levene, as Neva Small's grandfather, used a full-blooded urban Jewish accent.

Levene had an odd role, as he never took part in the action. Playing a street peddler, he simply occupied the stage "in one" during set changes to joke around at the audience and converse with Small and, at one

---

* Technically, Rashumsky was not entirely an invention, having been loosely modeled on Boris Thomashefsky, a leading actor-manager of that place and time. Still, Preston's Villa, Franklin, and Sennett, presented by name, were bound to *some* historical illusion. With Nathan Rashumsky, Merrill was free to improvise.

point, with Preston. Levene's solo bits were set pieces, as if Merrill had been saving up little Jewish presentations all through his career and now wanted to spend them, one after another. In one such, Levene and Small had a little talk made entirely of questions ("How should I feel?"), and in another, Levene marveled at a sudden death in the neighborhood:

> LEVENE: You remember Epstein the grocer? Sure, you do. A skinny, tiny fella with a crooked back? When he walked, one leg dragged. *Gone!* Just like that! (Incredulous) He was a *picture of health*!

In fact, no one in the cast had a lead in any real sense except Preston and Small. Below Preston's headline and Small's featured billing, the poster heralded eleven players' names. Aside from the non-singing Levene and Klemperer, this group included a number of acting singers, such as Bernice Massi, Richard Muenz, and Walter Charles. Yet none of them was in the score. Every song went to Preston, Small, and the chorus, except for an occasional short solo during the three onstage performances at Rashumsky's Grand Tivoli Theatre: *Romeo and Juliet*, *Young Avrom Lincoln*, and *Huckleberry Finn*.

This was because Merrill had written a two-person story, and there was no place for any other character to sing in it. Perhaps Merrill wanted the ensemble to form a generalized background for his tale of a man resisting his age, an actor refusing to retire. Small is far too young for him, and too trusting and honest as well. He's a scoundrel. That was to be the show's conflict, along with the pressure on Preston to choose more appropriate roles.

These turned out to be makeweights. The show's appeal lay entirely in the Preston charm as he dodges and pretends. It's Harold Hill taking Small to a weekend in Atlantic City, where he not only seduces but cheats on her. She runs, he finds her, and he insists that they stay together:

> LEAH: (excited) Will you marry me?
> NATHAN: Yes.
> LEAH: (more excited) When?
> NATHAN: Eventually.

Merrill's score was much better than his book, even if limited largely to the love plot and ensemble numbers. "Do I Make You Happy?" was Preston's big ballad, but Small had an arresting establishing number in "A Girl With Too Much Heart" and, much later, the very dramatic "What Do I Do Now?" In fact, the score accidentally made Small the show's protagonist. For instance, she had the intensely yearning "A Place in the World," which she sings from the wings while watching Preston performing. Moments before, Merrill had been goofing on Yiddish theatre, having Preston's Avrom Lincoln make a campaign promise to "turn the state of Illinois into a homeland for the Jews." But now he has Small singing over the play's dialogue—over even Preston's lines—as if distinguishing Small's feelings as something stirring and ingenuous amid the hilarity. It's hard for us to leap from Harold Hill in Atlantic City to this. What wonderful music! But the story is cockeyed. "I always think there's a band," the Music Man tells us. Yet now it's Small who thinks there's a band. Whose story is this?

Remember the failure on which the creators later realize that they were each working on different ideas of the same show? That happened here: Merrill *alone* was writing several different shows. And it is our loss, for the score is never less than melodious and sometimes brilliantly theatrical. "Sew a Button" found Small working in the garment industry, surrounded by women singing a dark-hued waltz with a socialist undertow in the lyrics. Into this came Small, to sing another of her yearning ballads against the women's chorus in quodlibet style. It's superb music-making, but it confuses us. The working women seem so unhappy, so importunate—are we supposed to worry about them, too?

Where did Preston fit into the music? He had the charm stuff, of course, including his absurd manifestation as Huckleberry Finn. But think of Preston's songs in *The Music Man*, how well they travel between his con-man surface and the attitudes below. He had nothing comparable in *The Prince of Grand Street,* though one number, "Look at Me," suggests the darker show that Merrill might have written for a character he so obviously adores.

"Look at Me" begins as Preston's solo, then takes in Small and the entire singing ensemble, and finally breaks into a dance that ends Act One. It's a magnificent, desperate, insistent plea of a song, one of the very few existential numbers in the musical's history. At least, it seems to be.

It's not entirely clear what the song is about, as it's more a feeling than a direct statement. Still, the needy music clarifies the moment even if the lyrics don't. It's at once terrific and confusing, like so much of this entertaining but hopelessly misconceived show. It makes one wish that Merrill had written the work for production by Hal Prince, for Prince would have guided Merrill to an idealization of his theme. Then Broadway would have seen what a top-rank talent Merrill was.

These three shows, whatever their other qualities, do point up a recurring problem in this era: the loss of professional acumen by professionals. In decades past, we find every major name suffering failure now and again, but not usually through blatantly crucial errors of judgment. We think of certain notable flops by, say, George Abbott—*Beat the Band* and *Barefoot Boy With Cheek*. A Cole Porter flop between *Kiss Me, Kate* and *Can-Can*—*Out Of This World*. A Rodgers and Hart flop—*Higher and Higher*. A Rodgers and Hammerstein flop—*Pipe Dream*. But these weren't "don't" musicals. They simply ended up being not good enough.

The modern-day "don't" musical invented itself after shows that sounded like terrible ideas in advance turned out to be *Oklahoma!* or *West Side Story*. After that, how was anyone to know what a terrible idea was anymore?

True, Buster Davis must have been so eager to be graduated from musical director to author that his ambition blinded him to *Doctor Jazz*'s lack of content. And the magic of that Pagnol film would mesmerize anyone, perhaps. But surely Bob Merrill must have known that his show had only two characters in an uncomfortable *Don Pasquale* romance; and a musical-comedy feeling but a selection of musical-play numbers; and a score tilted to favor the singing lead over the dramatic lead.

Where does one go from here? How about to the worst idea yet? But this one doesn't die on the road. When this one closed, it was the longest-running show in Broadway history.

14

Don't Pop the Head, Cassie!

THREE CLASSICS

In the early-middle 1970s, Ed Kleban performed a number for Lehman Engel's class in writing for the musical theatre—the "BMI Workshop" made familiar in *A Class Act* (2000). Normally a composer-lyricist, Kleban explained that he was writing only lyrics, with a composer not in the class, for a show about applicants for jobs in a Broadway chorus. Before he sang the number "(Everything is beautiful) At the Ballet," Kleban warned the BMI group that, in this show, the action did not consist of conventional audition material. Instead, the auditioners would talk about their personal lives. So the class know-it-all leaned over to the girl on his right and whispered, "That show will run a week."

I was off by fifteen years. But Kleban was not a sharp performer of his own material, especially not a vocal demonstration piece like "Ballet." And doesn't *A Chorus Line* (1975), described in outline before one experiences it, sound like something that is too crazy to run? What do actors' personal lives have to do with their talent?

Of course, what Ed didn't tell us that day is that *A Chorus Line* is, like *Follies*, not to be taken literally. To someone like Michael Bennett, who lived to make theatre and made theatre to live, everything is an audition for—as the show puts it—"somewhere exciting to go." Not everyone will get there: the show closes with some of the hopefuls being chosen and some being rejected. But it is interesting that the metaphorical aspect of *Follies* somehow eludes many of its audience, while fifteen years of ticket buyers managed to take in the symbolic aspect of *A Chorus Line*. Maybe it was because Robin Wagner's set was so clearly unreal. Not abstract, just not possible: black box, white line, magic turning mirrors, and a finale of golden dancers before a sunburst in what is unmistakably a fantasy curtain call. What Ed should have said way back in that BMI class is that the characters speak of their secret hopes because the audition isn't for a job. It's for life.

Of course, Ed Kleban (and his composer partner, Marvin Hamlisch) may not have known that at the time. *A Chorus Line* is famously the show created as much by performers as by writers. It began not as entertainment but rather as a kind of taped therapy session, a dancers' all-night chill. Bennett was present. And I bet he knew that there was a show in those tapes long before anyone else did. He had a genius instinct for theatre—how it works, where it was, whither it's going. This is why Bennett was so in demand by shows in tryout distress: he knew *how it works*. He couldn't rewrite, despite his *Seesaw* book credit. But he could tell where rewriting was needed—what, in the audition for success, was not performing adequately.

Bennett must have envisioned the entire show that first night. He had only to collect more of these confessional tapes, have the more interesting sections fashioned into dialogue and song, then stage, cut, refine, and open.

"Who am I, anyway?," one of Kleban's lyrics, could be the motto of the bizarre development of this show in its workshop, as dancers spilled out their most personal stories and then had to audition for the privilege of playing themselves; as time passed and some left and others came in; as Joseph Papp proved his importance as a New York culture baron by giving Bennett money and space when any commercial manager would have balked.

Typically, along with the untested Hamlisch and Kleban, Bennett assigned the book to Nicholas Dante, also untested. Dante, one of the dancers, had contributed his tale as an alienated gay teen who was working in a seedy drag theatre, and Bennett thought this backstory absolutely essential. But Dante nourished writing ambitions, and Bennett sensed that he might lose the rights to Dante's saga if Dante didn't get the bookwriting job. Bennett signed Dante on, figuring that he could always bring in a more experienced writer to collaborate. This Bennett eventually did, adding James Kirkwood, not untested but more successful as novelist than playwright (and, in a typical Michael Bennett manipulation stunt, the author of one of Dante's favorite reads—so how could Dante refuse?).

By this time, the show was on its feet and very much nearing its final form. Some in the cast felt that Kirkwood clarified and sharpened; others assumed he was there simply to ensure audience empathy for the role of Cassie.

Cassie (Donna McKechnie) is the most noticeable of the audition lineup, because her personal story ties her to Zach (Robert LuPone), the director running the auditions. They're ex-lovers, which is one conflict. But the second conflict is more worrying: Cassie is gifted but unemployed. We know, of course, that if this were the 1920s she'd be enjoying a robust career, perhaps as a chatty sidekick or, with luck, taking custody of heroine parts. Americans were theatregoers to a fault in those days; and there were Ziegfelds who could make a show on anyone they liked, which meant employment for two hundred other people, not to mention a new score by Rodgers and Hart or the Gershwins.

So there's a tiny bit of *Follies* in *A Chorus Line*, because it lives in the time that *Follies* is greatly afraid of: when the theatres come down and the work thins out.

And yet Bennett knew that his plotless one-acter needed a throughline besides Who Gets Hired. So that first conflict is strongly played. Maybe Bennett wanted *his* story, too, included: because LuPone was groomed to resemble Bennett, and Bennett had had some history with McKechnie, and the gifted McKechnie was, in 1975, unemployed.

Others in the line draw our interest. Nicholas Dante's character, Paul (Sammy Williams), is at first shy and hidden, then takes the theatre apart with his story, the only major autobiographical narrative not set into song. Sheila (Carole—later Kelly—Bishop) is smart and funny, but also so tough that we wonder if she realizes that she is being judged on how she comes across as a person. Morales (Priscilla Lopez) wins every heart as the girl up against the poisonous acting teacher in "Nothing," one of those numbers so disarming in its helpless innocence that one cannot anticipate the wicked twist ending.

Bennett, too, disarmed: not on stage, but in life. He was able so to focus on an individual that some had the impression that no one in the business had ever listened to them before. Men and women alike fell under his spell. It was partly because his choreography and direction made his casts feel ennobled, perfected; and partly because he knew such a racy personal life that many wanted to feel included. Michael Bennett himself was an audition for life; that in itself allowed him to manipulate just about everyone. One could always run him off, of course. But then one was out of the audition, maybe even out of show biz, which could be thought of as a Michael Bennett production. Those buoyed up by his favor felt as redeemed as those whom he turned on felt destroyed.

There was no other director-choreographer like this one. There were wonderful choreographers who also directed, like Agnes de Mille and Michael Kidd. There was Gower Champion, who with David Merrick created a form that dominated sixties musical comedy. There was even one who also had a genius for envisioning out of raw material a finished piece and deleting whatever wouldn't work, and that was Joe Layton. But there was no director-choreographer with Bennett's gift for exalting talent to its utmost except Jerome Robbins. And Robbins, unlike Bennett, was hated by everyone who worked with him. Bennett could arouse intense resentment, but also adoration. No one got anything out of Jerome Robbins' favor, but then Robbins never favored anyone. Jerome Robbins was the Wicked Witch of the West. Michael Bennett was the Wizard of Oz.

What better proves this than *A Chorus Line*'s famous anthology performance on September 29, 1983, celebrating the show's surpassing the record as Broadway's longest-running title? Almost all the original players took part, along with many members of various productions from, literally, the world stage of *A Chorus Line*—something like three hundred fifty people in all, now showcased and now en masse. Bennett laid it all out in four days. The traffic management alone is staggering; but Bennett made the event more than a gala: an emotional celebration of the very *civilization* of theatre, of its sublimation in music, of the audacity of Broadway. Who else could cause one's life to pass before one's eyes in two hours of musical comedy?

No question, the show's triumph was Bennett's. This must be the least beloved score of all the top classics, and, contradicting the show-biz myth that a smash makes stars, *A Chorus Line* did little for its players. Ten years into the run, *The New York Times* ran a "Where are they now?" follow-up on the original cast, with tiny representations of their figures from the poster logo next to paragraphs on their activities. Some had received a boost from the show, but some weren't even in show biz anymore. Updating to the present, we find that many have achieved success, but probably were going to, anyway. Donna McKechnie, Kelly Bishop,

Pamela Blair, and Priscilla Lopez pursued worthy careers. Thomas J. (now Thommie) Walsh, Baayork Lee, and Wayne Cilento are prominent choreographers. Michel Stuart co-produced *Nine* (1982) and *The Tap Dance Kid* (1983). Lee and Walsh even conducted a therapy session to match the one that launched the project by publishing a book (with their former *Line* fellows) on the experience, and on Life After Michael.

A long-awaited offshoot of the show appeared in 1985. This was *A Chorus Line*: the movie. The option had been kicked around Hollywood for years, assigned to various writers and directors who could not satisfy anyone's idea of how to film this most theatrical of theatre pieces. Finally, Richard Attenborough won the Oscar as director of *Gandhi*, and Attenborough was interested in *A Chorus Line*. As actor and then director, the English Attenborough was not associated with musicals—but he did make a superb film out of *Oh, What a Lovely War*, the English musical's equivalent of the most theatrical of theatre pieces.

So Attenborough must have the imagination to pull it off. And his choreographer, Jeffrey Hornaday, had the lush and trendy moves for *Flashdance* (1983), a runaway hit. It sounded sensible.

Alas, Attenborough literalized and clichéd the show. In his version, the characters are simply auditioning for chorus jobs. Simply. Literal. Nothing. It is a tremendous deflation of what Bennett conjured up in his black box. The dancing was Vegas. The cast, though it included Broadway replacements, was uninteresting, and emphasized youth over professional dedication. Attenborough's writer, Arnold Schulman, built up the Zach-Cassie subplot as if the show were a backstage romance, and Attenborough's Zach was the idiot Michael Douglas, who introduced the illiterate "nucular" into the culture in the movie *The China Syndrome*. Who is less persuasive than Douglas as a director-choreographer casting a show? Rex the Wonder Horse?

Ironically, it was Bennett himself who figured out how to film *A Chorus Line*, and he did it—once again, in no time at all flat—at the 1976 Tony Awards show. Asking for one extra camera for the taping of *A Chorus Line*'s opening sequence and the finale, Bennett edited on the run, drinking in the action while moving from screen to screen. He jumped, pivoted, close-upped: for instance on Cassie, distractedly staring at Zach while the others sang their "I hope I get it!" lines. Throughout the dancing audition, Bennett kept the screen feeding on character information—the different levels of talent, the worried or merely persevering looks. Again, a few stood out among the crowd—but then, that's Bennett's view of show biz/life, isn't it?

Above all, there was Cassie, so overqualified for this call; even the way she stood on stage told us that she absolutely belongs there, and not in the chorus. Zach, too, impressed with his efficient command: because if this is life, he's God. When the last eliminations were completed, the line of seventeen applicants came striding forward from upstage, a community formed of chaos. At their halfway point, the lights went out as punctuational warning to the audience. The first sequence is over and applause is permitted: and the lights came up again on the seventeen, stretched across the white line, holding their résumé shots in front of their faces. Who am I, anyway? And the Tony audience went crazy.

Of course, Bennett should have been the director of the *Chorus Line* movie. But he would not have made the film that Hollywood expected a smash Broadway musical to turn into. Bennett would have filmed that smash Broadway musical.

He knew film, Bennett. He knew show biz, life in America. Those last few minutes of *A Chorus Line*'s realistic action, before the starburst finale knocks in, give us a slow build to fade-out: Zach makes his choices about who lives and who dies. Those whose names he calls shall step forward. Those summoned smile: they live. He names Morales—no, a mistake, please step back. She is devastated, as are we, not realizing that it's a splendid Michael Bennett trick. The forward line is not Saved, after all. They are headed for the hell of bartending and table-waiting. Sheila, the last of the damned to depart, retrieves her bag at stage left and starts off to the right, pausing to give Zach a murderous look. Did anyone else after Kelly Bishop project quite the uncontaminated hatred that Sheila feels for the man who took her confession and then refused to absolve her? As Zach monotonously informs his new hirelings of the boilerplate business, each reacts in his or her own way, one reaching up beatifically to bounce her wrists together. D. W. Griffith himself did not fade to black on so transcendent a narrative's end.

Unfortunately, *A Chorus Line*'s gestation instituted the workshop as not only a cheap alternative to the Boston tryout but a thing in itself. Shows could be workshopped over and over in private, less theatre than masturbation.

I prefer the tryout. Write it, do it, fix it. Bring it to New York and open it: *Annie* (1977). To be fair, this was a five-year voyage of write, do, and fix, for not everyone saw the potential of what was to be one of the biggest musical-comedy hits of all time. Martin Charnin was the first to reckon this show's possibilities, after happening upon a republication of some of the original sequences of Harold Gray's comic strip *Little Orphan Annie*.

By now, most Americans probably take the musical's version of Gray's characters as authentic: the dauntless, good-hearted kid heroine with the homeless mutt, the gruffly tender "Daddy" Warbucks, the villains and sweethearts and lovable brood of orphan girls. In fact, the world that Gray created is nothing like this at all, and one wonders exactly what musical Charnin had in mind at first. For it appears that somewhere along the way, the material—drawn from what was in its heyday an elementally American cultural entity—was softened, arguably vandalized.

Famously far to the right in his politics, Gray was more precisely a believer in individualist self-reliance, charity to the disadvantaged, and punishment of the wicked in the mortal sphere. When he launched the strip in 1924, Gray was still sifting his ingredients, many of them derivative, not least of the comically stupid *Moon Mullins*, which had started in 1923. However, by the Depression years Gray had found his proper stage, one that could hardly suggest a musical comedy. Gray's atmosphere is gloomy. His backgrounds, whether interior or exterior, are interchangeable. His animation is perfunctory, as if all existence unfolded in a slow-mo confrontation of stick figures. His view of human nature is misanthropic; the few well-intentioned people are assailed on all sides by criminals, hypocrites, and incompetents. In fact, as Gray sees it, law-abiding people cannot depend on the state for justice and, when under attack, must get justice for themselves. In one strip, thieves trick their way into Warbucks' residence with the intention of killing him and his staff and stripping the house of valuables. When Warbucks gets the drop on them, they simply surrender, counting on the usual bit of jail time. Warbucks has them dragged off to be hanged by his employees. And Annie, rushing into Warbucks' arms, cries, "Oh 'Daddy'!"

The constant separation and reunion of Annie and Warbucks gave the strip structure. But Annie is less a heroine than an emcee, gleaning moralistic commentary from other characters for the reader's edification.

Her adventures are often based on the exploits of others; she just gets taken along. True, she is fearless in the face of the most depraved evil. And she never ages in her white-trimmed red dress and her pupil-less eyes and topping of curly red hair.

Where's the musical in this dour and drab world? Thomas Meehan wrote the book and Charnin the lyrics, to Charles Strouse's music. They set it in New York in the Depression, when the division between the impoverished working class and the bourgeoisie was intense. Prime Harold Gray timeplace, one might think. No: Gray was not class-conscious. He judged individuals on how they treated other people, not on who their grandparents were.

Little of his original strip informed the musical. Warbucks' major henchmen, the seven-foot Sikh, Punjab, and the bizarre Asp, were not on hand. Nor were Warbucks' and Annie's many derisive comments on Franklin Delano Roosevelt. The president was in the show, but he held Warbucks' respect—even if, in a daring joke that few would get, Warbucks closed a phone conversation with Roosevelt on the line "Give my regards to Lucy."* The orphanage keeper who detains Annie in one episode of the strip, Miss Asthma, was in the musical (renamed Miss Hannigan), as was Annie's dog, Sandy. Of course, the show used a cute trained theatre dog, not anything like the four-legged golem that Gray drew. By the time that Goodspeed Opera House mounted *Annie*, in 1976, it stood somewhere between Harold Gray and musical comedy. Then Mike Nichols saw it.

I have to guess that Nichols, who loved the show, thought that the more it favored Gray the less well it worked. When it abandoned Gray for sheer fun, it shone. If there's a *faithful* musical in *Little Orphan Annie*, it would have to be written by Frankenstein's Uncle Cy, and no one wants to see that. But there is a *Little Orphan Annie* in the American musical. All that Strouse, Charnin, and Meehan had to do was find her.

Harold Gray was now gone. Mike Nichols, as producer—an unusual role for this comic and director—led the writing team forward to yesterday, to

---

* What reader caught this reference? Lucy Mercer was Roosevelt's lifelong girl friend. The family forced him to give her up, and he made the sacrifice for his political career, but only at first. The pair found ways to reunite just as Annie and Warbucks always did, and Lucy was one of the very few maintaining watch at F.D.R.'s deathbed. The author salutes her, the true choice of this most historical of American men.

the kind of musical that held the stage when *Little Orphan Annie* was a daily read instead of something one chanced upon in archival republication. Gray maintained the strip till his death in 1968, and others continued it well into the 1970s. But it had long before lost its national impact.

The *Annie* that arrived on Broadway is a fifties musical: the heavy scene plot, complete with incidental music accompanying the blips in the action and then fading out as each new place appears; the sixteen-person chorus doubling and tripling in small roles; the overture medley of happy tunes launched by a canon of trumpet and trombone on "Tomorrow" that says, This will be Public Melody Number One; the scene leading up to a song, followed by a dance, followed by the next scene, instead of the seventies blending of score into script and script into score; the view of life as a natural vindication of the good and defeat of the bad.

Harold Gray would retort that there is nothing natural about it; one must strive for it, as the bad never stop coming at one. But I stand with Nichols, for the *Annie* that he drew out of the Goodspeed version felt like the return of an indispensable item that I hadn't known about before: someone wonderful I missed. So it isn't really a fifties musical. It is what a fifties musical would have been like if the 1950s had lasted for twenty-seven years.

Annie is familiar and novel; that's how musical comedy used to work. The story patterns are familiar, but the characters aren't. That creates openings for new fun. And the kinds of feelings that initiate the vocal spots are familiar, but their content won't be. So the score, too, is new. The heroine's establishing song in *Annie* in fact establishes *the show*, which originally began with a big Depression number out on the street, "Apples." But the piece isn't about the Depression; it's about the kid. So, in revision, the curtain went up on the orphanage dormitory after lights-out. Thus, Annie (Andrea McArdle) can demonstrate her leadership capability by comforting the youngest girl, meanwhile sharing with us her vulnerability, in "Maybe."

Ballads are tricky in a show without a true Boy Meets Girl. *Annie* has a few, but it's stronger in up-tunes and curiosities, such as the orphans' "It's the Hard-Knock Life," with its distinguishing syncopations; or, for the denizens of a Hooverville, "We'd Like To Thank You," a kind of bitter cakewalk. The villainous Miss Hannigan (Dorothy Loudon) has her character number, built on a dangerously evil minor ninth chord, and

Warbucks (Reid Shelton) enjoys a list song with Annie, "I Don't Need Anything But You," that takes us back to the swinging 1930s. So does "You're Never Fully Dressed Without a Smile," marked "Tempo di Ted Lewis," and backed by a close-harmony girls' trio. "Ah," says the Lewis knockoff, as they step up to the mike, "the lovely Boylan Sisters."

The large number of ensembles typifies *Annie*'s antique flavor, as in "N.Y.C.," a gradual crescendo of a production number; or "I Think I'm Going To Like It Here," Annie's welcome at Warbucks' mansion and a showpiece for the chorus; or the White House reprise of "Tomorrow," when F.D.R. brings cabinet members Cordell Hull, Harold L. Ickes, Frances Perkins, Henry Morgenthau, and Harry L. Hopkins—all identified as such in the program—into the vocal score.* It's astonishing how big a show this is, when is makes do with only twenty-two people in all. An extremely comparable show of the actual 1950s, *Li'l Abner*, employed a cast of fifty-seven.

Interesting, too, is how nicely the nearly six-year run tooted along with various replacements. The joyless 1982 movie is stuffed with stars: Albert Finney and Ann Reinking as the good grown-ups, Carol Burnett, Tim Curry, and Bernadette Peters as the bad grown-ups, Edward Herrmann as F.D.R., and Geoffrey Holder as Punjab. (The Asp is on hand, too, played by Roger Minami.) Indeed, the movie is stuffed, altogether. A handful of new songs braces the ear, including one from an early version of the show, "We Got Annie." That incomparable master of the film musical John Huston was enlisted as director. Warbucks' mansion rises with visible overkill from Manhattan pavement as a white Taj Mahal, and Radio City Music Hall is selfishly bought out so that Warbucks and his suite can take in a film without the bothersome encumbrance of fellow moviegoers. Producer Ray Stark must have been determined to top the *Chorus Line* movie.

The stage show, ironically, won its success through a sort of good-sized simplicity. Its only star part was Miss Hannigan, and, at that, only because Dorothy Loudon made it one. Meehan's book does give her something more to play than the other characters have. Annie is the kid hero;

---

* Mistake! *Annie* takes place in late 1933, when, indeed, Hull was secretary of state, Ickes secretary of the interior, and Perkins secretary of labor. However, Morgenthau did not succeed William H. Woodin at Treasury till 1934, and Hopkins didn't take over as secretary of commerce till 1939.

Warbucks' assistant Grace Farrell (Sandy Faison) is his unappreciated admirer. There's not much more room than those captions in such roles; and F.D.R. is a cigarette holder and a wheelchair.

But Loudon found something in Miss Hannigan even while getting the laughs. She is involved in a conspiracy to murder Annie, but the show is essentially innocent—or, let's say, not entirely real. So Miss Hannigan is an acting challenge: to put together in one's mind just how Miss Hannigan got this debased by her disappointments, and to play that while keeping it all on the cartoon level. Like Elaine Stritch's Joanne in *Company*, Loudon's Miss Hannigan was a thrilling event in an up-and-down career. At last, in the words of Colleen Dewhurst at her first successful Tony Awards, "Mother has a hit."

We should probably ask why a show that is in effect nothing more than a capable musical comedy became such a landmark in the musical's geography. Admittedly, many capable shows have been huge hits—*Grease*, for example. Perhaps *Annie* is more than capable. It never falters, for one thing. It starts very immediately and does not let up; many shows start up too slowly or lose content in the second half.

Annie does have weaknesses in composition. The lyrics are sometimes banal, and there are too few character songs. Some may regret the almost total absence of Harold Gray. Even his visualization of the heroine, featured in the show's logo, was avoided, except in the final scene, when McArdle came high-kicking down the stairs of Warbucks' mansion in the strip's curly hair and red dress.

On the other hand, *Annie* did reclaim a noble tradition that had fallen into disuse by 1977: that of the inventively busy musical comedy, the result of a high collaborative effort to find crazy wonder in the material. Everybody has an idea—not just director Charnin but producer Nichols, choreographer Peter Gennaro, and just about anyone else in the house. This is not the kind of collaboration that makes a *Gypsy* or *My Fair Lady*. It makes a *Damn Yankees* or *Hello, Dolly!*. *Annie* is filled with those little touches that keep the level of surprise and delight high—the orphan girls, whom we thought asleep, joining in on the plangent last utterance of the title word in the last phrase of "Maybe"; the irruption into the gala, *molto fortissimo* climax of "N.Y.C." by a grouch yelling, "Quiet!"; the authentically observed radio program for the Ted Lewis "Smile" number, with the ventriloquist and dummy, the sound-effects man, and one zany touch in an announcer proudly wearing a Lone Ranger mask; or F.D.R.'s elegant silencing of his cabinet during the "Tomorrow" reprise with "Solo for the president!"

None of this challenges the discoveries of the great seventies shows—*Chicago*, *A Chorus Line*, the five Sondheim titles. But that's the point: *Annie* was rediscovery, a return to what American know-how and imagination made of the form that Europeans invented. It was not supposed to generate unique masterpieces every time, but rather unique formats of protean potential. What's wonderful about *Annie* is not that it made history, but that it didn't have to.

Sweeney Todd, the Demon Barber of Fleet Street (1979) had to, because this one is a unique masterpiece. It is also an opera, and occupies—like *Porgy and Bess*—an odd niche in the musical's history. At that, its niche in opera history is odd, too: as a melodrama with the timing and coincidence of farce in its last half hour, just when its dire plot gets particularly ghoulish.

Nevertheless, while it does have some spoken dialogue and a great deal of underscored dialogue, everything in *Sweeney Todd* that can possibly be sung is indeed vocal material. That is the definition of opera.

Sondheim's eighth show as composer-lyricist (counting the at that point unproduced *Saturday Night*) stems from a Victorian horror play, *The String of Pearls; or The Fiend of Fleet Street* (1847), by George Dibdin Pitt. Christopher Bond, an actor in an English repertory company that was about to stage the work, had the task of refashioning this ludicrous and sloppy antique into something with point and playing content for the modern actor. By his own admission, Bond borrowed the retaliation-for-the-victimization-of-one's-sweetheart theme in Cyril Tourneur's *The Revenger's Tragedy* and the escape from-prison-to-seek-revenge theme from Dumas *père*'s *The Count of Monte Cristo*, to motivate the protagonist and to consider the culpability of the powerful.

A horror buff, Sondheim saw Bond's *Sweeney Todd* in London while preparing the Angela Lansbury *Gypsy*, and heard in its madder music the formulations for the first Sondheim opera. Bogged down in trying to set Bond as one sets an opera text, Sondheim finally turned to Hugh Wheeler for a script based on Bond. This Sondheim simply absorbed into music, leaving as dialogue the very bits and pieces of a play. The show was billed as "a musical thriller," not an opera. Still, we note that for the first time,

Sondheim the composer is trying out the morphing Leitmotiven and repetitions of melodic cells that are the hallmarks of the Classy Opera Guys, such as Leoš Janáček and Benjamin Britten. Not that Sondheim has actually heard their output: in the club of geniuses, one doesn't have to meet to agree.

Sondheim had flirted with this brand of composition before—the rising three-note theme of B-D-E that highlights *Pacific Overtures*' opening returns to propell its finale. But *Sweeney Todd* actively reuses or revamps its ur-themes. "The Ballad of Sweeney Todd" has hardly ended when the sailor Anthony enters singing the melody that launched the Ballad, over different harmony. The eerily compulsive ostinato that runs through the Ballad becomes the ostinato for Todd's "There Was a Barber and His Wife," the music suddenly calmed except for the repeated stabbing of an augmented seventh. The Beggar Woman's theme turns into a minuet for the flashback of her rape at Judge Turpin's party. The traditional *Dies Irae* melody that slams into hearing during the Ballad is inverted for Sweeney's song when he is reunited with his razors. That was a prayer for the dead; this is a salute to the killers.

Here is craftsmanship of highest order. But what insists on *Sweeney Todd*'s generical identity as an opera is its vocal casting. These are heroic roles for the most part: grand and intense. Is there another male lead in a musical as difficult for the singing actor to encompass? Is anything even close?

Not that Todd is a faceted or comprehensive character. On the contrary, by the time he appears he has closed up whatever nuances his nature once cultivated. He lives exclusively to have revenge on the men who destroyed his life. He is brusque, sarcastic, malevolent. He is that most dangerous of embittered men: the wronged innocent with nothing left to lose. But he is no longer Dibdin's fiend, who murders because to do anything less in a Victorian horror play is to waste the audience's time. This Todd murders first out of self-defense. He would have stopped at the second and third murders, of the judge and beadle who thoroughly require this truer justice than they themselves serve. But when the judge escapes the punishment whose expectation has sustained Todd through fifteen years of misery, he snaps. His mad scene, called "Epiphany," hurtles from a syncopated clanging to a hysteria of what feels like a thousand tiny screams to a heavily accented $\frac{4}{4}$ on "They all deserve to die!," the sound of a mind unhinged yet working out a logic all its own. The Beggar

Woman's theme reappears in a keening for Todd's family, repeatedly broken into by percussive bits as he stares at the audience, ordering them to step up to his judgment.

Mrs. Lovett, on the other hand, can be sung by a Broadway voice, because some of her role has the flavor of musical comedy, or perhaps music hall. Of all the characters, she is the only one with low comic numbers. While this suggests an odd foil for the brooding Todd, it is actually Mrs. Lovett who incites his murder spree by offering to dispose of the corpses as food. Till that point, Todd has threatened to kill indiscriminately only in mad outburst. Mrs. Lovett makes Todd her instrument in the development of her business, and thus can bring him into one of "her" comic numbers, the first-act finale, "A Little Priest." No doubt Christopher Bond sees the last sight of Act One (used as the logo drawing on the posters) as an emblem of capitalism: Todd wielding a cleaver and Mrs. Lovett a rolling pin. Open for business.

What's odd about this is that Mrs. Lovett isn't in it for the profit any more than Todd is. She's in it for him, for love; and we have to imagine this woman waiting all those years in the crazy wish that somehow the transported Todd would return. What other reason could there be for her not having pawned his silver working tools but that she hoped to see him again? "So it is you," she says, as he wails helplessly at the recounting of his wife's destruction. The stage directions tell us that she says it "coolly." Of course she does. This isn't surprise. She knew who he was the moment he walked into her shop; she has been living for it for fifteen years.

In a way, Mrs. Lovett combines the wistful patience of Desiree Armfeldt with the obsessive intensity of Fosca in Sondheim's *Passion* (1994). The role does repay work by opera singers, though such major actors as Dorothy Loudon (a Broadway replacement) and Julia McKenzie (on a BBC concert) have also distinguished themselves. Still, aficionados feel that Angela Lansbury's creation of the part is never to be challenged for the pathos that informed her portrayal even as she exuberantly fulfilled its comic potential. The absurdly coquettish "By the Sea," so often a quagmire for the opera ladies (not least because it's a real test of breath control while demanding better-than-opera diction), put Lansbury into flight.

Versatility is the essential quality of a great Mrs. Lovett, far more so than for other Big Rep parts such as Mrs. Anna or Rose. She must project a terrible regret when, in "Not While I'm Around," she realizes that the first murder victim's assistant, Toby, is about to sleuth out what happened and so must be murdered. And she suffers this realization even while singing, "Nothing's gonna harm you." On the other end of the acting scale, she must present a kind of unyielding anti-naturalism in the show's last seconds, when she and Todd, about to exit, break out of character (or do they?) to turn and look meaningfully at each other. That moment of Brechtian "It's only a play" gesture is a hallmark of the concept show, at once so firmly defined and so ambiguous, so seething with social values yet so much larger than politics. No work as loaded with content as *Sweeney Todd* is "only" anything.

Of the original cast, Len Cariou (succeeded by George Hearn) alone matched Lansbury's greatness. The others—Victor Garber, Sarah Rice, Ken Jennings, Edmund Lyndeck, Jack Eric Williams, Merle Louise—varied in quality. But only the biggest talents can withstand the dwarfing of so expansive a production. Against a backdrop of urban riverside, with a working catwalk and factory roofing overhead, the action utilized the Uris stage area from wing to wing. Even when the chorus was fully deployed, there seemed too few of them.

Ironically, some thought the show overproduced. No. The set, designed by Eugene Lee, was big, yes. The staging itself was tight—not spare, but more a series of tableaus than a grandstanding pageant. By now aware that resisting Sondheim imperiled one's credentials, the critics generally raved—except, of course, Walter Kerr. It was Kerr's misfortune to lack ear; all he could handle was ditties. Anything more sophisticated than De Sylva, Brown, and Henderson simply didn't *sound*. Rather than work around this defect, however, Kerr habitually panned shows with extra music, finding some imaginary fault as his excuse. With *Sweeney Todd*, Kerr complained that "we haven't been lured into sharing [the authors'] complex, macabre, assiduously offbeat vision." Remember the producer in *Merrily We Roll Along*, played by Jason Alexander, the one who dismisses the creative work he hears with "There's not a tune you can hum"? That's Walter Kerr.

Isn't it time to free ourselves of this canard? Hummability does not define good music. Bach? Beethoven? Berlioz? There is as well an educating humiliation in learning that others can hum what you can't. Moreover, how were these eager hummers planning to get into a number like "Kiss Me," one of the finest pieces in the *Sweeney Todd* score, but a set of dialogues, at first for two characters, then another two, then all four? Which part of this quartet were they intending to hum? And is their humming more important than the urgency of plot action that hurries this piece along, as the young lovers prepare to elope and the two villains set off for what Todd hopes will be the culmination of his revenge plot?

Rather than get their humming in, wouldn't they rather enjoy the way the composer creates suspense with a single chord, $E^{maj.7}$, under a fluttering melody that hovers around the second of the scale, an effect that shimmers with deadly sin? Aren't they interested in how even the hideous Beadle Bamford can find his way into the music, in the quartet's middle section, when he solos in "Ladies in Their Sensitivities," so unctuous in its dirty formality? Or, to put it still another way, does anyone really care what Walter Kerr hums?

Sweeney Todd's original New York run tallied 558 performances, and it swept the Tonys for Best Musical, Score, Book, Direction, Actor, Actress, Set, and Franne Lee's Costume Design. No, it didn't pay off. Now that we're a few months away from the end of the Third Age, listen to two rules of the Fourth Age: one, Nothing pays off anymore except junk. And, two, It doesn't matter.

Or, yes, it matters to the people who put up the capital. They really are angels, after all. Now I have some good news and some bad news for you. People love to say, "Shit happens." Here's what also happens: *A Chorus Line*, *Annie*, and *Sweeney Todd*. The odds were against them, though the first two made fortunes worldwide in the end. Still, they didn't sound like hits in description. Even *The Producers* didn't sound, at its announcement, like a hit. It's not the idea: it's the execution. It's Michael Bennett, Charles Strouse, Angela Lansbury. It's they do this because they have to. Because it matters; and after them everything will be Britney Spears and Adam Sandler. That's why the Golden Age is ending.

And that was the good news.

15

PLEASE SIGN THE BOOK ON YOUR WAY OUT THE DOOR

THE 1979–80 SEASON

We've seen enough vexations in these pages to end any Golden Age, and here's the result: the musicals produced on Broadway from autumn 1979 to the end of summer in 1980 included only *three* new American book musicals with new scores—and two of them were awful.

Revivals of course played a part, trying to make up for the paucity of vital new work and reassuring producers who lack the sense even to know what's vital today. The *Hair* imitations all bombed: so let's do *Peter Pan, The Most Happy Fella, Oklahoma!*. What else is a sure thing these days?

Peter Pan opened the season, on September 6, in its first return since Mary Martin played the original of this musical adaptation in 1954. As always, the program kept the secret of who exactly had trimmed down James M. Barrie for the inclusion of the Mark Charlap–Carolyn Leigh songs. These had been joined by a few more, by Jule Styne and Betty Comden and Adolph Green, during the troubled tryout, when a doctoring Jerome Robbins turned a play with songs into a full-scale musical. Though Robbins' name was invoked, this was a new staging, by Rob Iscove. It started as an unimportant regional tour, but did so well that Ron Field was brought in to glitz it for Broadway. The Mr. Darling/Captain Hook was George Rose–in–a–box. But Sandy Duncan's Peter, kitted out with a green laser beam for Tinker Bell, enchanted the town, not least when she blithely flew right up to the balcony of the Lunt-Fontanne for her curtain call. A hit.

The Most Happy Fella, which arrived in October after a mounting at the Minnesota Opera Theater, failed. There was nothing wrong with it— on the contrary, like the triumphant 1976 *Porgy and Bess*, it was produced by Sherwin M. Goldman and directed by Jack O'Brien in the same loving and restorative manner. Giorgio Tozzi led the capable cast; maybe the roles need more than capable. We saw the same problem with *Sweeney Todd*. Apparently, these Broadway operas aren't easy to cast once the stars are signed, because the secondary parts are then left to secondary talents. Why wasn't this a problem in 1956, when *The Most Happy Fella* had its premiere? Are we running out of even the dandy supplementary people that musical comedy could take for granted, the Susan Johnsons who might never achieve full stardom but are still excellent company?

At least *Oklahoma!* remained a champion. A Christmas present two weeks before the holiday, it was a faithful revival in this age of desecrations. Oscar's son William Hammerstein directed, Gemze de Lappe supervised the retention of the original de Mille choroegraphy, and even the original conductor, Jay Blackton, led the orchestra in Robert Russell Bennett's 1943 scoring. And it was a proper *Oklahoma!*: now dark, now joyous; now so regional in attitude, then thrillingly nationalistic.

A noteworthy innovation was the casting of romantic hero Martin Vidnovic as the villainous Jud Fry, suggesting that Laurey's quandary is a confusion between the hot guy who worries you and the sweet guy who bores. Laurence Guittard's wooden Curly supported this conundrum (though his replacement, Joel Higgins, livened things up), and Christine Andreas played a fascinating Laurey, very soprano, very headstrong and ambivalent, an authentic Hammerstein heroine. The second couple, Harry Groener and Christine Ebersole, were excellent, precisely the pairing of male dancer and girl comic that was originally intended. Critic Erick Neher notes that Ebersole "may not carry a show but invariably steals one," and so it was here. In its first open-run revival since 1943 and numerous limited-engagement institutional seasons, *Oklahoma!* looked great and felt good. Best of all, its old songs were being used as they were meant to be: in *Oklahoma!*.

That wasn't true of a great many other old songs. "(Our) Love Is Here To Stay," "That Old Black Magic," "Ain't She Sweet," "I've Got a Gal in Kalamazoo," and other helpless numbers were drafted into *The 1940's Radio Hour*, which showed up in October after development by companies in New Haven and Washington, D.C. Note that, once again, the regions were keeping the Broadway season from imploding; note as well another pathetic Lizzy Flop conception credit, for Walton Jones taped his name onto the poster three times, as writer, as director, and in "based on an idea by Walton Jones and Carol Lees."

Why is it always the duds that have to be thus "conceived"? *The 1940's Radio Hour* treated, in real time, a broadcast from a low-rent studio in the old Astor Hotel. I see it as an excuse for the eight thousandth drab unit set and no intermission, the cliché equipment of the seventies musical. But Walton Jones and Carol Lees saw it as a way of getting a play out of the interacting personalities of the singers, players, and crew: the grouchy doorman actually called "Pops" (Arny Freeman), the frantic announcer (Josef Sommer), the too-good-for-the-job-but-happy-to-be-there singer (Mary Cleere Haran), the black singer (Dee Dee Bridgewater), the cheesy Frank Sinatra imitation (Jeff Keller), the starry-eyed delivery boy from the local drug store (Jack Hallett), and so on.

The problem is, no matter how interesting these characters may be, there won't be any character songs for them in this potpourri of standards. So this isn't a musical any more than *Dancin'* was. That was a dance piece. And *The 1940's Radio Hour* is . . . what? A song piece?

It's a testament to the performers that the show lasted three months, because it had to run entirely on their talent. There was but one interesting event in the writing, a sketch in which an "elocution expert" coaches the announcer in diction. The joke is that the expert not only has a terrible accent but invents words. He wants his subject to try the line "Betty Botter baked a batch of buttered brownies." Each time, the announcer scarcely gets to "Botter" before the expert stops him:

> DICTION COACH: Remember, in diction you must use ya woid which gives you da proper trelmedge in tha mask area. Suppose you use a woid and people don't understand. You got gels with an equaline and vibins in your nose. Don't let that happen. Let your lips be felma.

Actually, not every show with a "conceived by" credit was a dud: *Sugar Babies* opened the night after *Radio Hour*, "conceived by Ralph G. Allen [its book writer] and Harry Rigby [its co-producer]." Isn't the conceiving part of the job of producer, as which Rigby was also credited, and of writer, as which Allen, too, had his primary credit? Whence this ludicrous need to milk an extra credit out of the poster? Why is it that people at the top of the profession do not routinely request this pourboire no matter how much conceiving they do?

Sugar Babies is a revival of burlesque, in the later meaning of the word: smutty jokes, low comedy, and strippers. Everyone knows why vaudeville died: radio. But no one knows why burlesque died—that is, if there was any cause beyond the enmity of the authorities, who were forever passing laws about what it could do and where. (For instance, it was outlawed in Philadelphia, but the interested simply crossed the Delaware River to see it in Camden, New Jersey.)

Burlesque was tame by today's standards, but very knowing. The jokes aren't any old smut at all; they play on its inevitability, on the relentless erotic hunger of the average man. One thing that burlesque never had was good music—but *Sugar Babies* was Big Broadway, and it featured about a half-dozen good old songs and plenty of new ones in the old style. Composer Jimmy McHugh was the featured author, seconded by composer-lyricist Arthur Malvin and with Jay Livingston and Ray Evans contributing a New Dance Sensation, "The Sugar Baby Bounce."

Another thing that burlesque never had was major show-biz stars. Early burlesque, of course, had Weber and Fields and Lillian Russell, but *this* burlesque is what the second act of *Gypsy* sinks into. Any stars created by burlesque got out of it quickly, as Gypsy Rose Lee did.

So *Sugar Babies*, despite a desire to create burlesque in fair spirit, did employ stars, Mickey Rooney and Ann Miller. This is a far-fetched pair, for neither had any burlesque background, and one had done little (Miller) and the other nothing (Rooney) on Broadway. Still, they were authentic showbiz characters, he with his rambunctious versatility and dancing Ann with her "Hit it, boys!" belt and her wonderful ability to tell a joke with perfect timing even while leaving the impression that she herself doesn't get it.

They had solid entrances, too. Rooney opened the show, all by himself, turning to the audience from silhouette and, after taking his welcome applause, launching "A Good Old Burlesque Show." Miller's entrance was delayed for a Train Sequence, opened by the girls in nighties for a trip on a sleeper in "In Louisiana." A train dance followed, with a cardboard train. Then conductors pushed on a baggage cart topped with luggage and Miller, who leaped off, crashed into "I Feel a Song Comin' On," then tore off her dress to reveal a tap skirt for the Ann Miller Dance. The two stars of course got an eleven o'clock number, a Jimmy McHugh medley with Rooney at the piano.

This was not just any revue with a burlesque overlay: this really was a tour through burlesque styles. The sketches recalled many a tradition and were filled with venerable shtick. An announcement from the stage:

> CHARACTER MAN: Starting next Thursday and every Thursday thereafter is Mothers' Night. So all you ladies who want to be mothers should meet the manager in his office after the show.

A hotel sketch:

> CLERK: (answering phone) This is the Broken Arms Hotel. Front desk. What's that? You say you've got a leak in your bathtub? Well, go right ahead. You paid for the room.

Miller as a schoolteacher, smacking naughty Mickey with a ruler:

> TEACHER: Mickey, what's the difference between prose and poetry?
> MICKEY: That's easy. The pros stand on the corner.

Rooney in pastel drag topped by a blond fright wig, as Hortense, recounting a sad biography:

> HORTENSE: I overheard the Colonel say to Brock, "Is that Hortense?" And Brock replied, "She looks pretty relaxed to me."

The musical staging, by Ernest Flatt, revived such old burlesque tropes as the swing number, the sister act, the fan dance, the vaudeville dog act. It was all fast and funny and it ended with a patriotic number, "You Can't Blame Your Uncle Sammy," from as far back as 1924, staged with the entire company in red, white, and blue, with a flag background and Miller as the Statue of Liberty. In a season filled with interesting new shows, *Sugar Babies* would have made for a lively museum. It was nostalgia for the old and education for the young, and it had, to its credit, a scholar's archeological precision and a spare-no-expense production. However, in a season made almost entirely of old stuff, *Sugar Babies* was more old stuff.

A staging of the Walt Disney *Snow White and the Seven Dwarfs* cartoon that fall at Radio City Music Hall is technically not subject to our survey. But we include it as a harbinger of the Disney Company's presence on Broadway in the years leading up to millennium. Of Disney's three productions to date of this writing, two were also stagings of cartoons, and while this *Snow White* was not a Disney offering, the firm must have been following the show's development and reception with interest.

The show was reasonably faithful to the movie, even unto putting Mary Jo Salerno in the yellow skirt and black bodice with red-and-gray armlets and matching headband seen on the heroine in the 1937 film. All the Frank Churchill–Larry Morey songs (and much of the original scoring) were retained, with two new numbers by Jay Blackton and Joe Cook. "Welcome To the Kingdom (of once-upon-a-time)" was the opening chorus, in a pseudo–Jerome Kern Waltz; and the Prince (Richard Bowne), little more than a cipher in the cartoon, was expanded with a ballad, "Will I Ever See Her Again."

There were a few deviations from text, mainly to fill the giant Music Hall stage and give the chorus something to do. So the Queen (Anne Francine) started the story off with a court ceremony, village girls helped Snow White with "I'm Wishing," and the forest scenes abounded with dancers in cunning animal getups. Interestingly, where the Disney people would seek out theatre innovators such as director Julie Taymor and designer Bob Crowley in *their* Broadway ventures, this *Snow White* used dependable journeymen, and the director-choreographer was Frank Wagner, a never-made-it who specialized in off-Broadway revue.

After the revivals and new shows made of old parts, the first half of the 1979–80 season knew only two new story musicals. *Comin' Uptown* was a black version of Charles Dickens' *A Christmas Carol*. The fourth collaboration of producer Philip Rose and word man Peter Udell, *Comin' Uptown* saw composer Gary Geld leave the concern, to be succeeded by Garry Sherman. Like *The Wiz*, the show got its fun from jiving a classic with Harlemania. So the ghost of Christmas Past is a boxer in gold lamé robe over white satin trunks, escorted by three trophy babes, who sing backup for his "Get Your Act Together"; and when the reformed Scrooge brings Christmas dinner to Bob Cratchit's family, all he can find open is a Chinese take-out place and a Jewish delicatessen.

The critics cheered Gregory Hines' Scrooge and were appreciative of the trouble that Robin Wagner had gone to with the sets. But these one-joke burlesques (in the older sense of the word) need stronger scores than this one's to attract a public for a lengthy stay. And did anyone really want to see Gregory Hines as a slumlord?

The other new story show was an English pop opera by Andrew Lloyd Webber and Tim Rice, *Evita*. A late September entry, *Evita* differed from *Jesus Christ Superstar* in coming over in a production that was already running in London. However, the Hal Prince–Larry Fuller staging, designed by Timothy O'Brien and Tazeena Firth, was quite unlike the campy splendor with which Tom O'Horgan and his team profaned *Superstar*. If anything, Prince's gang graced the Argentinian adventuress with the highest compliment that Broadway can pay: a high-art concept production with sophisticated stage groupings, projections, and a baffling twist ending. But then, the piece itself was written conceptually, as a two-disc dramatic song cycle that took place less in actual "scenes" than in a phantasmagoria of history.

Just like *Cabaret*, the show had an emcee, billed simply as Che (Guevara, we presume), who has La Gioconda's ability to turn up at will anywhere the action is, and always in his guerrilla fatigues. Certain sequences occur in multiple locations simultaneously—at one point, Evita and Juan Perón are seen in their bedroom with the Argentinian people strung along the area just behind them. Even in small ways, the staging that Prince thought up for the album's transfer to the theatre defies fourth-wall naturalism. On the discs, the opening funeral sequence includes The Voice of Eva singing an anticipation of "Don't Cry For Me, Argentina." Prince assigned this to a girl in the crowd of mourners—Just any girl at all, but played, of course, by the same actress who plays Evita.

One thing that Prince could not maneuver around was the astonishing structural similarity between *Superstar* and *Evita*. For Che is like Judas in hectoring the audience on the protagonist's hypocrisy, while a third lead—earlier, Mary; here, Juan Perón—never quite gets what all the yelling is about. There are many obvious shifts in form, especially in the change from a lot of rock in *Superstar* to rather little in *Evita*. We hear a piano rave-up in "Rainbow Tour" and an electric-guitar riff to launch "She Is a Diamond," and Che's outbursts match the *Superstar* sound style in general (though he is never as frantic as Judas). However, the Latin-lover "On This Night of a Thousand Stars," the parade of bed partners in "Good Night and Thank You," another Latin number in "I'd Be Surprisingly Good For You," and the "Waltz for Eva and Che" would be unthinkable in *Jesus Christ Superstar*. This suggests that Lloyd Webber was trying to establish his own New Music to harmonize theatre and pop.

All the same, there they still are: the rampaging narrator, the don't-touch-me central figure, and the clueless whore/general. It's virtually blasphemy to follow Jesus with Evita thus, not least because to some in Argentina she was an uncanonized saint. It's a devil of a role, intense, very long, and vocally so demanding that producers Robert Stigwood and David Land had to hire an alternate for the matinées. In London, Elaine Paige, David Essex, and Joss Ackland led the cast; New York saw Patti LuPone, Mandy Patinkin, and Bob Gunton. The critics were divided—some hated it while others loathed it—but the high-powered staging, the fascinatingly ghastly Eva, and the flying carpet of a score put the show over as an instant hit. In particular, *Evita* installed Patti LuPone as one of the era's most electric and versatile talents.*

Be careful what you wish for, they say. *Evita* is what writers on theatre were wishing for, whether they knew it or not, when they kept crabbing about Broadway's conservative musical aesthetics. *Jesus Christ Superstar* was an accident, a pop album that managed to become a show. But *Evita* was written by two men who had enjoyed an international stage hit with that show. So they knew that the LPs were simply a tryout for a staging. *Superstar* was a one-off. *Evita* was the New Music theatre piece that you had all been ranting about in the late 1960s. *Hair*? No: another one-off. *Georgy* wasn't it. *Purlie* wasn't it.

Evita was it—and, but for the lack of a single decent new book musical by American authors, the first half of the 1979–80 season was thus energized. Broadway couldn't write new shows, but it could put them on: *Evita*'s entire production team, in London as here, was American.

Then came the season's second half—more revivals, more junk. The English musical *Canterbury Tales* moved downtown, briefly, from Equity

---

* Now that she is queen of Broadway is finally the time to correct a common error. Her family name is not LuPone, but Pone. Patti Lu's siblings are Robert Lu, William Lu, and Jubilation T. Corn.

Library Theatre. *West Side Story*, in the original Jerome Robbins staging, with Ken Marshall, Jossie de Guzman, Debbie Allen, James J. Mellon, and Hector Jaime Mercado, was a hit. This work, at least, they do not fool with, though the summer brought in a hit *Camelot* with Richard Burton absolutely starred as the wraith of Richard Burton, the shadow, the never self. King Zombie. Otherwise, it was *Camelot* in a unit set with a mixture of correct performances (for instance in Richard Muenz's sin-of-pride Lancelot) and cartoon performances (Robert Fox's oily Mordred; no, Mordred's an ascetic hypocrite, not a silent-movie Sweeney Todd). It was perhaps the worst big-budget revival that Broadway had seen, till it returned a year later with Richard Harris in *Hamelot*.

Two Lizzy Flop "conceived" shows, *Reggae* and *Musical Chairs*, were quick failures. *Reggae* was the black flimflam that comes along almost annually in this decade, amateurish in both writing and staging, though not in its casting. The setting was Jamaica, where star pop singer Sheryl Lee Ralph met ganja farmer Philip Michael Thomas. They were menaced by thugs led by Obba Babatunde and saved by Rastafarians. As so often with a "conceived" show, one person took three poster credits—"story by," a book co-credit, and a score co-credit. Altogether, nine people were listed as having written *Reggae*. But if it took only two men to write *Show Boat*, why does it take nine to write *Reggae*? Moreover, as electronic amplification had by the late 1970s become universal on Broadway, why was *Reggae*'s so, again, amateurish that on opening night the speakers picked up a broadcast of a Knicks game?

But "*Reggae* is no longer the worst musical of the 1979–80 season," wrote Frank Rich in the *Times* in his report on *Musical Chairs*. This show was not unlike *A Chorus Line: The Audience*, for its set presented theatre seats and its cast played theatregoers talking about their lives. There were three critics (one gay), two single women, two couples, the playwright, his ex-wife, and so on. The show was excoriated, though it did get praise from *Variety*, the *New York Post*, and *Show Business*. However, *The New Yorker* walked out—an act of violence—and, for one of the two weeks that it played, *Musical Chairs* sold 7.5 percent of the house.

At least these two bombs had to be written. *Happy New Year*, which came along in late April, had only to be arranged, by Burt Shevelove, from Philip Barry's *Holiday* and the Cole Porter catalogue. It was perhaps inevitable that someone get to *Holiday* sooner or later, but who would have thought it would be Cole Porter some fifteen years after his death? Barry's tale of a vital young man (here, Michael Scott) who finally ditches his stuffy fiancée (Kimberly Farr) for her vital sister (Leslie Denniston) is the stuff that musical comedy dotes on. And, for an ensemble, one need only bring in pretty young people of "the Stork Club set" (as the program had it) for a party scene.

Porter and Barry would seem a match, because Barry insistently wrote about the kind of people that Cole Porter was. *Happy New Year* takes place in the townhouse owned by the fiancée's family—and they don't rent out to meet the mortgage. These people aren't just wealthy. They're the word they themselves never use: rich. And Cole Porter was: rich. And so were all those friends of his that kept turning up in his list songs.

However, Cole Porter didn't write about rich characters. Porter's musicals were full largely of the finaglers and crooks habitually played by William Gaxton, Ethel Merman, Jimmy Durante, Bert Lahr. Yes, there's a role for Fred Astaire; but *Gay Divorce*'s Guy Holden isn't rich. He's a novelist.

So assigning Merman's "Ridin' High" and "Red, Hot and Blue" to Philip Barry's characters simply doesn't work. Have we so lost grip on our own show-biz traditions that the adept Burt Shevelove doesn't hear in these two jazzy up-tunes Porter's assessment of Merman as a cultural breakaway in the history of the American stage heroine? Merman is the dame for whom Porter rhymes "Stravinsky's" with "Minsky's." She's even the dame who made it possible in the first place. Merman doesn't sing what rich people sing.

At least some of *Happy New Year* reclaimed semi-forgot songs and a few out-and-out novelties, including the wonderful "Let's Make It a Night," dropped from *Silk Stockings* (1955). There it was meant for the three comic commissars and a Luella Gear/Helen Broderick type, planning a tour of the sleaziest dives in Paris. For these comic characters, the number is a spoof, mock shocking. But it completely destroys the joke when this protective shell is removed and the number is sung by the vital sister and two of the Stork Club boys. Now it's shocking, when the characters aren't supposed to shock. (Some cute history was made here nonetheless, in that Leslie Denniston was flanked by Lara Teeter and Tim Flavin, who both went on to play the male lead in the Natalia Makarova *On Your Toes* revival, respectively in New York and London.)

Worst of all, while dropping some of Barry's characters to streamline for moderns, Shevelove retained the most dated aspect of Barry, his coy wordplay that is supposed to sound whimsical and smart but comes off as affected and stupid. Let's ponder this bit of dialogue spoken by the hero and the girl he'll end up marrying, during their wholly inappropriate singing of "Let's Be Buddies":

LINDA: Give me a break.
JOHNNY: Here 'tis. One good turn.
LINDA: Deserves another. Fred.
JOHNNY: Adele.
LINDA: Tennis, anyone?

A few days later brought another work cannibalizing old show biz for new, *A Day in Hollywood/A Night in the Ukraine*. This double bill was comprised of, first, a revue goofing on old Hollywood and including the coming-attractions trailer for a Marx Brothers movie, which then comprised the second half of the evening. The show had already been seen in London but was considerably revised for Broadway and is in any case the work of an American librettist and lyricist (Dick Vosburgh) and a South African composer (Frank Lazarus), with contributions by other Americans (Jerry Herman for three numbers, a medley of hits by Richard A. Whiting) and an American director-choreographer and his co-choreographer (Tommy Tune, Thommie Walsh).

So it's really an American concoction, on a highly American theme at that; but it's also rather a lot of names for a little thing of a show. Theatregoers reveled in one number in which old-time movie stars were imitated on a miniature stage showing only their feet—Tom Mix's cowboy boots, Sonja Henie's skates, Judy Garland's ruby slippers as she is menaced by Bela Lugosi in Dracula's cape, Mickey and Minnie Mouse in their yellow clodhoppers (and tails). The pit consisted of two pianos and a bass, though some of the performers filled in onstage. David Garrison blew after-hours clarinet for Kate Draper's "Too Marvelous For Words," and Garrison and Stephen James played those portable sawed-off keyboards that one blows into, which made them look as if they were eating Vladimir Horowitz. There were only two sets, first the lobby of Grauman's Chinese Theatre (with the cast dressed as ushers) and then the setting for the Marx Brothers "film," loosely based on Chekhov's *The Bear*.

Small—reduced from what musicals used to be, really—had started as a survival expedient and become a working aesthetic. Unit sets, palm court groups instead of orchestras, small casts, and replicas of stars, such as Garrison, Lazarus, and Priscilla Lopez playing Groucho, Chico, and Harpo. This is all but admitting that Broadway cannot create new stars, because the public now raises up its idols in other venues.

Hollywood/Ukraine was a hit. Some of the first half was sophomoric parody, like that tired old "Let's get Nelson Eddy" thing, in Herman's *complainte* for Jeanette MacDonald, "Nelson." Why don't writers go after some of the true freaks of old Hollywood, like Wallace Beery? It is also not the wittiest act on earth to set the endless no-nos of the Production Code to a tap number. There was too much of this obvious stuff, which must have sounded like a good idea because everyone in the audience would catch the jokes. But what shot-up targets these are. One number got all its fun from spouting examples of cliché genre dialogue. They're funny in their movies because the generical context makes a line such as "Oh please, Judge, my Tony is a good boy" ghastly yet strangely necessary. Take away the context and the line has no reason to be uttered except to let people feel superior to something.

The *Night in the Ukraine* takeoff worked better, particularly because Tune and the performers kept it sly and frisky. Then, too, the parody was a perfect echo of the originals, as in the opening few minutes:

> CHICO: (to male servant) Hey, Sasha! Joost think—tonight Mrs.-a Pavlenko she's-a finally go out and have-a some fun. . . . It's the first time she's-a leave-a the house since she getta to be a widow. . . . (To audience) Well, atsa da plot—now let's get on widda jokes. (To female servant) Hey, Masha . . . When Mrs. Pavlenko's husband, he droppa dead, it sure was some big surprise.
>
> MASHA: Yes—he'd never done *that* before!
>
> CHICO: (To audience) Well, if at's one of the jokes, let's get back to the plot!

Unquestionably entertaining, this Marx Brothers revival was even so old art, and a Golden Age isn't old.

Barnum, which opened the night before *Hollywood/Ukraine*, was the one good new book musical with a new score. Mark Bramble conceived it and fought for it for years but is too big a man to demand a concept credit. That must be why *Barnum* ran two years on Broadway and traveled the world: England, Australia, Germany, Italy, Spain, the Netherlands, and even France, generally disdainful of foreign musicals.

All right, that wasn't why. The saga of Phineas Taylor Barnum (Jim Dale), showman, was staged by Joe Layton in a simulation of that showiest of show-biz genres, the circus. Side-show barkers touted the crowd outside the theatre and in the lobby before the performance. A ringmaster (William C. Witter), who flew into the show from a platform way above stage left by swinging down a rope, narrated in the stentorian italics of the tanbark captain; and the players juggled, rode the unicycle, flew the trapeze, walked the high wire. Barnum's midget star, General Tom Thumb (Leonard John Crofoot), danced between two Tower of London beefeaters twice his height (stilt-walkers, of course) and under Jumbo the elephant (so huge that we saw only its legs as it marched in). David Mitchell's set of ropes and ladders overhanging three touring wagons clearly laid the action under the big top. Theoni V. Aldredge's costumes ran from real-life frock coats and high-collared dresses to circus tights and clown pajamas, with Barnum at last a resplendent circus king in white breeches and vest, black boots, and red tailcoat.

The show was a circus dazzle of a musical right from the start, when a woman in a theatre box that was actually part of the set suddenly got up to go home. Dale argued with her; she won. "Good day, Mister Barnum," she said with finality; but he rushed over to a trampoline, bounced up, and took a kiss from her. It was his wife, Charity (Glenn Close), who spends her role in the show ever disapproving of Barnum's "noble art of humbug" and trying to get him out of show biz. A forgiving spouse, she regrets but tolerates his affair with one of his attractions, opera soprano Jenny Lind (Marianne Tatum). Charity even gets Phineas into politics. But she dies, and Barnum then puts his freak show, vaudeville, and concert past behind him for ultimate completion in the creation of the Barnum & Bailey Circus, as the cast throngs the aisles for the champion rouser in a mostly rousing score, "Join the Circus."

With lyrics by Michael Stewart to Cy Coleman's music, *Barnum* had exactly the brand of songs this unique event needed. Bramble's book is tight and fast-moving, seldom dwelling on emotional values as Barnum asserts the ambitious American's right to entrepreneurial self-fulfillment. He's a hustler, selling culture without having any himself. But it worked: when he died, in 1891, he was worth five million dollars.

Obviously, the *Barnum* score couldn't rival Sondheim's intricately layered psychological readings or the edgy narrations of *A Chorus Line*. *Barnum* needs *songs*, as rhythmic as the swing of trapeze artists and as bright as calliope noise. Two ballads—"The Colors of My Life" and "Love Makes Such Fools of Us All"—were still moments in the joyful uproar of "There Is a Sucker Born Ev'ry Minute"; the quodlibet with patter section, "One Brick at a Time"; the Barnums' jazz-country duet, "I Like Your Style"; "Come Follow the Band"; and "The Prince of Humbug."

Some felt that the story, however much from chronicle, was simply an excuse for the production. Still, the show started with Bramble's wish to transform circus fun into musical-comedy devilry. This had never been done before. Previous musicals with a circus background either featured actual circus attractions (such as *Jumbo*, in 1935, which had a *real* elephant onstage) or absorbed a bit of circus color into an otherwise regulation musical (such as *Are You With It?*, in 1945). *Barnum* really lived in a *stylization* of circus, as when a tiff between Barnum and Charity, ever bristling with schemes of reform, was played out as if Barnum and his staff were taming a wild animal. The Ringmaster even threatened her with the tiger-master's chair.

Of course, it's easy to fault a musical's book when that musical is designed to turn what would have been its book material into entertainment by other means. *Barnum* is what Bramble dreamed it would be: a musical made of circus. So he turned over his "book rights," so to say, to director Layton, who laid out a narrative more in live action than in speech, in song and dance and stunts and tricks. Another Bramble book, co-written with Michael Stewart, gave us a very different kind of show at the tail end of the season,* though this, too, was a work in which

---

* I take "season" in its traditional usage, dating back to before the implementation of air-conditioning, when many theatres closed during the summer and all the star performers went on vacation. Though the use of giant (and noisy) fans came into limited use by the 1910s, the season as such ran from September 1 through the following August, until the Tony Awards committee assigned artificial dates for annual eligibility. The aim was simply to position the televised awards show for maximum PR effect, but it created an unnatural jurisdiction that confounds history.

the director-choreographer proves so crucial that, as some see it, the presentation matters but the writing doesn't.

42nd Street is the reason why we keep getting flop stagings of movie musicals.* Its tally of 3,486 performances on Broadway, its lengthy stay at London's Drury Lane, and its hit revival that opened but thirteen years after the original closed all contribute to this show's mystique. The last of the David Merrick–Gower Champion super-musicals, it shouldn't have mystique. It doesn't even have a new score, though Bramble and Stewart did ask Jerry Herman before going back to the four numbers written by Harry Warren and Al Dubin for the Warner Bros. film and adding in others from the Warren-Dubin backstager catalogue.

"Based on the novel by Bradford Ropes," the credits read. No, *42nd Street* is based on the 1933 movie made from the novel, but in a simplistic rendering that polishes a piece of hard-luck realism into a pastel dancefest. The movie is really about a showman with a terminal heart condition, determined to deliver one last smash before he dies. Stewart and Bramble eliminated this throughline, turning the complex character played by Warner Baxter into a cartoon martinet (Jerry Orbach). His star, a trembly Bebe Daniels in the film, is now the icy Tammy Grimes. The chorus girl who goes on for the crippled star to save the show—Ruby Keeler casually immortalizing one of American show biz's most essential roles—was now the tensely efficient Wanda Richert.

So we're losing some of the film's charm but also its detailed look at backstage life. On the other hand, the movie typifies Hollywood's ignorance of what a genius showman actually *does* in getting up a hit show. All we really see Baxter do during rehearsals is shout at the chorus because they aren't performing the choreographer's vapid combinations with enough energy. That's the secret behind great showmanship? C'mon, snap into it?

Stewart, Bramble, and Champion knew that this is balderdash; but their solution is not much better. After the woman half (Carole Cook) of the eccentric writing duo screams her way through a taste of the "Shadow Waltz," Orbach, with a knowing condescension, tells his staff to "try it in three-quarter time" and "down a tone." Oh, that's the secret—change the key signature.

---

* And *Thoroughly Modern Millie* (2002) is the reason why we'll be getting plenty more. I can't wait for the staging of *The Great Gabbo*; can you?

Slimming the director down from the movie's neurotic protagonist to the stage show's dour cipher made for the characterological inconsistencies that sometimes corrupted George Abbott shows. When Richert is involved in an accident that lames Grimes, Orbach abruptly fires Richert without finding out who really was at fault. Not long after, he is encouraging her to take over Grimes' part as if he had always believed in Richert. *What?*

I'm quibbling with a hit because this show falsely led some people to think that the musical was still in trim in an age of recycled music and recycled stories and recycled stars. Even given the use of old songs, *42nd Street* seemed the newest of shows on the most basic of themes: making a hit on Broadway. At the decade's end, it appeared to speak the reply to *Follies* at the decade's start. You're wrong—show-biz tradition is still with us, still vital, still ready to change form and bounce back.

There was nothing tired about *42nd Street*. It was another of those shows that made one envy the entire cast for the fun they must be having. They live one's dreams, rushing off after one big number to change costumes for the next. One unexpected boon was the way the songs fit the book, for now some of the old Warren-Dubin presentation numbers had turned into story and even character songs.

Granted, half the score is sung "onstage," in rehearsal or performance— the "Shadow Waltz," "You're Getting To Be a Habit With Me," "Dames," "We're in the Money," "Shuffle Off To Buffalo," and the title song. Even "About a Quarter To Nine," which functions as a charm number, is actually a last-minute coaching session by Grimes of her replacement, Richert.

However, "Go Into Your Dance" blew into the stage show from the forgotten Al Jolson–Ruby Keeler film of the same title as a perfect sixties-seventies change-of-scenery number, a Champion specialty. It takes us from the theatre to a lunch spot, tapping all the way, in a message that could serve as the show's motto. Dance was being drained out of the musical by pop operas and serious subject matter—and this is why Champion raised his curtain to pause at about twenty-four inches above the deck to show some forty-five pairs of dancing feet. It was to return his form to first principles, to revive the musical as treat instead of the musical as a black family escaping the ghetto or the musical as let's burn Joan of Arc.

"Lullaby of Broadway," so self-contained a sequence in its source, *Gold Diggers of 1935*, that it's virtually a one-act movie, turned beautifully into a story number. The scene is the center-city Philadelphia train station, whence the heroine will flee from being fired out of the tryout of *Pretty Lady*. She is a strange mixture of dejected and determined, and is waiting for the train that will take her back to her home city of Allentown, about sixty miles to the northwest.

The lights pick her up alone, sitting on her suitcase, a small figure in a great imposing space framed by staircases running down right and left to meet in the center. The director enters. As I've said, he will now pull his character inside out, appealing to her to rejoin show biz—in fact, to save it. But she will not forgive metropolitan life, and *Pretty Lady*, and the director in particular for having shattered her dream. This is the *Chorus Line* scene we never saw: Zach and one of Michael Bennett's protégés after the rejection.

But *A Chorus Line* is a musical play: revelation. *42nd Street* is a musical comedy: fantasy. So now the whole cast comes running down those stairs, and finally . . . but it isn't what happens that matters; the suspense of dénouement is for shows like *A Chorus Line*. What matters here is how the show brings us in on the resolution of the problem, how it welcomes us into the joy. We know that metropolitan life is tough. That's what the *Pretty Lady*s are for: to soothe our pain. The heroine must save show biz, and—so *A Chorus Line* has taught us—she will herself be Saved.

Naturally, it's "Lullaby of Broadway" that the director and then the various principals and finally everyone present will sing to get Wanda Richert off that suitcase and back to the theatre. As with all this show's numbers, no special insertions were needed to cue in the refrain. Jerry Orbach just opened up on "Come on along and listen to," and the current was *on*. Orbach's surprisingly ample baritone seemed almost too good a voice for an actor this accomplished, especially given the unemotional demeanor that he had to affect for the role. The number built till it filled the auditorium with pleasure. Came then a classic moment: Orbach took Richert's hand to lead the cast in a final cakewalk refrain starting with giant *tenuti* on the first two notes, fifty-one voices letting go with fierce commitment.

It is worth noting that Harry Warren and Al Dubin wrote so many song hits for Warner Bros. that much of the score was standards or nearly so. There were three odd items. Another scene-changer took the *Pretty Lady* company from New York to Philadelphia in "Getting Out of Town." This was originally a pop number by Warren and Mort Dixon called "Got To Go To Town," the lyrics unchanged but some of them assigned to specific characters to create a plot number. "I Know Now," Tammy Grimes' torch number, dropped in from *The Singing Marine* to set up her later lack of disappointment when, *force majeure*, she leaves show biz to star in a private romance. (The Australian production substituted the more familiar "I Only Have Eyes For You," and the innovation has held through *42nd Street* productions generally, including the 2001 Broadway revival.) Yet another plot number "(There's a) Sunny Side To Every Situation," with lyrics by Johnny Mercer, was found in *Hard To Get*, like *The Singing Marine* one of the many forgotten movies that Dick Powell made in the 1930s. Champion staged "Sunny Side," the second-act opening, with the *Pretty Lady* chorus members singing individual lines as they contemplate unemployment in a stack of dressing rooms.

Note that each of the three songs, absorbed into *42nd Street*, evinced generical qualities of the Merrick-Champion format. Although set designer Robin Wagner gave the show a trendy new look with a big open space capable of accommodating spare clutter when necessary, this was an old-fashioned show. "Getting Out of Town" not only covers a change of scenery but exploits it as part of the visual entertainment. "I Know Now," too motionless for the restless Champion, is dovetailed into a party scene. "Sunny Side" gives the second act its all but essential opening chorus—"Hello, Good Morning," "The Farmer and the Cowman," "How Do You Raise a Barn?"

One element was missing—the utter Merrick-Champion star. Orbach and Grimes got major yet ambiguous billing, for Merrick had adopted a poster logo in the soon-to-be-influential pop opera style: one pictorial image (here, a pretty lady) against a solid color field (in Merrick's favorite red), and no names featured. It prepares us for such later incarnations as *Cats*' green eyes against black or *The Phantom of the Opera*'s mask and rose duo, though the style dates back to the medallion of praying angels used for *Jesus Christ Superstar*.

So *42nd Street*'s window cards suggested an ensemble show without leads of professional authority, a bald misstatement. *Barnum* also used one piece of art against one color—Tony Walton's line drawing of an ecstatic hero, arms upraised before a sheet of circus yellow. But *Barnum*'s posters idolized Jim Dale.

42nd Street worked differently. It had stars but was not made on them and gave them nothing to dazzle with comparable to Dale's greatest-show-on-earth stunts. And *42nd Street* never had trouble finding replacements or kitting out other productions; neither did *Barnum*. The talent was still with us. The shows, too: with the expansive vocal arrangements; the tricks with shadows and mirrors; the show curtain (which was the *42nd Street* pretty lady, beguiling against her, yes, David Merrick red); the spectacle, such as a costume parade in "Dames" so rich that as the number neared its end the girls were racing out in their summer-colors dress-and-hat ensembles to hit the stage before the music stopped.

The shows were still with us! Merrick would destroy you for a Cracker Jack prize if the mood struck him, but like all great showmen he spent the money. Ziegfeld, Cohan and Harris, Mr. J. J. Shubert, Charles Dillingham, Arthur Hammerstein: they spent the money on the creative, staging, and performing talent, the sets and costumes, and everything else. Ziegfeld was spendthrift and Mr. J. J. Shubert as close as a vise; still, these are the men who made the musical when the musical was created.

So if Merrick was still there to do what they did, the musical enjoyed correct ownership: because Merrick was there to give Gower Champion a theatre. And Champion was there to tell the stories. Too many seventies musicals assumed that all the stories had been told and invented alternatives to storytelling in novelty settings, incongruous music, and weirdo characters. *42nd Street*'s strength lay in its confidence in an old story—one of the oldest, in fact: if one wills it hard enough, and cultivates the talent and puts in the effort, one will get there, because that's how democracy works. It helps to be young and cute, of course, but it really does provide for everyone. That's why they call it "democracy."

One might expect Merrick to rush this sure-thing smash to its premiere. On the contrary. Perhaps reckoning that this must be his last big one, Merrick toyed with press and public, scheduling run-throughs of the finished show without admitting theatregoers and issuing gnomic comments to the media. In fact, Merrick had secretly staged an intervention in his own production by demanding a major structural change in the set design. It was expensive and it delayed the premiere, but it was Merrick's show in the most literal sense: he had put up the entire 2.5 million capitalization out of his own pocket. That's how sure he was.

Some thought it a reckless gamble because of Champion's poor track record after *I Do! I Do!* in 1966. Indeed, Champion had become the worst thing one can become in this business: desperate. This is what doubtless led him to attach his name to a long shot like *Rockabye Hamlet*. Champion may even have tried to take over *Chicago* during its early stages when Fosse suffered his heart attack (for which Fosse repaid Champion with an unflattering portrait in Fosse's autobiographical film *All That Jazz*).

There was this, too: of all the leading director-choreographers, Champion was the least willing to experiment. De Mille's *Allegro*, Robbins' *West Side Story*, Layton's *No Strings*, Fosse's *Chicago*, Bennett's *A Chorus Line:* this is important history. Champion never did a historically important show. Even so, he himself was historically important as the one who crystalized musical-comedy format, purifying the form in *Hello, Dolly!* so that the unfocused high spirits of such seminal works as *Lady, Be Good!* and *Anything Goes* were definitively centered. The musical *play* received its definition back in the 1940s. But not till consistency of character development was routined in musical comedy could Champion bring forth the masterpiece in the form. *Hello, Dolly!* formulates an absolute balance of the musical's three basic elements—song, dance, and humor—in the ultimate musical-comedy plotline, which is: everybody conquers his flaw and learns the art of happiness.

42nd Street was not on *Dolly!*'s level of accomplishment. The main reason was the score, for no matter how cleverly the numbers were sliced into the action, the Warren-Dubin songbook could not offer Champion anything on the level of "Ribbons Down My Back" or "It Only Takes a Moment," in which Jerry Herman extrapolates character while glorifying salient points in the musical's worldview. "Ribbons" sings of the expectation of something wonderful about to occur. And "Moment" is the occurrence.

Still, *42nd Street*'s abundance of choreography and the speed with which Champion moved from number to number made the show play marvelously when it finally admitted a paying public. Merrick wasn't finished with his pranking, however, canceling one preview at the last moment because, he said, "a rat got into the generator." (He had spotted a reporter in the audience.) And another preview was interrupted by a bomb scare during the second act, when the audience was invited outside to enjoy a second intermission while the theatre was searched.

Finally, on August 25, 1980, *42nd Street* opened. Its audience was set for a hit—better, the kind of hit that no one in the business need be jealous of. Show people get resentful of colleagues who are enjoying a reign, not of those trying to recover from a dethronement, as Champion was. And the show itself was not an artistic breakthrough, so no one with pretensions could feel that he'd lost a hard-on contest.

In fact, *42nd Street* was a throwback. Late in *Camelot*, when King Arthur pauses to rest in the Enchanted Forest, he calls out to the long-vanished Merlyn, "Do you remember how often we walked this valley when I was a boy?" Unbeknown to the king, his dream of an ideal system, so painstakingly actualized, is being shattered even as he speaks; and he says, "Do you know what I miss of those days? Not my youth. My innocence."

That is what informed *42nd Street*'s immense success: its return to innocence, even to youth as well. It was a revival in this decade of revivals, but, for once, a fresh one. When Jerry Orbach topped off the show with a wryly sardonic reprise of the last few lines of the title song and the curtain fell, the audience broke into one of the few genuine ovations of the modern era.

Then David Merrick came out and told them that Gower Champion was dead: and the Golden Age was over.

INDEX

Aaron, Paul, 60, 170
Abbott, George, 60, 117, 185–87, 216
Ackland, Joss, 240
Act, The, **182–83**
Adams, Lee, 54–56, 82–83, 86
Adler, Renata, 9, 124
Adler, Richard, 99, 147, 186
Agress, Ted, 101
Ainsley, Paul, 16
Ain't Misbehavin', **173**
Aint Supposed To Die a Natural Death, 72
Albert, Donnie Ray, 153
Alden, Christopher, 171
Aldredge, Theoni V., 245
Alexander, C. K., 154
Alexander, Jason, 231
Alfred, William, 87–89
Ali, Muhammad, 49
Allegro, 25, 26, 31, 252
Allen, Betty, 159
Allen, Debbie, 241
Allen, Jay, 82
Allen, Peter, 117
Allen, Rae, 12
Allen, Jonelle, 10
Allen, Ralph G., 235–37
Allmon, Clint, 198
Allyson, June, 143
Alvarez, Carmen, 120
Ambassador, **80–82**, 86
Ameche, Don, 143
Anderson, Carl, 15–16, 33
Andreas, Christine, 152
Andres, Barbara, 99, 169
Andrews, George Lee, 105, 106, 202
Andrews, Maxene, 58, 59
Andrews, Patty, 58, 59
Angel, **181–82**
Annie, **223–28**
Annie Get Your Gun, 32, 42, 101
Anthony, Joseph, 49
Anything Goes, 6, 252
Applause, **54–56**, 56, 82
Arkin, Alan, 60
Arlen, Steve, 88, 89
Arnaz, Lucie, 201
Aronson, Boris, 25, 29, 39, 102, 105, 131, 138
Arrighi, Luciana, 83
Attenborough, Richard, 221
Attles, Joseph, 172
Atwell, Rick, 179
Auberjonois, René, 51, 116
Avian, Bob, 42, 111

Babatunde, Obba, 241
Bacall, Lauren, 54, 55, 56

Back Country, **163**
Backus, Richard, 118
Baker's Wife, The, **209–13**
Balanchine, George, 153
Ballard, Kaye, 45, 59, 60, 60n
Ballroom, 39, 179, **190–92**
Balthrop, Carmen, 159
Bar Mitzvah Boy, 86
Baragrey, John, 70
Barbeau, Adrienne, 76
Barcelo, Randy, 16
Barclay, Jered, 119
Bari, Lynn, 41
Barlow, Anne Marie, 81
Barnes, Cheryl, 175
Barnes, Clive, 162, 209
Barnum, **245–46**
Barrett, Joe, 164
Barrie, Barbara, 28, 116
Barry, John, 92
Barry, Philip, 241–42
Bart, Lionel, 110
Bartlett, D'Jamin, 102
Bartlett, Michael, 41, 57
Bates, Alan, 22, 189
Battle, Kathleen, 159
Bay, Howard, 88
Bayer, Carole, 22, 200–201
Beach, Gary, 181
Beatles, The, 175–76
Beckham, Willard, 181
Beggar on Horseback, 21–22
Behrman, S. N., 193
Benjamin, P. J., 178
Bennett, Michael, 25, 28, 29, 33, 38, 39, 39–40, 40n, 50, 99, 110, 111–13, 113, 137, 190–92, 217–22, 252
Bennett, Robert Russell, 234
Benson, Robby, 189
Benthall, Michael, 50
Berg, Gertrude, 59, 60, 61
Bergen, Polly, 45–46
Bergman, Alan, 191
Bergman, Marilyn, 191
Berkeley, Busby, 141
Berkman, John, 37, 44, 64
Berlin, Irving, 1, 3
Berlin To Broadway With Kurt Weill, **168**
Berman, Shelly, 182
Bernstein, Leonard, 94, 134, 135, 139, 158
Berry, Eric, 109
Berry, John, 207, 210
Best Little Whorehouse in Texas, The, 161, **197–99**
Big Time Buck White (play), 49
Bigelow, Susan, 174
Birch, Patricia, 58, 76, 186, 201

INDEX

Birkenhead, Susan, 174
Bishop (Kelly), Carole, 219, 220
Björnson, Maria, 42
Black Crook, The, 2
Blackton, Jay, 234, 238
Blaine, Vivian, 29, 41, 61–62
Blair, Pamela, 221
Blake, Eubie, 173
Blanchard, Cayce, 171
Blank, Lawrence J., 163
Blier, Steven, 171
Blood Red Roses, **162**
Bobbie, Walter, 76, 137
Bock, Jerry, 93, 94
  See also Apple Tree, The; Body Beautiful, The; Fiddler on the Roof; Fiorello!; Rothschilds, The; She Loves Me; Tenderloin
Body Beautiful, The, 93
Bonazzi, Elaine, 156
Bond, Christopher, 228
Booth, Shirley, 120
Bostwick, Barry, 76, 117, 196
Boublil, Alain, 14
Boulez, Pierre, 20, 20n, 21
Bowne, Richard, 238
Boy Friend, The, 42, **149**
Boy Meets Boy, **164**
Brackman, Jacob, 189
Bramble, Mark, 193, 245, 245–46, 246–47
Breakfast at Tiffany's, 65
Breaux, Marc, 115
Brecht, Bertolt, 19, 156
Brennan, Jimmy, 169, 187–88
Brice, Carol, 70
Bridgewater, Dee Dee, 235
Brittan, Robert, 124–25
Broderick, Matthew, 51
Brooks, David, 118
Brooks, Donald, 146
Brown, Georgia, 188, 189
Brown, Michael, 118
Brown, Oscar, Jr., 49
Brown, Steve, 162
Brown, William F., 75
Browning, Susan, 96
Bryan, Wayne, 146, 169
Brynner, Yul, 121–22
Bubbling Brown Sugar, **172**, **173**
Buck White, **49**
Bufano, Rocco, 12–13
Burgess, Anthony, 121
Burns, David, 58, 115
Burns, Philip, 162
Burns, Ralph, 53
Burr, Charles, 165
Burrows, Abe, 145
Burton, Richard, 241
Bury, John, 13
Bye Bye Birdie, 55n

Cabaret, 6, 35, 78, 102
Cabin in the Sky, 12, 72–73
Cacoyannis, Michael, 120
Cahn, Sammy, 169, 173
Calbes, Eleanor, 115

Callan, Chris, 149
Camelot, 32, 122, **241**, 253
Campbell, Patton, 83
Can-Can, 75, 93
Candide, 25, 26, 135, **147**
Canterbury Tales, **240–41**
Capalbo, Carmen, 156–57
Capers, Virginia, 125
Capote, Truman, 69–70, 71
Cariou, Len, 102, 105n, 106, 231
Carlo, Monte, 177–78
Carmelina, **188–89**
Carmines, Al, 62, 163
Carne, Judy, 149
Carnelia, Craig, 174
Carousel, 31, 92, 102, 104
Carroll, David, 169
Carroll, Vinnette, 73, 172–73
Carson, Jeanie, 162
Carter, Desmond, 80
Carter, Dixie, 119
Carter, Nell, 12, 173
Carter, Ralph, 12, 13, 125
Casey, Warren, 76
Cason, Barbara, 169
Castle, John, 22
Catlett, Mary Jo, 117, 118, 148, 162, 179, 180
Cecil, Jonathan, 171
Chadman, Christopher, 153–54
Champion, Gower, 62–64, 65–69, 68, 72, 91, 182, 183, 220, 247, 248, 250, 251–53
Champion, Marge, 46
Channing, Carol, 62n, 148
Chapman, Alan, 31
Chapman, William, 100
Charisse, Zan, 151
Charlap, Moose, 233
Charles, Maria, 42
Charles, Walter, 214
Charmin, Martin, 56, 184, 223, 224, 227
Cherry, **61–62**
Chicago, 3, 22, 115, 127, **128–31**, 136, 137, 252
Chorus Line, A, 39, 40n, 137, 190–91, 192, 201, **217–22**, 252
Christopherson, Stefanianne, 165
Christy, **163**
Churchill, Frank, 238
Cilento, Wayne, 221
Clayburgh, Jill, 109
Close, Glenn, 245
Coca, Imogene, 202, 203, 205
Coco, 39, **49–51**, 56, 86
Coe, George, 202–3, 205
Cohan, George M., 3, 6, 8, 110
Cohen, Margery, 168
Cole, **171–72**
Cole, Kay, 175
Coleman, Cy, 110, 197, 202–4, 245
Collins, Dorothy, 36, 44–45
Colson, C. David, 24
Comden, Betty, 41, 54, 202, 204–5, 233
Comin' Uptown, **238–39**
Company, **25–31**, 33, 35, 62, 112
Condos, Steve, 63, 64
Conklin, John, 100

Connecticut Yankee, A, 140, 143
Contrast, The, **162**
Coogan, Jack, 207
Cook, Barbara, 46, 70
Cook, Carole, 247
Cook, Joe, 238
Cook, Roderick, 168–69
Coote, Robert, 151
Corsaro, Frank, 16, 135, 159
Coullet, Rhonda, 196
Coward, Noël, 110, 168–69, 171
Cowardy Custard, **171**
Cox, Catherine, 186
Cox, Richard, 183, 184
Cox, William, 186
Craig, David, 40–41
Crazy For You, 101
Crofoot, Leonard John, 245
Crom, Rick, 31, 99
Cronyn, Hume, 118
Crowley, Bob, 238
Cry For Us All, **87–89**, 178
Cryer, David, 61–62, 149
Cryer, Gretchen, 164
Cullum, John, 100, 104, 202, 205
Curtis, Keene, 13, 94, 210
Cyrano, **121**, 122

Dale, Clamma, 153
Dale, Grover, 111, 175
Dale, Jim, 245, 251
Damn Yankees, 99
Dancin', **173–74**
Daniels, William, 105n
Danner, Blythe, 46
Danner, Harry, 149
Dante, Nicholas, 218–19
Darcel, Denise, 41
Darrieux, Danielle, 51, 80, 81
David, Mack, 60
Davila, Diana, 11
Davis, Buster, 141n, 142, 207–8, 216
Davis, Clifton, 10
Davis, Ossie, 23
Davis, Sammy, Jr., 153
Day in Hollywood/A Night in the Ukraine, The, 243–44
De Carlo, Yvonne, 41
de Guzman, Jossie, 241
De Koven, Reginald, 3
de Lappe, Gemze, 234
de Mille, Agnes, 220, 234, 252
De Shields, Andre, 75, 173
Dear Oscar, **117**
Dear World, 67, 194
del Valle, Peter, 163
DeMain, John, 153
Demas, Carole, 76, 210
Demy, Jacques, 165–66
Dench, Judi, 85
Dennen, Barry, 16
Denniston, Leslie, 242
Desert Song, The, **149**
Desmond, Johnny, 63
DeSylva, B. G., 145
Dexter, John, 157

Diamond, Neil, 174
Diener, Joan, 88, 89, 121
Dietz, Howard, 80, 170
Different Times, **117–18**
Dittman, Dean, 202–3, 205
Dixon, Ed, 171
Dixon, Gale, 50
Dixon, Mort, 250
Do Re Mi, 55n
Do I Hear a Waltz?, 56
Doctor Jazz, **207–9**
Doctor Selavy's Magic Theatre, 19, **20**, 22
Dodge, Jerry, 67, 68
Doing It For Sugar. See Sugar
Don't Bother Me, I Can't Cope, **73**
Dont Play Us Cheap!, 72, **72–73**
Donnelly, Ruth, 143
D'Orsay, Fifi, 41
Drake, Alfred, 122, 123, 124, 169
Draper, Kate, 243
Dreamgirls, 39, 113, 192
Dubey, Matt, 71
Dude, 10, **11–13**, 13n
Duncan, Sandy, 149, 233
Dunn, Don, 141, 141n
Dunn, Michael, 12

Ebb, Fred, 57, 58, 129, 182–83
Ebersole, Christine, 234
Elephant Steps, 19, **20**
Elias, Alix, 11
Elliman, Yvonne, 15, 16
Elliott, Patricia, 102
Elmer Gantry (novel), 51, 52
Elmslie, Kenward, 69
Englander, Ludwig, 3
Essex, David, 240
Ettlinger, Don, 80, 81
Eubie!, 173
Evanko, Ed, 99
Evans, Harvey, 36, 41, 119
Evans, Ray, 236
Evita, **239–40**

F. Jasmine Adams, **163**
Fagan, Scott, 117
Faggot, The, **163**
Faison, George, 75, 135
Faison, Sandy, 227
Falana, Lola, 207, 208–9
Farr, Kimberly, 242
Farrar, John, 78
Fashion, **162**
Faye, Alice, 145, 146–47
Fearnley, John, 169
Feingold, Michael, 155
Feld, Eliot, 93
Feldshuh, Tovah, 169, 179
Fenholt, Jeff, 15, 16
Feuer, Cy, 184
Feuillade, Louis, 21
Fiddler on the Roof, 9, 93, 94, 153, 209
Fieger, Addy O., 117
Field, Ron, 55, 149, 150, 189, 233
Fields, Dorothy, 110

INDEX

Finian's Rainbow, 3, 93
Finn, William, 37
Fiorello!, 93, 94
Firth, Tazeena, 239
Fischoff, George, 22
Fisher, Jules, 175
Fisher, Robert, 53
Flatt, Ernest, 237
Flavin, Tim, 242
Follies, 30, **34–47**, 58, 104, 105
Foote, Horton, 83
Ford, Chip, 101
Ford, Nancy, 164
Foreman, Richard, 19–22, 154
Forrest, George, 121, 148
Forsythe, Henderson, 198, 199
Fortus, Daniel, 53, 61
42nd Street, **247–53**
Fosse, Bob, 97, 108–10, 113, 128–29, 137, 173–74, 252
Frankel, Gene, 154
Franklin, Nancy, 47
Freedman, Gerald, 193, 195, 196
Freeman, Al, Jr., 120
Freeman, Arny, 235
Freeman, Damita Jo, 183
Freeman, Stan, 115
Frey, Leonard, 92
Friedman, Gary William, 161, 183
Frings, Ketti, 182
Fuller, Dean, 71
Fuller, Larry, 170, 203, 239
Fuller, Penny, 55, 98–99, 99
Funny Thing Happened on the Way To the Forum, A, 147
Funny Girl, 22, 79
Furth, George, 25, 26, 112, 183

Gable, June, 147
Gabrielle, Caryl, 117
Gaetano, Nicholas, 201
Gallagher, Helen, 88, 89, 142, 208
Gallegly, David, 164
Gantry, **51–52**, 56
Garber, Victor, 231
Gardenia, Vincent, 191, 192
Garfinkle, Louis, 59–60
Garner, Jay, 96, 198
Garrett, Betty, 46
Garnett, Chip, 172
Garrett, Kelly, 169
Garrison, David, 243, 244
Gavin, John, 113
Gaynor, Charles, 141n
Geld, Gary, 23–25, 68, 100–101, 104, 181–82, 238
Gennaro, Peter, 49, 227
Gentlemen Prefer Blondes. See *Lorelei*
Gentry, Minnie, 72
George M!, 193
Georgy, **22–23**
Gere, Richard, 117
Gershwin, George, 1, 31, 80, 152, 167–68, 171
Gershwin, Ira, 1, 80
Gershwin!: A Celebration, **171**
Gesner, Clark, 179
Gibson, B. G., 175
Gibson, William, 110

Gielgud, John, 143
Gigi, **122–24**
Gilford, Jack, 141
Gillan, Ian, 15
Gillette, Anita, 48, 49
Gimbel, Norman, 165
Gingold, Hermione, 102, 106, 122
Girls Upstairs, The, **34–35**, 112. See also *Follies*
Gleason, Joanna, 197
Glickman, Will, 209
Glynn, Carlin, 198
Godspell, 108, 108n
Gohman, Don, 80, 82
Goldby, Derek, 93
Golden Apple, The, 25, 26, 71
Golden Boy, 82
Goldenberg, Billy, 191
Goldman, James, 34, 42–44, 112
Goldman, Sherwin M., 234
Goldsmith, Lee, 119
Gone With the Wind, **83–86**, 86
Good Companions, The, **85–86**
Good News, **145–47**
Goodbye Girl, The, 101
Goodtime Charley, **95–97**, 193
Gore, Christopher, 13, 98
Gorshin, Frank, 48
Got Tu Go Disco, **178**
Graff, Ilene, 197
Grand Tour, The, **193–95**
Grant, Micki, 73, 172–73, 174
Grass Harp, The, **69–71**, 79
Gray, Harold, 223–24, 227
Gray, Timothy, 146
Grean, Robin, 183
Grease, **76–78**, 156
Green, Adolph, 41, 54, 202, 204–5, 233
Greene, Ellen, 154
Grey, Joel, 95, 97, 137, 156, 193, 195
Grimes, Tammy, 247, 250
Groener, Harry, 234
Grossman, Larry, 53, 96, 97
Guare, John, 10, 11
Guillaume, Robert, 25
Guittard, Laurence, 102, 106, 165, 169, 234
Gunton, Bob, 155, 240
Guys and Dolls, 46n, 153
Gwynne, Fred, 182
Gypsy, 33, **150–51**, 228

Hackady, Hal, 53, 80, 96, 97
Hackett, Joan, 118
Hair, 11, 12
Half a Sixpence, 9
Hall, Carol, 198, 199
Hallelujah, Baby!, 3
Hamilton, Bonnie, 149
Hamilton, Margaret, 106
Hamlisch, Marvin, 200–201, 218
Hammerstein, Oscar, II, 1, 31, 185, 216
Hansberry, Lorraine, 124, 126n
Happy End, 155
Happy New Year, **241–43**
Haran, Mary Cleere, 235
Hardy, Joseph, 210

Harney, Ben, 159
Harnick, Sheldon, 93, 94, 98, 99, 126n, 165
  See also Apple Tree, The; Body Beautiful, The; Fiddler on the Roof; Fiorello!; Rex; Rothschilds, The; She Loves Me; Tenderloin
Harper, Wally, 145
Harris, Barbara, 95, 157
Harris, Richard, 241
Harrison, Gregory, 46
Harrold, Jack, 156
Hart, Lorenz, 1, 80, 169, 216
Hart, Melissa, 22, 190
Hart, Moss, 151
Harwood, Ronald, 85, 86
Hastings, Harold, 39
Hawkins, Ira, 150
Hayman, Lillian, 207, 208, 208–9
Haynes, Tiger, 75, 148
Hays, David, 83, 183
Hayworth, Rita, 54
Head, Murray, 15
Healy, David, 41–42
Hearn, George, 184–85, 231
Heckart, Eileen, 180
Heffernan, John, 24
Hello, Dolly!, 65–66, 79, 153, 194, 252
Hemsley, Sherman, 24
Henderson, Luther, 142, 163, 173, 207
Henderson, Ray, 145
Hendra, Tony, 71
Hendry, Tom, 20
Henner, Marilu, 58
Henning, Doug, 174–75
Hepburn, Katharine, 49–51
Herbert, Victor, 3, 6, 31–33, 121, 158
Herman, Jerry, 63, 65, 66, 67, 68, 132, 194, 243, 244, 247
  See also Dear World; Grand Tour, The; Hello, Dolly!; Dear World; Mack & Mabel; Mame; One of the Girls
Heuman, Barbara, 181
Hewett, Christopher, 186
Hiawatha, 2
Higgins, Joel, 101, 182, 186, 234
Hill, Sharon Lee, 212
Hines, Gregory, 239
Hirsch, Louis, 3
Hirson, Roger O., 108
Hitchcock, Raymond, 4, 5
Hobe (*Variety* critic), 153–54
Hodes, Gloria, 52
Hodges, Joy, 143n
Holder, Geoffrey, 75, 148
Holgate, Ron, 193
Holliday, David, 50–51, 52, 186
Holm, Celeste, 179
Holm, Hanya, 151
Holmes, Rupert, 110
Holt, Will, 58, 161, 183, 184, 186
Home Sweet Homer, **121–22**, 178
Hopkins, Linda, 170
Hornaday, Jeffrey, 221
Horne, Lena, 75
Hotel For Criminals, 19, **20–21**
Hoty, Dee, 45

Howard, Ken, 107, 111, 112, 134, 136
Hunt, Peter H., 97
Hurwit, Lawrence, 119
Husmann, Ron, 115, 149
Hynes, Elizabeth, 156
Hytner, Nicholas, 151

I and Albert, **82–83**, 86
I Love My Wife, **196–97**, **199–200**
I Remember Mama, **184–85**
In Person. See Act, The
Inge, William, 62
Ingram, Michael, 178
Irene, **143**, **144–45**
Irving, George S., 144, 187
Ivey, Judith, 46, 46n

Jackson, Anne, 118
Jackson, Ernestine, 125
Jackson, Michael, 75
Jackson, Nagle, 179
Jacob, Abe, 175
Jacob, Bill, 48
Jacob, Patti, 48
Jacobs, Jim, 76
James, Bob, 116
James, Stephen, 243
Jennings, John, 110
Jennings, Ken, 231
Jepson, Helen, 152
Jerome, Timothy, 210
Jesus Christ Superstar, **14–19**, 86, 97, 239, 240
Jimmy, **48–49**
John, Tom H., 75
Johnny Johnson, **154**
Johns, Glynis, 103
Johnson, Louis, 159
Johnson, Susan, 41
Johnston, Justine, 41, 57
Jones, Dean, 25
Jones, Tom, 161
Jones, Walton, 235
Joplin, Scott, 65, 158–60
Joseph, Stephen M., 161
Joyce, Elaine, 64
Julia, Raul, 10, 13, 153, 154

Kael, Pauline, 9, 10, 12
Kahn, Madeline, 56, 202, 203–4, 205
Kaiser, Georg, 155, 156
Kalem, T. E., 11, 176
Kalfin, Robert, 155
Kander, John, 57, 129, 182–83
Karnilova, Maria, 122–23
Karr, Pattie, 120
Kasha, Lawrence, 115
Kass, Jerome, 191
Kaufman, George S., 14, 21
Kava, Caroline, 154
Kay, Hershy, 139, 186, 203
Kaye, Danny, 57
Kaye, Judy, 205
Kaye, Stubby, 146
Kazan, Lainie, 107, 111, 113
Keel, Howard, 80–82, 80n

INDEX

Keeler, Ruby, 141, 142, 143, 146, 247
Keller, Jeff, 235
Kelly, David Patrick, 175
Kelly, Patsy, 141, 142, 143, 144
Kercheval, Ken, 168
Kern, Jerome, 1, 3, 6, 31, 32, 113, 153
Kerr, Walter, 121, 130, 152, 159, 231
Kert, Larry, 28, 28n, 30
Keyes, Evelyn, 143
Kidd, Michael, 46n, 93, 220
Kikuta, Kazuo, 83
Kimbrough, Charles, 28
King, Larry L., 198, 199
King, Mabel, 75
King and I, The, 31, 79, 153
King Dodo, 4–5, 36
King of Hearts, **189–90**
Kirk, Lisa, 65, 68
Kirkwood, James, 218–19
Kismet. See Timbuktu!
Kissel, Howard, 134
Kitt, Eartha, 148–49
Kleban, Ed, 217–18
Klein, Robert, 201
Klemperer, Werner, 213, 214
Kline, Kevin, 196, 202
Klotz, Florence, 39, 105, 132
Kneeland, Richard, 117
Knight, Shirley, 155
Kookoolis, Joseph Martinez, 117
Kupferman, Meyer, 83
Kupperman, Alvin, 53
Kurnitz, Julie, 53

Lacey, Florence, 194
LaChiusa, Michael John, 37
Lady, Be Good!, 5, 6, 252
Lady in the Dark, 35
Laffing Room Only, 6
Lahr, Bert, 5
Lahr, John, 22
Lail, Barbara, 146
Lamb, Gil, 58
Lambert, Mark, 103
Lancaster, Lucie, 58
Land, David, 240
Lander, Judy, 168
Lang, Barbara, 196
Lane, Burton, 188–89
Lane, Nathan, 51
Lang, Philip J., 81, 55
Langella, Frank, 95
Lanning, Jerry, 119, 151, 168
Lansbury, Angela, 90, 91, 150, 150–51, 179, 230–31
Larson, Jonathan, 31
Last Sweet Days of Isaac, **164**
Layton, Joe, 83, 84, 184, 245, 246, 252
Lazarus, Frank, 243, 244
Lebowsky, Stanley, 52
Lee, Baayork, 111, 221
Lee, Eugene, 12, 231
Lee, Franne, 12, 232
Lee, Michele, 111
Lees, Carol, 235
Legrand, Michel, 165

Lehew, Stephen, 169
Leigh, Adele, 42
Leigh, Mitch, 88, 89, 121, 122, 178–79
Leighton, Margaret, 106
Lemmon, Shirley, 169
Lenya, Lotte, 57, 154, 156, 157
Leonard, Richard, 169
Lerner, Alan Jay, 50, 89, 91, 94, 122, 123, 134, 135, 188–89
    See also Carmelina; Coco; Gigi; Lolita, My Love; Love Life; 1600 Pennsylvania Avenue
Lester, Edwin, 122
Let's Face It!, 57
Letter For Queen Victoria, A, 68
Levene, Sam, 213, 214
Levin, Herman, 116
Levy, Jacques, 163
Lewin, John, 162
Lewine, Richard, 169
Lewis, Bobo, 174
Lewis, Michael J., 121
Lewis, Sinclair, 51, 52
Li'l Abner, 3, 55n, 93
Lieutenant, The, 68
Linden, Hal, 93, 147–48
Link, Peter, 120, 189
Little Johnny Jones, 6
Little Night Music, A, 30, **101–6**, 105n
Livingston, Jay, 236
Livingston, Jerry, 60
Livingston, Robert H., 161
Lloyd, Christopher, 155
Lloyd, Jack, 145
Lloyd Webber, Andrew, 14, 17, 18–19, 86, 97, 239–40
Locke, Sam, 62, 62n
Lockhart, Jamie, 196
Loesser, Frank, 64
Loewe, Frederick, 122, 123
Logan, Joshua, 120
Lolita, My Love, **89–93**
Long, Avon, 73, 172
Long, William Ivey, 137
Look to the Lilies, **120**, 122
Look Homeward, Angel. See Angel
Lopez, Priscilla, 219, 221, 244
Lorelei, **148**
Lost in the Stars, **154**
Loudon, Dorothy, 30, 90, 92, 179, 191, 192, 225, 226, 227, 230
Louise, Merle, 231
Louisiana Purchase, 3
Love Life, 6, 25, 26, 118, 135
Lovely Ladies, Kind Gentlemen, **114–15**, 116
Lovers, **163**
Lum, Alvin, 11
Lumet, Sidney, 75
Lund, Art, 61–62
Lupe, La, 11
LuPone, Patti, 196, 210, 240, 240n
LuPone, Robert, 219
Lyndeck, Edmund, 231
Lysistrata, **120**, 122

McAfee, Diana, 55
McArdle, Andrea, 225

McCarthy, Joseph, 143
McCarty, Mary, 37, 38, 129
McConnell, Ty, 162
McCullers, Carson, 163
MacDermot, Galt, 10–14, 13n, 105
McGillin, Howard, 68
McGinnis, Joe, 116
McGreevey, Annie, 175
McHugh, Jimmy, 236, 237
Mack & Mabel, **65–69**, 194
McKayle, Donald, 135, 207
McKechnie, Donna, 28, **44**, 45, 149–50, 219, 220
McKenzie, Julia, 42, 44, 172, 206, 230
Mackintosh, Cameron, 41–42, 43
McMartin, John, 36
McNair, Barbara, 147–48
McQueen, Armelia, 173
Magic Show, The, **174–75**, 211
Mahagonny, **156–58**
Mallory, Victoria, 101
Maltby, Richard, Jr., 121, 173
Malvin, Arthur, 236
Mame, 194
Man of La Mancha, 64, 88, 92, 153, 178
Manchester, Melissa, 174
Mandan, Robert, 54
Mandelbaum, Ken, 98
Manheim, Ralph, 154
Mankiewicz, Joseph L., 54
Mankiewicz, Tom, 22
Mansur, Susan, 198, 199
Marcovicci, Andrea, 98
Marre, Albert, 88, 89, 121, 122
Marshall, Garry, 145, 213
Marshall, Kathleen, 45
Marshall, Ken, 241
Marshall, Larry, 153
Martin, Barney, 129
Martin, Helen, 24, 126
Martin, Hugh, 146
Martin, Leila, 94
Martin, Millicent, 172
Masiell, Joe, 118
Massey, Daniel, 12, 41
Massi, Bernice, 214
Masterson, Peter, 198
Mata Hari, 46
Mathis, Sherry, 186
Me and Bessie, **170**
Me Nobody Knows, The, **161**
Meehan, Thomas, 184, 223, 224
Meet Me in St. Louis, 98
Meet the People, 52
Mellon, James J., 241
Melrose, Howard, 207
Mercado, Hector Jaime, 241
Mercer, Johnny, 85, 86, 250
Mercouri, Melina, 120, 122
Merman, Ethel, 5, 135, 150, 167–68, 183, 242
Merrick, David, 62–64, 65–69, 210, 220, 247, 251–53
Merrill, Bob, 63, 65, 91, 110, 213–16
   See also *Breakfast at Tiffany*; *Dangerous Christmas of Red Riding Hood, The*; *Pretty-belle*; *Prince of Grand Street, The*; *Sugar*
Merritt, Theresa, 163

Merry Widow, The, 4, 32
Meyers, Timothy, 76
Michaels, Sidney, 96
Mielziner, Jo, 63
Milford, Penelope, 101
Millar, Gertie, 80
Miller, Ann, 45, 236–37
Miller, Marilyn, 5, 57, 129
Miller, Ron, 62
Miller, Sharron, 148
Mills, John, 85, 86
Mills, Stephanie, 75
Minnelli, Liza, 65, 137, 182–83
Minnie's Boys, **52–53**
Mintz, Eli, 60n
Mitchell, David, 245
Mitchum, Robert, 110
Miyamoto, Amon, 138
Mlle. Modiste, 32
Molly, **59–61**, 81, 180
Monley, Adam, 212
Montevecchi, Liliane, 41, 45
Moody, Ron, 44
Moore, Melba, 23–24
Moore, Robert, 201
Moore, Tom, 58, 76
Mordente, Lisa, 183
Moreno, Rita, 51
Morey, Larry, 238
Morgan, J. L., 207
Morgan, Roger, 12
Morris, Anita, 175
Morris, Garrett, 72
Morrow, Karen, 70, 116
Morse, Robert, 63, 64, 187–88
Morton, Frederic, 93
Morton, Joe, 125
Moses, Gilbert, 72, 75, 135
Moss, Kathi, 76
Moss, Lawrence John, 188
Most Happy Fella, The, 102, **233–34**
Mowatt, Anna Cora, 162
Muenz, Richard, 214, 241
Mulcahy, Lance, 118
Murney, Christopher, 116
Murray, Don, 71–72, 204
Music Is, **185–87**
Musical Chairs, **241**
Musser, Tharon, 38, 39, 190, 192
My Fair Lady, 6, 104, 116, **151–52**, 190
My One and Only, 113

Nabokov, Vladimir, 89–90
Nash, N. Richard, 179
Natwick, Mildred, 58, 71
Naughton, James, 137, 197
Naughty Marietta, 6, 32, 33, 101
Neagle, Anna, 144
Neeley, Ted, 175
Nefertiti, **97–98**
Neher, Erick, 234
Neill, William, 156
Nelson, Barry, 182
Nelson, Gene, 36, 145
Nelson, Kenneth, 114–15, 171

Nemetz, Lenora, 174
Nemiroff, Robert, 125
Nervous Set, The, 55n
Neuwirth, Bebe, 137
Neville, John, 90, 91
New Moon, The, 101
New York, 141
New York Daily News, 61
New York Post, 149, 241
New York Times, 9, 195, 220, 241
New Yorker, The, 47, 241
Newman, Phyllis, 41, 45, 150
Newsday, 162
Newton, John, 119
Nicholls, Allan, 175
Nichols, Mike, 165, 224–25, 227
Nickerson, Shane, 109
Nine, 64, 113
1940's Radio Hour, The, **234–35**
No, No, Nanette, 58, **141–43**, 164, 181, 208
Noll, Christiane, 212
Nowhere To Go But Up, 48
Nunn, Trevor, 212
Nype, Russell, 30, 169

O'Brien, Frank, 10
O'Brien, Jack, 116, 153, 234
O'Brien, Margaret, 98
O'Brien, Timothy, 239
O'Connor, Caroline, 68
O'Haughey, M., 129
O'Horgan, Tom, 13, 16–19, 175, 176
O'Neil, Tricia, 57
O'Shea, Tessie, 180–81
Ockrent, Mike, 42
Odets, Clifford, 56
Oenslager, Donald, 146
Of Thee I Sing, 3, 75
Offenbach, Jacques, 2, 33, 206
Oh, Soon-Teck, 132
Oh! Calcutta!, 55
Oh Coward!, **168–69**
Oklahoma!, 9, 31, 52, 64, 115, **234**
On the Twentieth Century, 22, **201–6**
On the Town, 27, 112, **149–50**
Only Girl, The, 32
Oppenheimer, George, 162
Orbach, Jerry, 129, 247–48, 250, 253
Ostrow, Stuart, 109
Our Miss Gibbs, 80
Over Here!, **58–59**, 76

Pacific Overtures, 30, 127, 128, **131–34**, 136, 137–38, 229
Page, Ken, 173
Pagnol, Marcel, 209, 210
Paige, Elaine, 240
Pajama Game, The, 32, 33, **47–48**, 99, 109
Pal Joey, 6
Palmer, Peter, 148
Panko, Tom, 62
Park, **118–19**
Parry, William, 175
Parsons, Estelle, 157
Passion, 230

Patinkin, Mandy, 240
Patrick, John, 114, 115
Payne, John, 145
Pearl, Irwin, 53
Peck, Jon, 169
Pendleton, Austin, 164
Pène du Bois, Raoul, 142, 144
Perkins, Anthony, 30
Peter Pan, **233**
Peters, Bernadette, 62, 65, 150
Peters, Brock, 154
Peterson, Kurt, 36, 210
Philemon, 161
Pierson, Thomas, 210
Pinza, Carla, 10
Pippin, 107, **108–10**
Pippin, Donald, 55, 162
Pitchford, Dean, 165
Plain and Fancy, 40, 209
Platinum, 179, **183–84**
Plummer, Christopher, 121
Pope, Peggy, 207, 208–9
Porgy and Bess, 25, **143**, **152–53**
Porretta, Frank, 157
Porter, Cole, 1, 50–51, 80, 113, 171–72, 216, 241–42
Premice, Josephine, 172
Presnell, Harve, 84
Preston, Robert, 65, 67, 213–16
Prettybelle, 89, **90–91**
Previn, André, 49–51, 56, 85–86
Price, Gilbert, 134, 154
Priestley, J. B., 85, 86
Primrose, 80
Prince, Hal, 16, 25, 29, 33, 39, 99, 102, 106, 112, 134, 138, 156, 191, 202, 205, 239
Prince of Grand Street, The, **213–16**
Producers, The, 51
Prowse, Juliet, 41
Purlie, **23–25**

Quilley, Denis, 44
Quintero, José, 154

Raad, Gerry, 62
Rado, James, 12
Ragni, Gerome, 11–12, 13n
Rainbow Jones, 119
Raisin, 12, **124–26**
Raitt, John, 100
Rall, Tommy, 88, 89
Ralph, Sheryl Lee, 241
Ralston, Teri, 210, 211
Ramin, Sid, 139
Rampling, Charlotte, 22
Ramsay, Remak, 115, 149
Randall, Bob, 174
Rathburn, Roger, 141
Rayam, Curtis, 159
Raye, Martha, 57
Reams, Lee Roy, 54
Red Mill, The, 32, 143
Redfield, William, 12
Redgrave, Lynn, 22
Redhead, 6
Reed, Vivian, 172

Reggae, 241
Reiner, Carl, 187
Reinholt, George, 194
Reinking, Ann, 58, 95, 108, 137
Rex, **98–99**
Reynolds, Debbie, 143, 145, 146
Rice, Peter, 81
Rice, Sarah, 231
Rice, Tim, 14, 15, 16, 18, 18–19, 239
Rich, Frank, 36, 241
Richards, Jess, 149, 162
Richardson, Claibe, 69
Richardson, Ian, 152
Richert, Wanda, 247
Rigby, Harry, 141, 143, 145, 147, 235–36
Rigg, Diana, 41, 44, 106
Rio Rita, 52
Ritchard, Cyril, 63
Rittmann, Trude, 83, 124
Rivera, Chita, 129, 120, 137
Rivers, Larry, 157
Robber Bridegroom, The, **195–96**
Robbins, Jerome, 27, 149, 150, 153, 220, 233, 241, 252
Robbins, Rex, 151
Roberts, Joan, 45
Roberts, Judith, 165
Roberts, Pernell, 84
Roberts, Tony, 63, 64
Robinson, Phyllis, 88
Robison, David V., 118
Rockabye Hamlet, **178**, 252
Rodgers & Hart, **169–70**
Rodgers, Mary, 174
Rodgers, Richard, 1, 31, 56, 72, 80, 98, 99, 124, 169, 184, 185, 216
 See also *Allegro*; *Carousel*; *Do I Hear a Waltz*; *I Remember Mama*; *King and I, The*; *Oklahoma!*; *Rex*; *Sound of Music, The*; *South Pacific*; *Two By Two*
Rolph, Marti, 36
Romberg, Sigmund, 3, 149
Rome, Harold, 83, 84–85
Rooney, Mickey, 62, 236–37
Rosalinda, 52
Rose, George, 51, 151, 233
Rose, Philip, 23, 100, 238
Rose-Marie, 32, 101
Ross, Diana, 75
Ross, Jamie, 169
Ross, Judith, 13
Roth, Lillian, 58
Ross, Ted, 75
Rothschilds, The, **93–95**, 99
Roud, Richard, 210
Rounds, David, 129, 210
Routledge, Patricia, 134, 136–37, 171
Rubenstein, Barbara, 172
Rubin, Cyma, 141
Rubinstein, John, 107
Rudel, Julis, 156
Russell, Ken, 85–86
Russell, Nipsey, 75
Ryan, Charlene, 51
Ryan, Irene, 107

Saddler, Donald, 46, 145, 170, 195
St. Louis, Louis, 78
Saks, Gene, 197
Salerno, Mary Jo, 238
Sally, 57, 129
Sanders, George, 54
Sanders, Alma, 177–78
Sandifur, Virginia, 36, 71, 72, 169
Saratoga, 70
Saravà, **178–79**
Sato, Isao, 133
Saturday Night, 228
Sauter, Eddie, 23
Scardino, Don, 118, 182, 189–90
Scarlet, 83. See also *Gone With the Wind*
Schapiro, Herb, 161
Schisgal, Murray, 60
Schlesinger, John, 82, 83
Schmidt, Harvey, 161
Schönberg, Claude-Michel, 14
Schuller, Gunther, 159
Schulman, Arnold, 221
Schwartz, Arthur, 80, 170
Schwartz, Stephen, 108, 111–12, 174, 174, 175, 210–12
Scorsese, Martin, 182–83
Scott, Michael, 242
Seesaw, 99, 107, **110–13**
Sell, Janie, 58, 199
Selling of the President, The, **116**
Sennett, Mack, 65, 66
Serban, Andrei, 165
Seven Lively Arts, 51
1776, 9, 93
70, Girls, 70, **57–58**, 192
Sextet, **119**
Sgt. Pepper's Lonely Hearts Club Band on the Road, 175–76
Shapiro, Joseph, 101
Shapiro, Mel, 10
Sharma, Barbara, 199
Shavelson, Melville, 48
Shaw, Robert, 51–52
She Loves Me, 93
Shearer, Denny, 186
Shelton, Reid, 226
Shenandoah, 68, **100–101**, 104
Sherin, Edwin, 99, 111
Sherman, Garry, 238
Sherman, Richard M., 58
Sherman, Robert B., 58
Sherrin, Ned, 172
Shevelove, Burt, 141, 142, 141n, 170, 187, 241, 242
Shimoda, Yuki, 133-
Shimono, Sab, 133
Shine It On. See *Act, The*
Shire, David, 121
Show Boat, 6, 36, 55n, 101, 104, 113
Show Business, 241
Shubert, Mr. J. J., 121, 251
Shuffle Along, 72
Shull, Richard B., 53, 96
Shutta, Ethel, 41
Side By Side By Sondheim, **172**
Siepi, Cesare, 188, 189
Silverlake, **155–66**

INDEX

Silverman, Stanley, 19–22, 154
Silvers, Phil, 147, 150
Simmons, Jean, 106
Simon, Neil, 60, 200
Simon, Scott, 78
Simonette, Lys, 156
Siretta, Dan, 210
1600 Pennsylvania Avenue, **127–28, 134–37,** 139, 180
Sloane, A. Baldwin, 3
Small, Mary, 119
Small, Neva, 163, 181, 213, 214, 215
Smalls, Charlie, 75
Smith, **71–72,** 156, 204
Smith, Alexis, 36, 40, 46, 179, 183, 184
Smith, Oliver, 49, 151
Sneider, Vern J., 114
Snow White and the Seven Dwarfs, **238**
So Long, 174th Street, **187–88,** 192
Soeder, Fran, 138
Solly, Bill, 164
Some Like It Hot (film), 63, 64. *See also Sugar*
Something's Afoot, **180–81**
Sommer, Josef, 235
Sommers, Avery, 183
Sondheim, Stephen, 25, 28n, 30–31, 32–33, 37, 44, 101, 103n, 132, 134, 172, 228–29
  See also Company; Do I Hear a Waltz; Follies; Gypsy; Little Night Music, A; Pacific Overtures; Passion; Saturday Night; Sunday in the Park With George; Sweeney Todd, the Demon Barber of Fleet Street; West Side Story
Soon, **117**
Sorvino, Paul, 210
Soules, Dale, 175
Sound of Music, The (film), 78
Sousa, John Philip, 3n
South Pacific, 31
Spangler, David, 98
Spencer, Robert, 119
Sperling, Milton, 62
Spiro, Bernie, 163
Stadlen, Lewis J., 53, 147
Stanley, Kim, 34
Steele, Tommy, 9, 65
Stein, Joseph, 187, 190, 209
Sterner, Steve, 163
Sternhagen, Frances, 182
Stewart, Michael, 63, 65, 67, 68, 110, 111, 111–12, 193, 196–97, 245, 246–47
Stiers, David Ogden, 175
Stigwood, Robert, 15, 16, 175, 240
Stiller, Jerry, 10
Stimac, Anthony, 162
Stone, Fred, 9
Stone, Peter, 56, 63
Stop the World–I Want to Get Off, 153
Strachan, Alan, 171
Straiges, Tony, 148
Strauss, Johann, 2
Streep, Meryl, 155
Street Scene, 37
Stritch, Elaine, 25, 27, 29, 41, 61–62
Strouse, Charles, 54–56, 82–83, 86, 223–28
Stuart, Michel, 221

Stubbs, Una, 171
Student Prince, The, **149**
Styne, Jule, 63, 65, 86, 91, 120, 122, 233
  See also Bar Mitzvah Boy; Look to the Lilies; Peter Pan; Prettybelle; Sugar
Sugar, **62–65**
Sugar Babies, **235–37**
Sumac, Yma, 41
Sunday in the Park With George, 31
Swanson, Gloria, 34, 35
Sweeney Todd, the Demon Barber of Fleet Street, 30, 179, 228–32
Sweethearts, 32
Swenson, Swen, 60, 61

Tangerine, **177**
Tanner, Tony, 181
Tatum, Marianne, 245
Taube, Sven-Bertil, 82
Taylor, Clarice, 75
Taylor, James, 174
Taymor, Julie, 238
Tebelak, John-Michael, 108
Teeter, Lara, 242
Tenderloin, 93
Terkel, Studs, 174
Tesich, Steve, 190
Thacker, Russ, 70, 121
That's Entertainment, **170**
Theodore, Donna, 101
They're Playing Our Song, **200–201**
Thomas, Philip Michael, 241
Thomson, Virgil, 71
Threepenny Opera, The, 19, **154–55,** 155
Tibbett, Lawrence, 152
Tierney, Harry, 143
Timbuktu!, **148–49,** 153, 164
Time, 11, 59, 176
Tobias, Fred, 52
Tommy, 14, 15
Topol, 210
Toye, Wendy, 171
Tozzi, Giorgio, 234
Travolta, John, 58
Treemonisha, **158–60**
Trent, Bob, 143n
Tricks, **115–16**
Tucker, Robert, 210
Tune, Tommy, 111, 113, 195, 198, 199, 243
Tunick, Jonathan, 37, 96–97, 103n, 133
Tuotti, Joseph Dolan, 49
Two By Two, **56–57,** 164
Two For the Seesaw (play), 110–11, 113
Two Gentleman of Verona, **10–11,** 105
Tyler, Royall, 162

Udell, Peter, 23–25, 68, 100–101, 104, 181–82, 238–39
Uhry, Alfred, 195
Ullmann, Liv, 184, 185
Umbrellas of Cherbourg, The, **165–66**
Underwood, Franklin, 115
Unsinkable Molly Brown, The, 101
Urinetown, 3
Utter Glory of Morrissey Hall, The, **179–80,** 182

Vagabond, The, 101
Valenti, Michael, 162
Valli, Frankie, 78
Vamp, The, 62n
Van, Bobby, 142, 207, 208–9
van Dijk, Ad and Koen, 121
Van Peebles, Melvin, 72, 73
Van Ronk, Dave, 157
Vandis, Titos, 120
Variety, 153–54, 241
Varnay, Astrid, 157
Varrone, Gene, 187
Verdon, Gwen, 128–29, 137
Vereen, Ben, 16, 109
Very Good Eddie, 153
Vestoff, Virginia, 13
Via Galactica, 10, **11–14**
Vidnovic, Martin, 234
Vilanch, Bruce, 184
Villella, Edward, 153
Von Tilzer, Harry, 207
Vosburgh, Dick, 243

W.C., **62**
Wagner, Robin, 16, 63, 68, 157, 192, 203, 217, 239, 250
Walden, Stanley, 163
Waldman, Robert, 195
Walker, Don, 210
Wall Street Journal, 145
Wallach, Eli, 118
Waller, Fats, 173
Wallis, Shani, 41
Walsh, Thomas (Thommie) J., 111, 221, 243
Walton, Tony, 105, 109, 135, 250–51
Wand, Betty, 123
Warchus, Matthew, 45, 46
Ward, Donald, 164
Warner, Jack L., 49
Warren, Harry, 247, 249–50
Warren, Lesley Ann, 84
Warrick, Ruth, 144
Watling, Dilys, 22
Watson, Susan, 141
Watt, Douglas, 61, 119, 153
Watters, Hal, 168
Watts, Richard, Jr., 149
Wayland, Newton, 168
Wayne, Paula, 61–62
Webb, Marti, 86
Weber, Fredricka, 164
Weede, Robert, 88
Weidman, Jerome, 185
Weidman, John, 132, 138n
Weill, Kurt, 19, 21, 118, 154–58, 168
Werfel, Franz, 193

West, Bernie, 115
West Side Story, 33, **241**, 252
Wheeler, Hugh, 102, 138n, 156, 228
Where's Charley?, 153
White, Jane, 45
White, Onna, 97, 124, 174
White, Willard, 159
White House Cantata, A, 139
Whiting, Richard A., 243
Whoopee!, 153
Widney, Stone, 81
Wilder, Billy, 63, 64
Willett, John, 154
Williams, Jack Eric, 231
Williams, Jill, 119
Williams, Sammy, 219
Williams, Treat, 46, 58
Williamson, Nicol, 98, 99
Williford, Martha, 171
Willison, Walter, 57, 164
Willson, Meredith, 110
Wilson, Dolores, 88
Wilson, Edwin, 145
Wilson, Elizabeth, 154
Wilson, Julie, 48, 118
Wilson, Sandy, 110
Winters, Shelley, 52–53
Witter, William C., 245
Wittstein, Ed, 162
Wiz, The, 68, **73–76**
Wizard of Oz, The, 32, 74
Wodehouse, P. G., 1, 32
Woldin, Judd, 124–25
Wolfe, Karin, 123
Wolpe, Lenny, 212
Women's Wear Daily, 134
Wood, G, 163
Wood, Raymond, 164
Woodard, Charlaine, 173
Woodland, 4
Woods, Aubrey, 82
Words and Music, **169**
Working, **174**
Wright, Robert, 121, 148

Yancy, Emily, 134
Yeargan, Michael, 165
Yellen, Sherman, 93, 98
York, Rebecca, 169
Youmans, Vincent, 1
Your Arms Too Short To Box With God, **172–73**

Zaltzberg, Charlotte, 125
Ziegfeld, Florenz, 3, 57, 113, 251
Zipprodt, Patricia, 68, 109
Zorich, Louis, 96